INDIA'S NATIONAL SECURITY
Vision 2030

INDIA'S NATIONAL SECURITY
Vision 2030

Editors

R.K. ARORA

VINAY KAURA

PENTAGON PRESS LLP

INDIA'S NATIONAL SECURITY: VISION 2030

***Editors:* R.K. Arora and Vinay Kaura**

First Published in 2020

ISBN 978-93-90095-03-2

Published by
PENTAGON PRESS LLP
206, Peacock Lane, Shahpur Jat
New Delhi-110049
Phones: 011-64706243, 26491568
Telefax: 011-26490600
email: rajan@pentagonpress.in
website: www.pentagonpress.in

Printed at Aegean Offset Printers, Greater Noida, U.P.

CONTENTS

ACKNOWLEDGEMENTS

This volume would not have been possible without the generous support the editors have received from so many individuals. We are especially indebted to Dr. Bhupendra Singh, Director General of Police, Rajasthan; and Shri N.R.K. Reddy, Director General (Prisons) and Vice Chancellor of Sardar Patel University of Police, Security and Criminal Justice for their mentorship while we have been working on this project. Many thanks to Dr. Samir Saran, President of the Observer Research Foundation (ORF), for his support and friendship over the years.

We are grateful to all of those we have had the pleasure of working with during this and many other interesting projects on conflict resolution and national security issues. Although we are thankful to all in Sardar Patel University of Police, Security and Criminal Justice who helped us along the way, we want to specifically thank Anuj Tyagi and Himanshu Sharma.

As co-editors, we would like to express our sincere gratitude to all contributors not only for their submissions but also for their patience during the editorial and production process. We would also like to thank anonymous reviewers for their thoughtful and helpful comments. We are grateful to Ms. Mariam Karim Ahlawat, for her excellent translation of General Alain Lamballe's article from French into English.

This book could not have been imagined without the stimulation and challenge of many colleagues, and students. The SPUP has been regularly organizing executive programs on conflict and security studies for serving officials of police organisations of state and central governments. We are thankful to the participants of these programs for sharing their views on some of the issues mentioned in this volume. We are grateful to the many practitioners, policy analysts, and government officials who have supported us over the years.

The editors want to thank Shri Rajan, publisher at Pentagon Press, and his publishing team for their support and assistance in getting this book from concept into print. Lastly, this book would not have been possible without the support of our families. We hope that the contents and ideas from the chapters will inspire and motivate further debates on issues pertaining to India's national security.

R.K. ARORA
VINAY KAURA

INTRODUCTION

R.K. Arora and Vinay Kaura

It is not only the beginning of 2020, but also the opening of a new decade. Many important issues impacting us as a nation a decade earlier will develop at an accelerated pace in this new decade and change our politics, economy and society dramatically. According to an estimate by the United Nations, India's population will be the world's largest around 2027, surpassing that of China. In 2030, India will have 1.536 billion people, while China's population will be 1.464 billion. In terms of economic strength, by 2030 the size of China's economy will surpass that of the USA. India will rank third. We need to think about how to survive in the swiftly changing world in which intangible assets like data and ideas are likely to carry more weight than hard assets.

However, India will continue to face a complex set of challenges to its national security in the next decade. The definition of security itself has undergone a remarkable change with newer areas of threats emerging on the horizon. These threats call for a dynamic security architecture which is capable of dealing with these threats. Indians want their country to emerge truly as a great power. But without mitigating its security challenges and investing in human capital, India cannot hope to become a major power with innovative technological capability.

Immediately after independence in 1947, India faced a major threat from Pakistan whose illegal control over a part of Kashmir created a dispute between the two countries. To compound the economic problems at the time, India had to cope with the aftermath of the terrible communal violence. Pakistan's hatred towards India is manifested in the three Indo-Pak wars and the Kargil conflict, and the current low intensity war being conducted by state and non-state actors in Pakistan. In the name of religion, Pakistan's sponsorship of terrorism against India continues to create huge internal and external security problems.

After a decade of good neighbourly relations, China became a major external threat to India's territorial integrity. India's defeat in 1962 exposed glaring inadequacies in India's defence preparedness. Until the end of the previous century, scholars and practitioners often took a compartmentalised view of national security. Beyond Pakistan and China, Indians did not perceive any major external threat to security. Other threats such as communal conflicts, terrorism, naxalism and trafficking in weapons and drugs were viewed as threats to internal security. Some threats were not acknowledged at all. But soon, the view emerged that there was little distinction between internal and external security.

A closer examination of the threats to India's national security can reveal that there is an intimate connection. For instance, the threat of terrorism is linked with the threat of proliferation of arms and money laundering. The threat to the security of our sea-lanes is closely linked with the threat to energy security. Low intensity conflicts have an impact on social cohesion. Natural disasters can pose a serious threat to food security. Tense relations with a neighbouring country sharing rivers with India may affect our water security. Left-wing extremism is rooted in the exploitation of the tribal people.

Most external threats come from an unsettled boundary dispute with China and ongoing cross-border terrorism in the Union Territory of Jammu and Kashmir, sponsored and supported by Pakistan's ISI and Pakistan-based jihadist organizations like the Lashkar-e-Taiba and Jaish-e-Mohammad. This threat is significantly aggravated by the China-Pakistan military and nuclear nexus. The rise of China and its regional initiatives have begun to pose greater concern for India. Within the next decade, China will become a formidable military power, second only to the USA. A deepening nexus between China and Pakistan, a combination of an ascendant power and a hostile neighbour, is very dangerous for India, particularly in the context of India's ability to fight a two-front war with both Pakistan and China.

India's national security landscape seems inclined to conflict with developments in the neighbourhood. Some avoidable geopolitical dynamics have pushed Nepal and Myanmar more towards China's expanding orbit. The establishment of Chinese bases, coupled with logistics hubs, in the Indian Ocean is likely to diminish the Indian Navy's strategic advantages. India needs to effectively counter Chinese inroads into its maritime domain. India's recent gift of a 'Made in India' patrol vessel to the Maldives needs to be seen as part of New Delhi's efforts to emerge as the net security provider in the region amid China's increasing forays in the Indian Ocean.

Given India's vast coastline, the Indian Ocean is the most important strategic asset for India. This increases India's potential for domination in the region. The initiatives to strengthen a new maritime order in the Indian Ocean by creating new mechanisms will have long-term implications for the emerging security architecture in the Indo-Pacific region. At the same time, there are a number of maritime crimes and threats that confront India. The foremost among these crimes include smuggling, human trafficking, environmental crimes and espionage. The use of maritime routes by terrorists cannot be ruled out in the future as the lines between terrorism and piracy are beginning to be blurred.

When the Internet was created, no one had though that a new domain for conflict and competition was taking shape. But now, its negative side seems to be eclipsing its positive dimension. The might of a powerful nation can be challenged by a group of dedicated individuals well-versed with cyber technology; the more networked we become as a nation, the more vulnerable we become to cyber-attacks. The increasing dependence on cyber technology for governance, delivery of services and financial transactions has brought its own set of vulnerabilities.

We live in an era where digital information is created and used in cyberspace which, in turn, fuels the global economy. As admitted by India's foreign minister, data protection has now become an important part of national security. Therefore, India should step up efforts to ensure data privacy to become a world power in harnessing data. The digital domain has also become a target for India's enemies who will not shy away from sabotaging power plants, energy pipelines and water supplies. To deal with such threats, India should have a robust mechanism to ensure continuous functioning of the country's digital infrastructure. The challenges emanating from the cyber domain include interference in elections through the use of propaganda in social media. Although terrorist attacks through cyber means have not succeeded so far, things are changing very fast. There is an urgent need to evaluate India's cyber security vis-à-vis the espionage and surveillance from other countries.

The nexus between drugs and terrorism has emerged in recent years. Opium cultivation in the rural areas is a failure of many state governments in India. A major problem with respect to enforcement of drug laws lies in the fact that India does not have proper statistics regarding the total number of addicts in the country. Synthetic drugs, which are manufactured with almost no oversight, continue to pose threats. Another disturbing dimension relates to narco-terrorism which may give a new impetus to terrorism in Kashmir. There are reports that around one-fourth of narcotics being smuggled into Kashmir come via Punjab. While public attention has largely focussed on drug trafficking in Punjab, the situation in Kashmir is also becoming terrifying.

Some of India's southern states have become vulnerable to radicalisation with jihadist ideology and money coming from West Asian countries. The announcement that the ISIS has created a separate province to target Indian youth cannot be ignored. Some of the claims may appear exaggerated but the threat is real. The April 2019 Sri Lankan bombings, claimed by the ISIS, have underlined India's own jihadist threat. The Sri Lankan investigations have thrown valuable light on the growing cross-straits role of terrorist elements in Tamil Nadu and Kerala. India needs to draw appropriate lessons of what occurred in Sri Lanka. In fact, the Easter bombings underline the need to articulate a regional counter-terrorism strategy that not only deters the ISIS but also disrupts other terrorist networks, both at the national and regional levels. The strategy must involve the integration of information-sharing and intelligence inputs, tracking intercepts of terrorist groups, and monitoring their movements and activities for comprehensive analysis and coordination.

After the rise of the ISIS, a new trend has emerged in which individuals act on their own without any instructions from a central leadership. The non-state actors have increasingly started making use of cyberspace to pursue their goals. They are backed by more than one state and in order to challenge them, it is important to counter the state supporting them. Illiteracy and poverty is no longer the only contributing factors to terrorism and insurgency. Terrorists are coming from good educated and socio-economic backgrounds. Their education allows them to make efficient use of cyberspace. The path to radicalisation is mostly through the Internet, and time spent online listening to extremist propaganda will inevitably lead to extreme fanaticism.

The Supreme Court's verdict in the Ayodhya Ram Mandir-Babri Masjid dispute in favour of the Hindus has undoubtedly removed a major irritant in

Hindu-Muslim relations. However, the verdict is likely to have long-term implications on internal security since the ISIS, al-Qaeda or other home-grown terrorists may like to exploit the perceived grievances of Muslim youth. Many jihadist groups use social media platforms to fuel conspiracy theories online, and employ encrypted communications while inspiring lone actors to strike. Therefore, special attention would need to be given to maintain communal harmony in the country so that Muslims do not feel marginalized. At the same time, the rise in violent far-right tendencies in the country should also concern law enforcement and other government agencies.

Respect for national identity is an important feature of a citizen's dignity, and the role of political institutions is to protect this identity. Nationalism is thus a formidable force which can be harnessed for progress and prosperity. However, if defined in purely religious-ethnic-racial terms or if affiliated with xenophobia, it can also unleash potentially divisive impulses which could have a deleterious impact on social cohesion as well as national security. If religious identity replaces concepts such as civil rights, rule of law and constitutional values, this would be an encouragement to violence. Therefore, it would be dangerous to allow the far-right elements to have the monopoly of the Tricolour.

In August, the government abrogated Article 370 of the Constitution, which gave special status to Jammu and Kashmir. However, Kashmir's future is far from certain. In the context of Northeastern insurgencies, the underground outfits are getting support from a variety of sources. Local youths seeking jobs and money are joining cross-border insurgent groups. The Maoist insurgency based on Marxist-Leninist ideology is engaged in a violent struggle to overthrow the democratic structure of the Indian state. Terrorist attacks by home-grown insurgent groups in Maoist-infested areas and the north-eastern region have been disrupting peace and stability in the country. However, India's counter-insurgency strategy is not the product of well-defined doctrine or tactics, but is dictated by political factors.

In the Afghanistan-Pakistan region, terrorism remains a potent threat. India has no role in Afghan affairs and remains excluded from current talks involving the Taliban, the USA, Pakistan, Russia and China. This region is one of the most disturbed in the world and India has little say in any of the outcomes being discussed. Various terrorist groups pose formidable security challenges to India as the networking and inter-linkages among them have strengthened in recent years. The Pulwama terrorist attack in February 2019, which led to a retaliatory Indian airstrike on the Jaish-e-Mohammed's terror camp in Pakistan's Balakot, and the Uri terror attack in September 2016 which led to surgical strikes in Pakistan-occupied Kashmir, clearly underscore the potency of the terrorist infrastructure in Pakistan. India's security planners hoped that making public surgical strike and airstrike would send a stern signal to Pakistan about India's willingness to use military force to deter cross-border terrorism. It is true that since Pulwama, Pakistan has not staged any cross-border strike in India. However, cross-border infiltration is yet to stop completely. The trend to keep Pakistan under sustained pressure should continue.

The last couple of years have witnessed several terrorist attacks, exposing the vulnerability of India's borders. Such incidents raise concerns about India's border security system as well as the Intelligence architecture. In addition, India's Northeastern borders with Myanmar and Bangladesh remain vulnerable to the activities of insurgents, drugs traffickers and criminals. Trafficking of narcotics is also witnessing an increasing trend along India's international border with Myanmar. The influx of illegal Rohingyas into India may have national security dimensions as their continued stay could disturb social cohesion and create a fertile breeding ground for radicalisation. Supporting the democratic government in Bangladesh has been very useful for border security as well as Indo-Bangladesh relations. However, the Indo-Bangladesh border is very hard to patrol. Human trafficking, drug-trade and cattle smuggling are the most common cross-border crimes along the Indo-Bangladesh border. Counterfeit currency worth millions of rupees originating in Bangladesh is in circulation in India.

Though the government recognizes the need for modernisation of the border guarding forces and border security infrastructure, there are still many challenges to be addressed. Some shortcomings include gaps in the system at rivers, border systems working in unfavourable climatic conditions, and lack of progress in proper implementation of technological solutions. Communication between different paramilitary forces is also scarce, failing to provide a common operating procedure. The objectives of the BADP to improve the living conditions of the border populations have not been achieved fully. To secure the borders in India, a clever combination of modern technologies for border control and existing available resources is required to combat threats to the country. In addition to strengthening the security of the border, the government should also redouble its efforts to meaningfully engage the neighbouring countries to enhance national security.

The Indian Army depends on unmanned aerial vehicles (UAVs). The main advantage of using a UAV is that it acts as a force multiplier. Its extended range puts less pressure on human resources. However, there are significant limitations to the use of UAVs. The UAVs have a higher accident rate as compared to manned vehicles, and their cost of operation and maintenance is also significantly higher. Moreover, cyber attacks could be launched against the sensor nodes of UAVs by manipulating their functions. However, the real threat would emanate from UAVs operated by hostile individuals with the intention of causing harm. Although intelligence is a great preventive mechanism, the framework of counter-terrorism in India needs to change. A good counter-terrorism matrix should be based on both Intelligence and investigation-led foundations. There is a need for greater coordination and sharing of Intelligence among the various intelligence agencies in India.

The Government has announced the creation of the post of chief of defence staff (CDS). This decision has been rightly hailed as it has been a long-standing demand. The position of the CDS is likely to enhance coordination while providing coherence to the overall defence policy. However, the job to transform the Indian military will remain unfinished unless the CDS is empowered with the Ministry of Defence integrating military expertise into its policy-making apparatus. By launching the 'Make in India' initiative, the Government has recognised the importance of industrial power for national security. However, India must advance national security through fundamental reforms in the defence sector. Bigger military budget does not always mean greater national security. What really matters is how the money is spent to improve indigenous capabilities and prevent adversaries. There are persistent concerns on India's inability to develop indigenous defence capacity platforms. This issue was particularly raised by the former Army Chief, General V.P. Malik, during the Military Literature Festival in Chandigarh in December 2019, where he expressed disappointment over the lackadaisical attitude towards the defence needs of the country, emphasising the need for Parliament to debate the issue. There is also ambiguity and doubt around the aims laid down under 'Make in India' as far as defence acquisitions are concerned.

Though India must arm itself for self-defence, conventional weapons cannot, however, be adequate in countering unconventional threats, particularly in the cyber domain. The Indian military must gradually shift away from the conventional to the newest generation of warfare. Cyber warfare capabilities will surely hold the key for national security in the coming decade. The USA, Israel, China and Russia dominate cyberspace and artificial intelligence. India will have to devise new policy parameters to enhance capabilities in areas of artificial intelligence and cyber technology.

India's various federal and state police agencies are performing the commendable task of protecting both the state and society from all dangers. Almost every year, a considerable number of police personnel lay down their lives in the call of duty. However, the institutional architecture of internal security suffers from some structural flaws which adversely affect the ability of the government to govern effectively, jeopardizing national security in the process. Despite there being an urgent need to enhance internal security, the Indian security system is not evolving fast enough to meet the changing demands. Effective modernisation of the police forces cannot happen with a limited budget which does not guarantee good equipment and training. There are inadequate vehicles for the police, and the communications equipment used is also not very ideal for both policing and disaster management. The state governments need to be persuaded to accept their responsibilities to maintain internal security within their jurisdictions. Unfortunately, most of the states have not been able to establish efficient Intelligence machinery or maintain well-trained police forces to deal with the growing incidents of disturbance and violence. It is important for state police forces to increase their investment in modernising equipment and training.

India's judicial system is also one of the slowest in the world. An overburdened criminal-justice mechanism not only denies ordinary citizens easy access to secure their basic rights which are guaranteed by the Constitution but also hinders economic development and national security by fuelling unnecessary internal conflicts. In the absence of a robust and well-functioning criminal justice system, subversive elements and criminal syndicates are allowed to flourish with impunity.

India is a federal polity. Due to this constitutional mechanism, there are multiple concerns which need to be addressed before promulgating major reforms. However, this approach towards consensus-building leads to delays. Considering the hybrid nature of threats, time-bound interaction between all stakeholders is important, which calls for smooth communication channels between central and state agencies. Moreover, there is an enhanced need for institutionalised interface among various civil, law enforcement and the military agencies for tackling national security threats. It is within this context that the contributors to this volume debate and discuss India's national security challenges, future considerations and the road ahead. The chapters are organised around distinctive themes that help locate the current debates on the subject.

The volume is divided into eleven chapters. Chapter One titled "Conventionally and unconventionally assailed India in quest of security," by Brig. Gen. Alain Lamballe (Retd.), explains the diverse nature of threats India faces, while emphasising the need for some indispensible reforms. He argues that the Government has a strong mandate as well as the political vision to act without procrastination. Chapter Two by Admiral Arun Prakash (Retd.) discusses India's growing dependence on the maritime environment. While discussing recent developments on India's northern borders and the Indian Ocean Region, the author argues for a more active role for the Indian Navy and efforts to enhance the level of maritime consciousness amongst India's ruling class. Chapter Three titled "India's Quest for a Regional Security Architecture" by Christian Wagner traces the dynamics of inter-state cooperation on security in South Asia. He highlights the rising cooperation among security forces and the increase in legal instruments for countering non-traditional threats as a positive development for regional peace. In Chapter Four titled "Emerging Trends in India's National Security," Maj. Gen. Dhruv C. Katoch (Retd.) reflects on various aspects underpinning India's national security and predicts a more safe and secure regional security environment in the next decade. Chapter Five titled "From Strategic Lethargy to Strategic Stability: The Long Road to 2030," by M.J. Akbar traces the evolution of India's strategic thought since Independence. In his characteristic style, the author explains the important pillars of Prime Minister Narendra Modi's foreign policy as rooted in India's national interest, civilisational philosophy and the republican, democratic ethos of modernity. M.L. Kumawat, in Chapter Six titled "India's Internal Security: Threats and Solutions," discusses India's several internal security challenges and how to deal with them through police reforms and other policy initiatives. He also stresses the need to create an Internal Security Doctrine for India. Chapter Seven by R.K. Arora explains India's border security scenario, with specific reference to four important components of border security, and the need to integrate them for comprehensive border security. In Chapter Eight titled "India and the Global Order in Reset: The Effects of Uncertain Dynamism," Lt. Gen. Syed Ata Hasnain (Retd.) discusses uncertain global dynamics and India's role to secure its interests. In Chapter Nine titled "Security Challenges from the Neighbourhood," Professor S.D. Muni explains conventional and non-conventional threats in India's neighbourhood and concludes that no substantial reduction in these threats can be expected by 2030. Cautioning against growing religious and sectarian polarisation in many South Asian countries, he asks Indian leadership to take the lead in countering radicalisation by reaching out to the communities that feel alienated, both domestically and regionally. Chapter Ten titled "Problem of Illegal Migration from Bangladesh" by S.K. Sood traces the challenge of illegal migration from Bangladesh and its impact on India's national security. Chapter Eleven titled "India-Afghanistan Partnership, Counter Terrorism and Security in South Asia" by Vinay Kaura explains the significance of Indo-Afghan ties and how the exit of American troops from conflict-ridden Afghanistan will affect India's interests in South Asia.

Beyond doubt, much has been written about the topics touched upon in this volume. There are many books on similar themes. But how we frame the discussion on these issues is as important as the need to discuss them. The past cannot be a guide to the future. The goal of absolute safety or security cannot ever be realized. Thus, policy makers always seek that their country be as safe as possible. Realism explains that all states seek to ensure their safety and protect their interests, but the manner in which they do so depends on how their policy makers define threats to national security. Having been through several conflicts and national security crises, there is a growing recognition that India needs a robust national security system, one that is properly structured and devoid of ad-hocism.

It is important now to imagine 2030. We need to think about what kinds of security challenges India will face and what kind of solutions can emerge in the future. Given the hybrid nature of security threats that will confront India, there is an urgent need to enhance regional coordination and cooperation with neighbouring countries as it has become very important to forge relationships for meeting the existing and emerging security challenges. The threats India now confronts are largely unconventional. In the next decade, India needs to balance national security requirements with socio-economic priorities. It is hoped that the wide-ranging perspectives presented in this volume would add value to the evolving debates on India's national security vision for the next debate and resonate with readers, be they practitioners, researchers or citizens.

1

Conventionally and Unconventionally Assailed India in Quest of Security

Brig Gen Alain Lamballe (Retd.)

Confronted by all possible forms of strife, from nuclear conflicts to subversion, India should make concerted efforts to ensure its security on the borders and within its own territory. This chapter studies the conventional and unconventional threats that are likely to weigh heavily on India in the next ten years to come, and mentions the measures that it should adopt to forearm itself.

Threats that will Persist, and will Diversify

The length and the variety of the Indian borders as well as the size and diversity of its populations means that India has a vast exposure to the external world but which also leaves it open to multiple and various dangers.

India needs to defend 15,000 kilometres of terrestrial borders that it shares with six countries and 7,500 kilometres of maritime tracts with four countries. It also has to protect its exclusive economic zone of 2.4 million square kilometres.

Disruptive Pakistan

Western India faces Pakistan for over more than 3,000 kilometres including almost 1,000 kilometres in Kashmir, the territory disputed by the two countries.

Pakistan is the enemy country with whom wars have taken place on several occasions: 1947-48, 1965, 1971 and 1999. Pakistan has a strong army that is well equipped and well trained. The international frontiers have been completely fenced off by India along the line of control of Kashmir partially. On this line of control, a new form of combat has appeared without replacing regular artillery fire. There are elite Pakistani marksmen who have taken many victims with sniper rifles of American origin that allow them to fire up to 1,500 metres.

Pakistan not only constitutes a conventional threat, it also supports insurrectional and secessionist movements in Indian-administered Kashmir, taking advantage of internal troubles and confusion. The aid Pakistan gives to Kashmiri militants who are combating the Indian Army is likely to continue. In fact, supporting the troubles in Indian-administered Kashmir is of great advantage to Pakistan because it engages hundreds of millions of military and paramilitary forces of India, reducing, therefore, by as many, those deployed by India for the defence of its frontiers.

Pakistan supports radical movements that may or may not be affiliated to Indian groups and have the vocation to create trouble in different regions of India, mostly in Kashmir. The attack against the Parliament in New Delhi in 2001 and those in Mumbai in 2008 are glaring examples of this.

The bloody insurrection in Punjab in the 1970s and 1980s was crushed only in the 1990s. Pakistan may do everything it can to see that this movement starts again, by helping secessionist Sikh movements. The inter-services intelligence, or ISI, the key intelligence service of Pakistan, is also closely interested in the separatist movements of Northeast India. This is naturally more difficult since the birth of Bangladesh, but the Chinese are said to be helping. Besides, Pakistan allegedly infiltrates agents via Nepal into Indian territory because of the more porous borders. It is through these Nepalese borders that it sends fake Indian currency into India to destabilize the Indian economy.

Pakistan madrassas are not the only institutions to provide terrorists; some also come from universities. The profile of terrorists is now diversifying. They are more educated and more international in a certain way.

Its own galloping population may destabilize Pakistan. According to estimates, the population will be 400 million in 2050 and this will make it the fifth most populous country in the world. Islamic extremist groups are opposed to all forms of family planning estimating that greater numbers will help them to conquer the world, starting with India, where the population growth rate of the Hindus is lower.[1] Because of this, grave social troubles could occur as resources will be insufficient compared to requirements. Internal disorders will be provoked by migration towards Afghanistan which is less populated. Additionally, population growth will lead to a complete shortage of water which will be catastrophic. This shortage will be wrongly imputed to India being the uphill country, and could be the cause of a new war between India and Pakistan which will be started by the latter, the downhill country. Water-sharing will be a destabilizing factor in the bilateral relations of the two countries.

For several other reasons, a new war between India and Pakistan cannot be ruled out. The abrogation of the special status of Kashmir in August 2019 and the creation of two Union Territories—Ladakh and Jammu and Kashmir—(amputated from Ladakh) will aggravate insecurity in the short and medium term.

An armed conflict could be provoked by bloody terrorist acts perpetrated in India in Kashmir or in other places and attributed to Pakistan or to extremist movements that are given shelter in that country. The nuclear deterrent, nevertheless, will play a role in limiting Indian reprisals. A crushing victory by the Indian Army may actually provoke Pakistan to use nuclear arms, which it possesses. Pakistan has declared for all to hear that it can make first use of nuclear arms if the major interests of the country are threatened. The lack of clarity that exists concerning the definition of 'major interests,' reinforces the deterrent, because it is then difficult to define the nuclear threshold. The nuclear deterrence exercised by Pakistan is credible and strong because, unlike India, it finds itself in the hands of the military, which, under all circumstances, shows more determination. Furthermore, Pakistan is said to possess more arms than India. The atom has an equalizing effect, which annihilates in a certain manner, India's numeric superiority.

Pakistan would find itself more at liberty to follow this direction if it could count on aid from China. Certainly, China would not interfere militarily in Kashmir, but would leave doubt floating. The route linking Xinjiang to Punjab crossing Gilgit Baltistan and Khyber Pakhtunkhwa, linking Kashgar to Abbottabad, constitutes a major strategic axis permitting movement of troops and military material in addition to its interests of commercial exchange. As the road is being upgraded, it could be used the whole year round when tunnels are dug. Snowing-in will cease to be an obstacle. In reality, China could actually content itself by just doing some indefinite sabre-rattling on the border that is shared with India, of about 700 kilometres in Ladakh.

Powerful and Omnipresent China

A conflict between China and India appears improbable but India can, however, not ignore the threat weighing on it in the north, in the Himalayas from Kashmir up to Arunachal Pradesh.

Since the 1950s, China controls the northeast of Ladakh, although it was a part of historical Kashmir. It lays claim also to Arunachal Pradesh that it calls 'South Tibet'. All in all, the borders between India and China extend to about 3,500 kilometres which is an approximate number as it has not been properly delineated and is the object of litigation between the two countries.

The Indian staff should take into consideration the military capacities of China, and not only its intentions, that are liable to change very rapidly. Chinese potential in Tibet is considerable: ground and air units have been stationed there in large numbers. Besides, missile sites have been planted there as well. The army formations possess armaments and materials that are well adapted to mountainous terrain and high altitudes. The posts on the Indian borders at very high altitudes are very well managed: they have permanent electricity and adequate heating. They have low occupation in normal times as China does not feel really threatened by India. But they can, in case of tensions, house great numbers of soldiers for which they have been constructed. Reinforcements can be called in very rapidly because of an excellent network of roads in Tibet which reach even the most distant areas all along the border. In addition to these roads, there are also railway tracks that are increasing in number every day. The soldiers already positioned in the forward areas and those in the rear are very battle-ready, in winter as well as in summer. China has another advantage. A joint army air command based in Chengdu activated in peacetime and whose operational area includes Tibet and Xinjiang, would be capable of carrying out operations with great efficacy. Its functioning has been tested by huge manoeuvres organised regularly in these two western Chinese regions.

China also affirms its ambitions in the maritime domain. The Indian Ocean, through which a large part of its important exports and imports transit, is of great interest to China. China is developing relations with the maritime neighbours of India, mainly Pakistan, but also with Bangladesh and Sri Lanka. China is constructing and managing the port in Gwadar situated on the Baloch

Pakistan coast. In Bangladesh, China could construct a port in deep waters in the Sonadia island, off Cox's Bazar. In Myanmar, China has such a port at Kyaukpyu in the Arakan.

China has had to suffer certain disappointments in Sri Lanka. It will however, in the coming decades, be able to ensure the management of the deep water port that has been constructed in the south of the island at Hambantota while it has enlarged the port of Colombo from where various kinds of merchandise to and from India transit. In the same way, the Maldives arouses a similar aspiration. These appropriations reveal the desire to encircle India.

China exports submarines, planes, drones and tanks to Pakistan, which also receives aid to modernise its defence industry. Chinese launchers have placed in orbit two observation satellites and one communication satellite for Pakistan. Pakistan uses the Chinese Beidu Positioning System.

China has sold planes and submarines to Bangladesh and will later provide corvettes. A submarine base could be constructed by China in Cox's Bazar. Chinese equipment is also furnished to Nepal. Chinese and Nepalese armies are developing cooperation including common manoeuvres.

There have been indicators that China is sheltering and even arming militant and secessionist movements of Northeast India in their province of Yunan. Myanmar serves as the place of passage and even of refuge.

China excels in unconventional sectors. Its embassy in New Delhi knows where all the Chinese-Indian citizens live. It is true that many have left India to live in Europe, in Australia or Canada, or even in the USA. But a small community of Chinese still exists in Calcutta (now Kolkata), and one can find them in certain states of the Northeast, including Nagaland. Members of the Chinese embassy have visited them in the past. At least one Chinese ambassador has gone to Nagaland specially to meet a hotelier near Kohima. Among the 100,000 Tibetan refugees in India, it would be realistic to assume that Chinese agents have been infiltrated.

China is carrying out a cultural penetration operation in Ladakh where it sends Tibetan monks more or less surreptitiously. The aim is to present China in a favourable light. The Chinese wish to transform mindsets to convince the Ladakhis of their good intentions with regard to Buddhists and they give an example of the social and economic development of neighbouring Tibet. It is possible that the Ladakhis could be convinced and they would facilitate Chinese expansion. Chinese monks propagate their version of Tibetan Buddhism to the detriment of local ancestral practices and they promote Chinese language, Chinese customs and Chinese cuisine. On top of this, they are reinforcing, rather creating, tensions between the different sects of Buddhism in Ladakh. China's pretensions towards enlarging its territory in the west by the joining together of populations will be substantiated. China's aim is to control the Karakoram Pass, which is a point of passage between Xinjiang and Ladakh. In a certain manner, the Chinese, by the intermediary of some perfectly assimilated and controlled Tibetans, are sanitising Ladakh. One section of the youth is being indoctrinated. As in other places in India, the Chinese exercise with great talent their soft power: they are carrying out a veritable psychological warfare.

China could be interested more than ever in the Nepalese who have been living for a reasonably long time in India, mainly in Sikkim, in West Bengal and Assam but also in other northeastern states.

China also has a particular interest with regard to the Dravidian populations in the south of India. Political and economic leaders of the south Indian states are frequently invited to China and Chinese experts come to the south of India more frequently and in larger numbers than to the north of India. There is nothing to prove that Beijing wants to use its contacts to promote the nationalistic sentiments of the Dravidians, in particular, the Tamils, who are more inclined to defend their language and their culture. There is no proof either that China supports rapprochement between Tamil Nadu and the provinces in north and east Sri Lanka, which would be an early sign of a common political claim and indicator of a great independent Tamil state. China keeps itself updated, however, on the sentiments of the different populations. In the same spirit, China proposes provides aid to the Sri Lankan government to help develop the northern provinces that have suffered greatly from the Liberation Tigers of Tamil Eelam (LTTE) insurrections.

Chinese soft power exercised in the cultural domain, is transformed subsequently into hard power that could profoundly affect the minds of the people. China has started to penetrate the cinematographic milieu of India. The world of Indian cinema, Bollywood, is at risk of suffering the same fate as American cinema, Hollywood, which is partially under the control of the Chinese. It is losing its freedom of expression bit by bit.

The centres of Indian film production, mainly those in Hindi, are slowly beginning to be controlled by Chinese companies by way of financing and sharing of profits. Indian cinema is at risk of losing its specificity and its freedom of expression. This is what is at stake for India, and it must conserve that which has made its films so popular in the country as well as in the Diaspora in the world. For China, the stakes are both ideological, (that is, presenting a flattering image of its achievements and unfavourable image of the West and even of India) and also financial (raking in the benefits of these shows in Chinese cinema halls). These Chinese companies propose to finance Indian film production and lure them with sparkling benefits or advantages. Subsequently, they impose constraints on the content of the films, encourage themes that show India and the West in a bad light and disallow all negative interpretations of China. Indian film producers can be greatly tempted because then their films would be shown to larger audiences in China, evading the buying of rights elsewhere in the world as well, thanks to the Chinese distribution system. The profits would be divided between India and China. China would have two-fold gains at the level of propaganda and at the level of finance.

Indian producers have already started practising forms of auto censorship to please the Chinese which is going to lead to something detrimental to the image of India in the world and profitable to the perception of China. For now, China has authorised the screening of only two Indian films per annum but envisages increasing that number. This supposes naturally that the content of these films has to be politically correct for China. For the sake of reciprocity, Indians will be constrained to increase the number of Chinese films that are screened in India. In this manner, Chinese propaganda can be intensified, including in those sensitive areas such as Assam and its neighbouring states where the Indian nationalist sentiment is weak and where there are strong separatist tendencies.

Adopting a very elaborate global strategy China is carrying out a vast cultural offensive in India's neighbouring countries. Confucius institutes are springing up. Mandarin Chinese is taught more and more in Pakistan. It will be so in Nepal also, with the Chinese proposition of paying the salaries of professors who teach Mandarin. Already, private schools have rendered the teaching of Mandarin Chinese obligatory.

Friendly But Powerless Bangladesh

India possesses its longest border with Bangladesh, 4,095 kilometres, of which a thousand kilometres are along rivers. The borders were cordoned off by India for the major part and the sectors which are constituted by water bodies controlled by electronic sensors. Bangladesh is buying arms from China but poses no military threat to India. The danger here is different. Destabilization of the Indian border states may happen. Despite the fencing of the borders, which is as yet incomplete, there continues to be a clandestine migration of Bangladeshi Muslims into Assam and West Bengal. This migration modifies the ethnic and religious composition of these provinces or states. In spite of linguistic similarity, West Bengal is no longer the most suitable place for migration as it is overpopulated already, like Bangladesh itself. It is now towards Assam that the migrations of those that are leaving Bangladesh take place. Since then, the percentage of Muslims in Assam has become 30 per cent. In time, this could increase, if, ecological displacement is brought about by the rise of water levels in the Indian Ocean and migrations which are essentially economic, continue on a larger scale. Additionally, the illegal entry of Rohingyas, also Muslims, chased out of Myanmar and in a precarious situation in Bangladesh, increases the total number of refugees. Around 40,000 Rohingyas are allegedly now present in India. Surely, some are radicalised. Physically, they cannot be distinguished from Bangladeshis. If the number of Muslims in Assam keeps increasing, it is possible that claims for the reattachment of Northeast India to Bangladesh can start. A greater Bangladesh would mean a diminished India, and this would please China. New Delhi blames Dhaka for not stopping these clandestine migrations Actually, Dhaka denies them altogether. Besides, if the National Register of Citizens is put into force, it would generate grave troubles in Assam. According to the register, only those persons will be considered Indian citizens who came before midnight on 24 March 1971, the day before the Independence of Bangladesh. More than 4 million people do not fulfil the required conditions. What will become of them? Will they have to return to Bangladesh, where they largely come from? The country will not accept them as it denies illegal infiltration.

If this register is put into force, the terrain will become propitious for all sorts of protest movements which may or may not take recourse to terrorism. The situation may worsen if Nagaland decides to establish a similar register.

Migrations, Sometimes Linked to Terrorism

Population migrations in South Asia create tensions. This isn't new. In the 1960s, the Chakmas, originally from the Chittagong hill tracts of Bangladesh, sought refuge in Arunachal Pradesh and they are still there. Migratory movements are linked to internal troubles in the various countries of South Asia. Thus the Ahmediyas from Pakistan, with no affinity to extremist terrorists, migrate to Nepal being persecuted in their own land. Some subsequently reach India. Sometimes, international terrorists take advantage of these population movements. Among Bangladeshi migrants, malevolent elements on the payroll of Pakistan or China can be introduced. Among the 100,000 Tamils of Sri Lanka that have taken refuge in Tamil Nadu there are likely to be members of the erstwhile independence movement, the LTTE, defeated by the Sri Lankans in 2009, but not entirely eliminated. India, additionally, constitutes a place of retreat for the radical Islamists of Sri Lanka and the Maldives.

Among the Indian Diaspora can be found hidden members of terrorist organisations. The Sikhs, partisan to an independent Khalistan, are active in the UK and Canada. Large sums of money are collected, voluntarily or otherwise, and sent legally or illegally. This practice isn't likely to stop as the money transfers are made through channels that are very hard to detect.

The existence of a Diaspora in unstable countries poses the problem of security of another type, that of their eventual evacuation by civil or military means (in such cases, navy or air force).

Troubles in India: Internal and Transnational

Islamist movements are active in certain Indian states which are independent of the Kashmir movements. One finds them mainly in Assam and Kerala. Indian Muslim extremists sometimes leave for jihad in the Middle East. Those that return may carry on their battles with the Hindus. It can also be supposed that pilgrims that go to Mecca can return indoctrinated. As in Pakistan, recruitment can diversify into educated classes and not only in madrassas. The Islamic state, Daesh, is still not very present in India but is very active in Pakistan. It has been mentioned that in May 2019 two distinct *wilayats* were created, the *Wilayat-e-Hind* and the *Wilayat-e-Pakistan*, while the *Khorasan Wilayat* brings together Afghanistan and Central Asia. Aggressions between Shias and Sunnis are frequent in Pakistan but nonexistent in India. But will this always be the case? Twenty per cent of Muslims in both countries are Shias.

Radical Islamists in India are in contact not only with the neighbouring Islamic countries, Pakistan and Bangladesh, but also with the non-Muslim majority countries like Nepal and Sri Lanka. Islamist movements have in reality become transnational in South Asia.

Besides, Maoist insurrections are continuing in the central Indian states albeit losing intensity. The Maoists, however, continue recruitment from among the tribals and adivasis who live in the interior and poor regions, posing as guardians of their traditional mode of life against the powerful national and international firms that wish to exploit the mineral riches of the area. The Maoists also recruit from among the scheduled castes and the Dalits, a fraction of Indian society, still suffering because of ancestral prejudices. Maoist insurrectionists have difficulties in maintaining contact with the external movements as they are bang in the heart of the country. They have, however, succeeded in keeping in touch with the Nepalese Maoists ever since the latter carried out the battle against the Kathmandu regime.

Separatist movements in the north-east of India have no problems crossing international borders. They find shelter in Bhutan, Bangladesh and more often in Myanmar. They can easily serve as a relay between Indian Maoists and China.

Terrorist acts committed by Hindus against Muslims are rare. The most conspicuous case is that of the Malegaon riots in Maharashtra which saw 40 dead, mostly Muslims. Radical Islamists exploit these incidents to make known in India and outside, the discrimination suffered by the Muslim community which is very large, nearly 180 million, a minority compared to the Hindu population, but not isolated, as there are 550 million Muslims in south Asia. Those South Asian Muslims themselves are a part of the Umma extending from Morocco to the Philippines which makes up more than one-and-a-half billion followers of Sunni Islam and also Shias.

Terrorist organisations, mainly those that are part of what is known as Islamic terrorism, are becoming more and more adept at using modern means of communication, largely the Internet. Increasingly they are using modern techniques of encryption and communication. Social networks have given them greater visibility. Certainly, these clandestine organisations must possess their own media, classic or electronic. Internet viruses may paralyze entire sections of national activity such as water distribution, electricity, functioning of hospitals, transport, etc. The modus operandi of the terrorists may diversify to include commando-style, armed drone attacks on sensitive infrastructure such as hydroelectric dams, ports, airports and nuclear sites. They have modern equipment such as night vision apparatuses. Their power to create problems is therefore considerable. Isolated individuals or lone wolves/lone actors who are difficult to identify can multiply the attacks. Dangerous persons can apply for posts that will allow them to perpetrate disastrous designs. These could be bus drivers, metro staff, and security staff in strategic infrastructures. Poisoning of reservoirs and water bodies could be carried out for example during large religious festivals. Dangerous professions could be taken up by radicalised men such as is the case in the West. Suicide attacks could be carried out by women, even indoctrinated children.

Natural Catastrophes, a Grave Impact on Security

Global warming could cause population migrations within India, generating troubles which will be hard to control. Populations will be fleeing increasingly inhospitable regions to more suitable climes. Natural disasters are becoming more and more frequent. Earthquakes in the Himalayan zones and other places, floods in mountainous areas, and in the plains, cyclones and tsunamis on the east and west coasts of South Asia cause the loss of many human lives and material damage. They may affect the armed forces themselves, unable then to come to the aid of the affected people. Broken bridges, landslides will render roadways and railways unusable for indeterminate periods which would hamper all travel for the general population as well as for the military and paramilitary forces. Everywhere sites of strategic importance such as military headquarters, barracks, air bases, arms and ammunition depots, nuclear arms facilities, dams can be damaged or totally wiped out. On the coasts, desalination factories can be annihilated, naval bases and warships on the coasts may be affected too.

Such phenomena may affect only India or perhaps Pakistan and Bangladesh as well. If they occur only in one country they will possibly disadvantage that country for a reasonably long period as the balance of military forces in South Asia will be modified.

Dry spells will also yield consequences relating to security with the subsequent social upheavals they will generate. The rise in summer temperatures will bring about fires especially in forested areas. They will be doubly devastating as there will be no water to put them out. Retreating forests will be advantageous to security forces fighting against insurgents who will now be without refuge. There will be grave repercussions for natural life. Animals, including the most dangerous and savage tigers and elephants will then make incursions into human habitations in search of food causing deaths and damage to property. The human-animal conflict will be aggravated.

To a great extent, the forced displacement of populations will not know where the borders lie and cover international aspects. A part of Bangladesh may be swallowed by the rising waters of the Bay of Bengal, beyond even the Sunderbans. Two-thirds of the country is effectively five metres below sea level. The doomed populations will have no other choice but to flee to India.

New Areas of Conflict

Cyber space has opened new avenues of conflict which evolve perpetually. India seems vulnerable compared to China. The latter knows how to protect itself, close off everything that enters or exits. This isn't the case with India. Three levels of attack may be discerned: sabotage, espionage, and subversion. China excels in all three. It has, without a doubt, sleeping cells. It possesses the capability to sabotage Indian civil and military infrastructures and neutralise communication channels. It is already capable of obtaining valuable information on its potential adversaries of which India is one. It is a master in matters of influence. Its electronic networks complement its radio and television networks as well as print media.

China has full capability of observing India and its geostrategic environment. Its capabilities to cause harm will only increase. These will be greater as cooperation with Pakistan increases. India faces considerable challenges on all fronts: military, insurrectional, migratory, climatic, social and scientific.

Responses to Threats not Always Well Calibrated

Faced with multifaceted threats, military, terrorist and unconventional, India is making efforts to make adequate responses, but not being totally successful, as it lacks the means. The defence budget at less than 2 per cent of the GDP and is shockingly insufficient. In addition, the percentage assigned to revenue expenditure is 60 per cent for the entire armed forces and reaches 80 per cent for the army, which leaves very little funding for capital expenditure to modernise equipment and armaments. The picture is darker because the budget assigned to the interior civil security forces is much below what it ought to be.

There exists an intellectual paucity as well. In general, India lacks a strategic culture. Certain renowned government and independent think-tanks are working to remedy this. The creation of a National Defence University is highly desirable. Pakistan already has one in place. And China has multiple centres of geostrategic research. At the level of the government, the National Security Council, a purely consultatory body set up in 1998, meets extremely rarely although it requires to furnish elements of reflection and deliberation. In the same way, the Cabinet Committee on Security, a decision-making body, does not have sufficient data or analyses. There is no document defining the security politics that the government ought to be following. No White Paper on defence matters exists.

Some strategies ought to be decided upon for the training of military and paramilitary cadres. The various schools that impart training at various levels and in different areas need to be modernised. For this to be done, contacts with similar foreign establishments need to be built. This isn't done sufficiently. The Indian defence attachés posted in embassies across the world should invest more in developing international military relations, which are obviously sources of enrichment. Perhaps they do not have the necessary authorisation to be able to act in this way. Their lack of language skills also constitutes an obstacle. Indian military officers serving abroad are very often absent from colloquiums and discussions, unlike their Chinese counterparts, to cite only their example.

The Indian army is often enmeshed in the battle against terrorism and therefore diverted from its primary mission of defending the borders. Being engaged in counter insurgency activities mobilises great numbers of the workforce in the border areas of Kashmir and the Northeast. However, this battle-readiness of the officers and the ranks has a positive aspect. They are prepared to face dangers.

Indian aerial attacks were carried out on Pakistani soil in reprisal against terrorist attacks perpetrated in Kashmir by pro Pakistani militants. Their effectiveness is questionable. According to some analysts, the destabilising of the western Pakistani provinces is a means of immobilising Pakistani troops. Pakistani as well as foreign observers affirm that Indian intelligence services have already made such endeavours, not necessarily furnishing arms, but by sending funding to Baloch nationalist dissidents and the *Pashtun Tahafuz Movement* (movement for the protection of Pashtuns). The Indian consulates in Jalalabad and Kandahar and private Indian firms working in Afghanistan would be implicated. The reigning hostility in Gilgit-Baltistan between the local Shias and the recently-installed Sunnis could also weaken Pakistan and therefore be an advantage to India, but for the moment the situation is well under control by the Pakistani security forces and also by the visibly increasing hold of the Chinese.

In the east, Myanmar makes its case for dismantling the camps of Assamese and Naga secessionists that have been set up on its territory. The Tatmadaw strives to stop the furnishing of arms to certain groups by the *United Wa State Army*, an armed rebel group active on the Sino-Myanmar border. Myanmar aid however remains irregular and mostly ineffectual. To supplement this shortage, Indian army and paramilitary units have carried out reprisals in Myanmar, not always in consultation with the Myanmar authorities. Their success is disputable.

The army has succeeded till now in avoiding all involvement with the fight against the Maoist insurrection that is rife in the central parts of the country; the only intervention is by helicopters, essentially to evacuate the wounded. It is the Central Reserve Police Force (CRPF), the paramilitary force with the largest workforce, which assumes the responsibility of combating the Maoists.

To be able to combat these secessionist and ideological movements, the security forces must modernise their equipment. Drones could be used effectively to gather information. They could also be used in the surveillance of borders. The use of armed drones could be considered as well. India does not as yet have sufficient technology to be able to manufacture such sophisticated machinery. The observation satellites that India manufactures, some of them all-weather, also bring useful information for the security forces operating in the interiors and for those on the borders. India also possesses from now on a national global positioning system (GPS).

The three services suffer from penury of personnel, including of officers. Advertisements are absolutely necessary to present a more attractive image of the armed forces profession, the way it is done in Pakistan. Ammunitions stocks aren't sufficient for a long drawn out conflict. Weapon systems in the forces are lacking. The army does not possess sufficient artillery and helicopters.

The air force has only 32 squadrons although it requires 42. It has 38 kinds of aircraft which poses serious problems of maintenance. The maritime doctrine of 2015 clearly states the necessity of the presence of the Indian Navy in the Indian Ocean. For 2027, the Indian Navy envisages 212 warships and 458 aircraft. This objective will be very difficult to achieve. There is only one lone aircraft carrier in operation. Three aircraft carriers will be necessary: One based along the west coast and the other along the east coast, a third will guarantee naval permanence. This group of three aircraft carriers will be ready in 2030. The number of submarines is also insufficient. It will be difficult to swing naval warships from one coast to the other, from east to west and vice versa, and this will continue because the digging of a channel between South India and Sri Lanka which has been envisaged a long time ago, cannot be done in the coming decade. So circumvention by the south of the island of Sri Lanka will continue to be necessary. The naval bases of Mumbai on the western coast and that of Visakhapatnam on the eastern coast will remain co-located with commercial ports and this creates problems in their functioning. This inconvenience does not exist anymore with the base of Karwar, south of Goa on the west coast and will not exist on the east coast with the base being constructed in Rombili, south of Visakhapatnam.

India needs to import the major part of its arms for the three services, the army, the navy and the air force, because its defence industry does not perform well. Recent involvement of the private sector might improve the situation, but not in the short term.

India has proclaimed 'no first use' of nuclear arms which is conceivable with regard to Pakistan but not with regard to China which has powerful conventional armed forces. This politic supposes that the deterrent force includes, preferably, the three components of the army, air force and navy to avoid destruction of the majority of launching sites in case of a nuclear attack by the enemy. The missiles, Agni 3, have a reach of 3,000 kilometres, Agni 4 of 4,000 kilometres, and Agni 5 under construction, will have a greater reach up to 5,000 kilometres. The Agni 5 missiles can be more easily dispersed over Indian territory, which gives a better chance of survival faced with an enemy attack. The army presently operates Agni 3 missiles. The deployment of Agni 4 missiles should not be delayed. Agni 5 cannot be deployed in the near future. The supersonic cruise missiles, the Brahmas, which the army possesses, cannot attack distant targets because the reach is limited to 290 kilometres. These missiles are also available on board naval warships and will in the near future equip certain aircraft of the air force, which till now operates bombers.

A single nuclear launching submarine patrols the sea in an irregular episodic manner and additionally it is not really operational. A second submarine has been completed and a third is under construction. To render more credible the politics of the 'no first use' of nuclear arms India is seeking to build an anti-missile defence system. This is very difficult to achieve especially because the response time against the Pakistani for Chinese missiles would be short.

The reform of command structures which has been recommended for a long time now will appear increasingly necessary. The integration of military officers in the heart of the Defence Ministry is a necessity. A post of the chief of defence staff should be created. One should hope that the present reluctance in creating such a post on the civil side, particularly of the Defence Secretary, the highest functionary of the Ministry of Defence, as well as on the military side, specially the air force which fears a dilution of its means, will disappear.

The chief of defence staff will head the chiefs of staff of the army, air force and navy. At the moment, there is only an integrated defence staff under the authority of which are placed the Strategic Command and the Defence Intelligence Agency which is the intelligence service of the three forces and the Inter-Army Information Service.

Additionally joint commands of various theatres would be indispensable to replace the 17 higher commands which exist: 7 for the army out of which 3 are facing China, 7 for the air force and 3 for the navy. At the moment there is only one joint command in existence, that of the Andaman and Nicobar Islands. The actual existing complexity makes victory difficult and unpredictable.

Three operational theatres could be envisaged: the first would be destined to face China on the entire Himalayan range. It should be a joint army and air force command and commanded by an army general. The second would have for the responsibility of combat on the western border, against Pakistan; it would also be a joint army and air force command and so headed by an army general. A third operational theatre would group together army, air force and naval units and would have for its mission the defence of the maritime borders and their immediate ground surroundings. It should be placed under the command of an admiral. The generals at the head of the three operational theatres would have a certain liberty to take action.

Since no air marshal shall be given command of these three operational theatres, one air marshal should be given command of the Strategic Forces, presently divided between the three services—army, navy and air force. To put into action nuclear launching submarines, an admiral should be appointed as adjutant to the air marshal commanding the Strategic Forces. The latter would also have an adjutant from the army to be able to put into action the Agni missiles.

Three other joint commands, not geographical, but more thematic, will be created soon for Space defence (under the command of an air marshal), Cyber defence (under the command of an admiral) and Special Forces (under the command of an army general). Where Space is concerned, India has shown its technological abilities by destroying a satellite. Another joint command dedicated to logistics would be useful to economise on funds.

In matters of intelligence, integration is far from perfect. The school of intelligence of the army based in Pune in Maharashtra should become a joint services school and even accept interns from the paramilitary forces.

Indian preparations for a possible war with China in the Himalayas are extremely inadequate. Even before the beginning of battle, Indian soldiers find themselves in an extremely weak position. The forward posts are very badly equipped without any minimum comforts which should be indispensable in high altitudes. The land routes are sometimes badly conceived and too often impractical because of floods and landslides or even snows or avalanches. To make them useable throughout the year, they should be constructed on the slopes preferably not in the valleys which are regularly inundated. The passages which are the most snowed in should be abandoned and replaced by new roads through tunnels. Such tunnels being constructed in Himachal Pradesh and Kashmir between Manali and Leh and between Srinagar and Leh are taking too long a time to be completed. Certainly efforts are being made but they are quite insufficient. A west-to-east route will traverse Arunachal Pradesh and bridges that will permit the passage of heavy military convoys along with tanks have been recently constructed on the Brahmaputra. In this way, the transport of troops between Assam and Arunachal Pradesh will be facilitated and economic development will improve in the two states. Arunachal Pradesh has been claimed by China in totality and therefore needs more attention from Indian leaders. Real air bases need to be created as the existing runways do not permit the landing of large transport aircraft.

Civil security forces have diverse missions (surveillance of borders, of industrial infrastructure, of railways, of airports, ports, protection of strategic sites, of authorities, operations against insurgents, etc) and it is difficult for them to undergo a common training. They should be used only on the missions for which they have been trained. The Kashmir problem requires unique treatment. The civil security forces may give priority to recruiting locals.

The military and paramilitary forces must adopt new technologies based on artificial intelligence. China and the USA are highly advanced in this area. India should not be left behind. The use of robots to search for mines and hidden caches would increase the efficiency of the struggle against terrorists and reduce the number of mortalities in the security forces. Observation and attack drones will effective aids to the command. Terror outfits can however also procure drones. To protect oneself against these new aerial attacks there is a range of laser arms which can be used. Electronic warfare is also developing on both offensive as well as defensive fronts. Military headquarters have cognizance of this fact.

Internal social and economic problems continue to have consequences for security. Separatist movements will continue for a long time yet in Kashmir, and in the Northeast; the Maoist insurrection, although losing strength, may gather second wind in Bihar, Jharkhand, Chhattisgarh, Andhra Pradesh, Telangana, Madhya Pradesh, Maharashtra and Odisha.

Climate change will make it incumbent upon political parties to become more involved in order to meet the challenge. An urgent plan ought to be established in order to manage water resources. It should focus on recycling of used water, rainwater harvesting and replenishing groundwater. Inter-basin linkages which have been contemplated for a long time should be constructed, keeping in mind the political and ecological constraints. To the provisioning of water resources should be added measures to reduce demand. This can be achieved by a more rational drip irrigation system. Besides, the increase in population needs to be controlled. If these various measures aren't adopted, grave troubles will arise in villages, between different villages, in states and between states. Malevolent organisations could take advantage of these troubles to put in action their dark designs. A destabilising development due to terrorism would take place.

Civil administration should improve in order to face the challenges of the future. It is crucial to develop frontier regions giving priority to those on the China border because they are sparsely populated, isolated and lagging in social, educational and economic development, and are therefore vulnerable. New Delhi's action plans to improve all the frontier regions remain unsatisfactory. In Ladakh, which is a very sensitive area, seasoned functionaries ought to be placed and not inexperienced youngsters just out of Mussourie administration schools, as is the present case. The demands of the Ladakhis have been accepted. Ladakh has become an Union Territory in August 2019. This new status is not enough. Ladakh has two districts, Leh which is majority Buddhist, but where more and more Muslims are settling, and Kargil which is mostly Shia Muslim. In Ladakh, the overall the number of Shia Muslims is higher than that of the Buddhists and the latter resent this fact. Chinese activities could increase and propagate the idea that China can protect the Buddhists. The majority of Ladakhis continue to believe that their Buddhist brothers and sisters in Tibet do not have freedom and the practice of Buddhism is severely controlled in Tibet. But for how long?

The migration of other Indians to Kashmir was not permitted. With the abolition of the special status of Jammu and Kashmir which, without Ladakh, has become a Union Territory in August 2019, other Indians would be able to settle there, irrespective of their states of origin. These migrations would provoke protests from the Kashmir Muslims yet not so much reprobation from the international community, except of course, Pakistan. But with the abrogation of Article 370 later, the internal troubles in the state may be attenuated, even disappear altogether. To begin with, the return of the Pandits to the Valley, now exclusively Muslim, should be encouraged, with security assurances. Demographic modifications would improve security. There is a close relationship between demography and security. Demography can be an arm. To defend its politics, India could put forward the claim that Pakistan let Punjabis and Pashtuns settle in the part of Kashmir that it is under its administration. India could also state that China has reduced the Tibetans in Tibet and Uighurs of Xinjiang to silence by settling millions of Han there.

India makes efforts, with some success, to counter the Chinese installations in the Indian Ocean. In 1987, India did not hesitate to intervene in Sri Lanka, following an accord with the country, to try and put an end to the insurrection of the island's Tamils who wanted independence. This proved to be a failure but New Delhi has thus affirmed that it is willing to intervene across borders if it deems necessary. In 1988, India intervened successfully in the Maldives to end an attempted coup d'état. In future, India could again be ready to intervene if called upon by the governments of Sri Lanka or the Maldives. Actually, India should make it a priority to convince these governments not to harm its interests in any way, because the latter will be tempted by enticing Chinese offers.

India is securing its position in the international community which is beneficial for its security. It has now become part of the Australian Group regulating biological and chemical weapons, of the Wassenar Agreement regulating weapons and dual technologies and of *Missile Technology Control Regime* (MTCR) limiting the proliferation of missiles. But entry into the Nuclear Suppliers Group (NSG) is still closed to India because of opposition by China. In matters of counter terrorism, a dialogue has been started with the European Union and its member countries.

Past agreements with the USA consolidate the defensive and offensive positions of India. The *Logistics Exchange Memorandum of Agreement* (LEMOA) concluded in 2016 allows the Indian navy to use American infrastructures and vice versa. The *Communications Compatibility and Security Agreement* (COMCASA) signed in 2018 secures communications between Indian and American armed forces. A third agreement related to space is under discussion: the *Basic Exchange and Cooperation Agreement* (BECA).

The USA has imposed itself as a supplier of important armaments, which is new. This American hold will strengthen. The Americans have already sold maritime reconnaissance planes PI 8 Poséidon, ultra-light howitzers M-777, Apache attack helicopters, and Seahawk helicopters. To these weapon systems will be added others, including surveillance drones and later perhaps armed drones.

Common manoeuvres involving units of the army, air force and navy take place on a regular basis. The naval manoeuvre called Malabar, sometimes include Japanese ships.

Cooperation with the USA will become stronger as time goes by. Disengaging from Afghanistan, the USA will have less need of Pakistan. They will be tempted to have closer ties with India in the context of their deteriorating relations with China.

Russia continues to sell India arms but less than in the past. India acquired MiG 29 K loaded on aircraft carriers and will obtain performing surface-to-air SA 400 weapons systems, despite disapproval from America. India has also bought IL 76 to assure distance surveillance. The supersonic ballistic missiles, Brahmos ('Brah' for Brahmaputra and 'Mos' for Moskova) are manufactured jointly. Two frigates will be built in India with Russian transfer of technology. Further, a Russian nuclear attack submarine has been hired by the Indian Navy.

India and France signed in 2018 an agreement similar to the *Logistics Exchange Memorandum of Agreement* (LEMOA) signed with the USA. In this way, the Indian navy can benefit from refuelling in the Reunion, in Mayotte and in Djibouti. Six Scorpene submarines of French design constructed in the naval dockyards of Mumbai will equip the Indian navy; three are already in use. Common naval exercises called Varuna take place regularly between the two navies. The air force will acquire 36 Rafales. The *Indian Space Research Organisation* (ISRO) is cooperating with its French counterpart, the Centre National d'Études Spatiales (CNES) (The National Centre for Space Studies). This cooperation includes a military project for surveillance of the Indian Ocean.

Israel has become an important supplier. The two countries share common concerns in the fight against terrorism. Israel has worked successfully on tunnel detection systems which are interesting for India. Surface-to-air Barak 8 missiles have been delivered. Israeli radars equip the IL 76 AWACS aircraft. Armed drones may also be provided later.

In South-East Asia, Indonesia and more so, Singapore, have become privileged partners and will so remain, particularly in the maritime domain.

India could count on Bhutan's cooperation in a war against the insurrectional movements active in Assam, and the neighbouring states. In the past, combined police-military operations have taken place. Thimpu should state more firmly that it wishes to maintain the status quo on the Chinese border as long as it isn't clearly defined. It should in fact take into consideration the security interests of India that wishes to protect the narrow corridor between West Bengal and Assam. It ought to realise that Beijing is seeking to undo the strong ties existing between Bhutan and India. New Delhi on its part should take into consideration Bhutan's sovereignty and humour and understand the nationalistic susceptibilities of its citizens.

Due to the rapprochement between Kathmandu and Beijing, the cooperation of Nepal is more dubious. As for Bangladesh, it has dismantled a large number of the rear bases of separatist movements in the Northeast of India. Sri Lankan aid is acquired in the fight against Islamic extremists. Colombo also seeks India's assistance in the surveillance of separatist Tamil movements, and this it obtains from India. The Indian and Sri Lankan intelligence services are cooperating in the fight against all forms of terrorism.

Intelligence Services Hold the Highest Stakes?

Diverse intelligence services have specific missions. The *Intelligence Bureau* (IB) dating back to the British colonial era, is responsible for internal intelligence. It is therefore attached to the Union Home Ministry. It suffers from a paucity of personnel, especially regional language experts, such as the languages of tribals in the central part of the country and the Northeast. It ought to counter more effectively the Chinese propaganda and radical Islamist ideology, possibly with direct or indirect interventions with the print media and also television and radio.

The *Research and Analysis Wing* (RAW), created in 1968, is active outside the borders, and directly under the Prime Minister. It seeks especially to inform itself on the support received abroad by insurrectional movements active on

Indian territory. In order to achieve this aim, it is looking for cooperation with the intelligence services of friendly countries to monitor and possibly neutralise the most dangerous individuals. Cooperation functions well with the American and European services but less so with the Canadian services. Numerous deficiencies limit the capacities of the actions of the RAW, in particular the lack of experts in foreign languages including those of potential enemies (Urdu, Pushto, Chinese) and those where India has major interests (Arabic and Russian).

The *National Technical Research Organisation* (NTRO), set up in 2004, directly under the Prime Minister, gathers information in technical matters. The drones it possesses are improving listening capabilities. The *National Critical Information Infrastructure Protection Centre* (NCIIPC) created in 2014 to counter threats hovering over information systems, operates under the authority of the NTRO. The defensive and offensive capabilities in cyber space are insufficient. Recourse to specialists from the private sector would be necessary. India is vulnerable to cyber attacks. In an armed conflict, China would probably neutralise very rapidly government and services command networks.

In addition to these civilian organisations are the *Defence Intelligence Agency* (DIA), an inter-services intelligence institution created in 2002, and also the intelligence services of the army, navy and air force that have not been disbanded. In reality, the coordination between them is lamentable and the *Defence Intelligence Agency* has great difficulty in carrying out its missions.

In the past, the intelligence services has come under strong criticism. They had been unable to detect the Chinese army preparations in the months and years preceding the 1962 attack. They also failed to detect the Pakistani infiltration which triggered off the Kargil conflict in 1999. During the Indian military intervention in Sri Lanka from 1987 to 1990, their great lapse was a total lack of coordination, due, if truth be told, to the absence of a clear politics with regard to the Tamil insurgents. The intelligence services certainly learnt lessons from their failures, but as per several observers, their performance is still not up to the mark. Improvements are expected following better use of technical detection methods, especially satellites with a resolution within one metre. But research by human actors has progressed little, due to a lack of workforce and competencies. Since the end of 2018, intelligence services can control the Internet traffic of Indian citizens. The Aadhaar card system, based on biometrics, is also useful for them in identifying the entire population. These regulations have received unfavourable reactions from human rights associations.

Diplomacy in the Service of Security

India can boast of high quality diplomats. One from among them became the foreign affairs Minister. But the tool of diplomacy remains limited as the embassies haven't been sufficiently enhanced. A parallel diplomacy (*track 2 diplomacy*) involving erstwhile civil and military high officials, university researchers, diverse judiciary and scientific experts, constitutes a complementary body. It could be developed.

India denounces the indifference or the lack of firmness of the European countries and Canada vis-à-vis separatist Sikh militants. India is trying to put pressure on the international community so Pakistan satisfies the imperatives of the *Financial Action Task Force* (FATF), an organisation combating international terrorism financing.

The international community has a role to play to make India, Pakistan and Bangladesh realise the importance of population size. One billion and seven hundred million people live in South Asia. There is a population explosion. India as well as Pakistan ought to be receptive to the importance of the problem as has been already done in Bangladesh. Diplomats should work with demographers and scientists to put the brakes on the population explosion which generates tensions.

* * *

Asia is a continent of the future, which China, before imposing itself on the entire world, intends to dominate, taking the support of the neighbouring countries which it has subjugated, such as Pakistan to begin with. India must find its place in a region radically transformed by the growing power of China in all fields, the galloping population of Pakistan (multiplied by 7 since 1947) and that of Bangladesh more or less contained now (multiplied by 5 since 1947). In Pakistan, sectarian forms of Sunni and Shia Islam are active. From this country which has well equipped and well trained armed forces and a nuclear arsenal in the process of modernisation, radiate, towards neighbouring India, radical Islamist movements seeking to destabilise it by attacks in Kashmir and elsewhere.

Climate change concerns melting glaciers, diminishing groundwater tables, and changing monsoon patterns. The inadequacy of diminishing water resources and the needs of an increasing population and growing industrialisation would pose considerable security challenges. Grave troubles could be expected within provinces and between provinces. International water conflicts will also gain in intensity.

Confronted with internal and external threats, sometimes overlapping and likely to increase, India ought imperatively to make greater efforts to ensure the security of its citizens. This would include a substantial augmentation in the defence budget, but also a reorganisation of the armed forces command structures which are totally muddled. The three services should be equipped urgently with new generation materials and arms. In the immediate scenario, recourse to imports will become necessary, taking into consideration the infirmity of the defence industry. But in the long term, India should be capable of manufacturing the essential arms that it requires. It should not be left behind in high-tech. India's knowhow is well known in key areas such as information technology and space technology. But its glaring weaknesses are in the fields of aeronautics, naval and cybernetics. To improve these, contributions in technology to public and private enterprises, to arsenals and naval docks will be indispensible. Several countries are ready to cooperate. The Indian legislation however should be ready for liberalisation.

Paramilitary forces, which are mostly in the front lines in the battle against secessionist Islamic militants, radical Maoists, as well as in the guarding of borders, need greater attention. Local police forces will be increasingly needed with mounting social perils brought about by overpopulation and the lack of natural resources, primarily water.[2] In the coming years, the water issue will be at the heart of all security problems.

The armed forces and the paramilitary forces cannot work effectively without well-performing intelligence services. The latter need to fill their lacunae in personnel, the training of specialists, and equipment.

Faced with ecological threats, India needs to reinforce its infrastructure against natural catastrophes.

The government elected in 2019 has a free hand to carry out the indispensible reforms. It runs the country without having to answer to any alliance of parties. To face the considerable security challenges, the time has now come to act without procrastination whatever the economic constraints might be. It should not fail in its stately responsibilities.

Translated from the French by Mariam Karim Ahlawat.
(*French scholar, novelist, playwright*)

NOTES

1. See Alain Lamballe, *Asie du sud: bombes démographiques* in "Defense Nationale", Paris, Octobre 2017.
2. See Alain Lamballe, *L'eau en Asie du Sud: Confrontation ou cooperation?*, L'Harmattan, Paris, 2009.

2

India's Maritime Security: Challenges and Opportunities

Admiral Arun Prakash (Retd)

Our Forgotten Maritime Heritage

Many years ago, during a visit to Indonesia, I was shown around an old, Russian submarine, which had been converted into a museum. After an interesting walk-around, I asked my Indonesian guide what the submarine was named. 'Pasopati,' came the answer. I must have looked puzzled, because he explained, "It is another name for the Hindu god Shiva." Later I was to find that the motto of the Indonesian Navy was '*Jalaseva Jayamahe*,' Sanskrit for: 'On the Sea We Are Glorious'. In the heart of Bali I saw a magnificent statue depicting a scene from the *Mahabharata*; the final confrontation between Karna, son of Surya and Ghatotkach, son of Bhim.

My subsequent travels in SE Asia revealed many other cultural clues. The state emblems of both Indonesia and Thailand incorporate the *Garuda,* a humanoid bird from Hindu mythology. In monuments and paintings all over Indonesia, Thailand and Cambodia one comes across the recurrent theme of '*samudra manthan*', with *devas* and *asuras* churning the seas for *amrit*, with the serpent *Vasuki.*

While some of us may be aware of our close cultural linkages with SE Asia, most Indians have not given thought to how they were established, in foreign soil, so far from home? The answer is; that amongst our ancestors, were bold and proficient seafarers who, for centuries, ventured into the Bay of Bengal, as well as the Arabian Sea, to carry Indian art, culture, religions, languages—and trade—across thousands of miles of stormy seas. India has a great and ancient maritime tradition which has been forgotten, due to a malady that can be called 'sea blindness.'

The reason for our 'sea blindness' is, that as a nation, we have been indifferent to the reading as well as writing of history. Whatever little history we do study has been recorded by Western historians who dwell only on the maritime exploits of Greeks, Phoenicians, and Romans. Nowhere in any Western historical account does one find even a passing mention of the seafaring skills of ancient Indians.

The lone Indian voice in this arena is that of Sardar K.M. Panikkar, statesman, diplomat, and historian. According to him, due to the winds that accompany the cyclic SW and NE monsoons, it was the Indian Ocean and specifically the lands washed by the Arabian Sea which saw the first oceanic sailing activity. He clinches his extensive arguments by stating that, *"Millenniums before Columbus sailed the Atlantic and Magellan crossed the Pacific, the Indian Ocean had become a thoroughfare of commercial and cultural traffic between the west coast of India and the Middle East."*

He goes on to assert that Hindus mariners had in use a magnetic compass (*matsya yantra*) and possessed the skills to construct ocean-going ships, sturdy enough to venture into the distant reaches of the Arabian Sea. Panikkar then recounts the continuum of colonisation as well as cultural and religious osmosis by sea from India's east coast to SE Asia. Starting with the 4th century BCE Mauryan Empire, he traces Indian maritime activism through the Andhra, Pallava, Pandya, Chalukya and Chola dynasties. He concludes that Hindu influence could not have prevailed so far from home from the 5th to the 13th century without resolute and substantive maritime sustenance from the mother country.

By the early 11th century, however, Indian maritime power went into rapid decline, due to a prolonged naval conflict between the Sumatra-based Sri Vijaya Empire and the Chola rulers of South India. Thus, in 1498, when the Portuguese adventurer, Vasco da Gama, dropped anchor in Indian waters, the Sultanate of Delhi was ruled by the Afghan Lodhi dynasty, while southern India was divided between the Bahamini and Vijayanagaram kingdoms. Leave alone a navy, none of these rulers possessed the vision to think about the defence of India as a whole. But if a leadership-deficit was the primary cause of India losing its independence, neglect of technology was a crucial contributory factor.

During the 14th and 15th centuries, Europe had seen spectacular breakthroughs in the fields of shipbuilding and navigation. Not only had ships become larger and more seaworthy, they were equipped with sextants, compasses and charts for better navigation. While these inventions enabled safe long-distance voyages, it was the European superiority in weapon technology that tilted the balance in their favour. Thus, a few European warships carrying a battery of bronze cannons could repulse massed attacks by ill-armed native *ghurabs* and *gallivats* in Indian waters.

India's Maritime Awakening

It was against this backdrop that India's post-independence naval leadership struggled to remind their countrymen that India's security as well as prosperity was dependent on the oceans surrounding our peninsula. They were only partially successful, and the Indian Navy (IN) suffered neglect until it demonstrated, in the 1971 war, that the navy could be a powerful instrument of the state. The past two decades have, fortunately, witnessed certain key factors combining to bring about an awakening about the need to focus on maritime security.

Firstly, liberalisation during the 1990s brought India into the mainstream of world economy, which had become interlocked by the phenomenon of 'globalisation'. The dependence of India's economy on international trade and energy availability has grown dramatically highlighting the critical importance of Indian Ocean sea-lanes for our progress and prosperity.

Secondly, the upsurge of piracy and hijacking off Somalia in the past decade, clearly demonstrated the vulnerability of sea lanes and the serious consequences that disruption of shipping traffic could have on international trade and world economies. Closer home, the Mumbai terrorist strikes of November 2008 provided a grim reminder to India that its soft maritime underbelly could be neglected only at grave peril.

Finally, there was belated realisation in India's security circles that China's economic and military rise was likely to fuel its hegemonic ambitions and introduce animosity in its relations with neighbouring states. China has provided ample proof in the South China Sea and it seems a matter of time before the Indian Ocean could become an arena of maritime contention.

India's Maritime Interests

India occupies a dominant position in the IOR. Jutting a thousand kilometres into the ocean named after it, the Indian peninsula has a 7,500-km-long coastline containing 200 major and minor ports, with an exclusive economic zone of 2.5 million square km, rich with food and mineral resources.

As was just mentioned, India's economy is heavily dependent on foreign trade and energy imports, over 95 per cent of which come via Indian Ocean sea lanes. Located astride vital shipping lanes that run from the Persian Gulf to the Malacca Straits, India's island territories on both seaboards provide strategic maritime outposts with the Laccadive group lying across the Arabian Sea shipping lanes and the Andaman and Nicobar group keeping watch at the entrance to Malacca Straits.

India has a merchant fleet of about 1,200 vessels, displacing over 10 million tons. The waters of the Indian Ocean see over 100,000 merchantmen in transit, annually carrying cargo worth a trillion dollars. Both east-bound and west-bound shipping passes areas where it is vulnerable to interdiction or interference by state and non-state entities like pirates and terrorists. Nearly a hundred thousand Indian seafarers serve on ships of other nations, and their safety is always a concern. Thus, maintenance of 'good order at sea' is not only in India's interests, but has also become an international commitment.

While, the strategic importance of the Indian Ocean is self-evident, less well-known are India's rapidly growing interests in the Pacific. Almost, 55 per cent of India's trade with the greater Asia Pacific area transits through the South China Sea. The ONGC Videsh Ltd (OVL) is shipping crude oil extracted from its Russian Far East concessions to the Mangalore refinery. OVL has also been awarded offshore drilling rights in Vietnam's EEZ in the SCS, but work has been suspended due to China's maritime dispute with the Vietnamese.

In the 1990s, India had launched a vigorous 'Look East' policy in its quest for economic access to ASEAN nations. Upgraded to an 'Act East' policy, it has seen India establishing close rapport with Pacific nations such as Japan, Australia, Vietnam and Indonesia. Today, India's trading-links, investment and large Diaspora span an arc extending from Siberia in the east to Africa and Central

Asia in the west. Any attempts to dominate waters of the Indian or Pacific Oceans would represent a grave threat to India's vital interests.

As far back as 1890, American maritime strategist Admiral Mahan, acknowledging the importance of the Indian and Pacific oceans, had described them as future 'hinges of the world's geo-political destiny'. In his vision, control of this region could empower a maritime nation to influence political developments right across Asia and Europe. A hundred years, later, we find that the earlier expression, 'Asia-Pacific', is being replaced by a new term, the 'Indo-Pacific', which recognises the coupling of these two oceans by vital sea lanes. It also acknowledges some new realities such as a rising China and India and their overlapping interests across the Malacca Straits, India's emerging relationships with many Pacific nations and US interests across the region.

China's Maritime Rise

China, more than India, is reliant on the seas for its economic growth and has crafted a grand strategy based on a powerful navy to protect its seaborne trade and energy. In the early years of the last decade, China started making infrastructure investments in Indian Ocean ports as part of a coherent long-term strategy. By acquiring maritime footholds in Pakistan, Seychelles, Sri Lanka, Myanmar and Bangladesh, China was creating a network of facilities along its vulnerable sea lanes, which came to be known as the 'string of pearls'. With the subsequent launch of the 'Belt and Road Initiative', China has embarked upon a far more ambitious maritime agenda that will create a seamless swath of geo-political influence right across the Indo-Pacific.

Many other manifestations of China's unfolding grand strategy are emerging. Particularly worrisome is India's encirclement by a growing ring of Chinese power and influence. To the north garrisons, airfields and missile sites linked by modern road-rail networks underpin China's dominant posture on the Tibetan plateau. To our east, China's Yunan province will gain access to the Bay of Bengal via rail, highway and pipeline linking it to the deep-water port being built by China at Kyaukpyu in Myanmar. A parallel endeavour on India's western flank, dubbed the China-Pakistan Economic Corridor (CPEC), will create access to the Arabian Sea from Xinjiang to the Pakistani port of Gwadar via Gilgit-Baltistan.

Further west, China has set up its first overseas military base at Djibouti on the Bab el-Mandeb. To our south, China has built a new harbour in Hambantota and modernised Colombo port for Sri Lanka. All three ports could provide bases for PLA Navy ships and submarines deployed in the Indian Ocean.

China's Maritime Power

Ever since Xi Jinping designated the maritime domain as an essential building block of his 'China Dream', the Communist Party has brought sharp focus on it and overseen the systematic build-up of each element of national maritime power. The results are truly striking; China is today the world leader in shipbuilding and its 5,000-ship strong merchant marine ranks No.1 in the world. It also owns the largest number of coast guard vessels that protect the world's biggest fishing fleet.

Chinese shipyards are rapidly adding to its fleet of modern destroyers, frigates, diesel submarines and logistic support vessels. Its force of homebuilt nuclear submarines has been operationally deployed and its first aircraft carrier is at sea with more on the way. In a few years, the PLA Navy (PLAN) will overtake the US Navy in numbers and be second only in capability.

Looking landwards, heavy PLA deployment on the Tibetan plateau will ensure that the dice is loaded against India's land and air forces. Pakistan, enlisted by China as a 'cat's-paw' constitutes an integral part of the latter's foreign and security policies. In any conflict with India, the Sino-Pak axis will ensure that a second military front is opened for the other's benefit. The deployment of PLA Navy submarines in the Indian Ocean that commenced in 2013-14 was a clear indication that China seeks to not only gain strategic superiority across the Himalayas but also to establish maritime dominance in the Indian Ocean.

A Maritime Blueprint for the Future

As our decision-makers began to acknowledge the navy's role in state policy, a clear-cut roadmap became necessary to synergise our national maritime endeavours. During the past decade, the navy has promulgated a Maritime Doctrine as well as a Maritime Strategy with the aim of defining its aims, objectives, missions and force-architecture. These documents also serve the purpose of educating the political and security establishment, the bureaucracy, diplomats and the media about maritime security issues and the utility of naval forces in peace and in war.

The navy's share of the defence budget has traditionally remained well behind its sister services and tends to fluctuate from year to year. While fiscal stringency will demand a cautious approach, the approvals already accorded by the government to the Maritime Perspective Plan will place the IN amongst the top ranks of modern navies worldwide within the next decade or so. Let us look at how the navy's plans will be implemented.

Warship Building

One of the most significant decisions taken by the navy leadership, way back in the 1960s, was to initiate indigenous warship design and construction. Today, the navy's stature as well as operational capability owe much to the fact that its ships are largely designed and built at home.

There are four shipyards belonging to the MoD, one each in Mumbai, Kolkata, Goa and Vishakhapatnam, devoted to building naval vessels. They have, over the past five decades, constructed over 100 modern warships, including destroyers, frigates, submarines, corvettes, landing ships, tankers, patrol vessels, etc. A fifth shipyard, in Kochi, belonging to the Ministry of Shipping, has been engaged in building India's first aircraft carrier. In addition, a special facility has been established in Vishakhapatnam for building nuclear submarines.

While the navy derives great pride and satisfaction from the indigenous warship-building capability nurtured by it, there are a few areas of major concern. Firstly, a high proportion of the weapons, sensors and machinery that goes into these ships is imported and creates undesirable dependency on foreign sources. And secondly, the productivity of our shipyards remains low and will prevent the navy from reaching its required force levels within the given timeframes. Lastly, the exclusion of the private sector from defence production has hindered the progress of our warship building industry.

Submarines

In the case of submarine construction, India has lagged well behind China as well as Pakistan and our force is at a low of just 13 submarines against China's 70 and Pakistan's 15. We had undertaken the construction of two German designed submarines in 1990, but the programme was killed by shortsighted policymakers because of a corruption scandal. After a lapse of 15 years, another project to undertake construction of six Scorpene class French submarines was started in Mumbai. The first of these submarines has been delivered and the others will follow.

As an industrialised nation and a military power, the lack of submarine design and building competence has been a critical lacuna in India's maritime capability. The Indian Navy (IN) needs to create a force of at least 30 submarines to meet its operational commitments and the government must address this lacuna with a sense of urgency.

Aircraft Carriers

Coming to aircraft carriers; the IN acquired INS *Vikrant* in 1961 and for the past six decades, the aircraft carrier has formed the centrepiece of IN doctrine and strategy. After *Vikrant*, we acquired the *Viraat* from Britain and since 2013 we have been operating INS *Vikramaditya*, a former Russian carrier.

The navy started a project for design and construction of an indigenous aircraft carrier in the late 1980s but, for various reasons, construction was commenced only in 2005. The ship is nearing completion in Cochin Shipyard and may be delivered by 2020. It is likely to be followed by a larger carrier, for which specifications are being drawn up. If India's economic situation remains stable and there are no major technological problems, IN expects to have a force of three aircraft carriers at sea by 2030.

It is worth mentioning that China currently operates a former Russian aircraft carrier, and its first indigenously built carrier will soon be at sea. The PLA Navy plans to operate as many as six aircraft carriers by 2050 and some of them may be based in the Indian Ocean. It is also producing its own carrier-based aircraft.

Naval Aviation

Intense maritime activity in the Indian Ocean and the huge area that has to be kept under surveillance requires substantial maritime reconnaissance and anti-submarine warfare capabilities. The IN has evolved a multi-layered surveillance capability with a mix of long and medium-range aircraft as well as unmanned aerial vehicles (UAV). A new squadron of Boeing P-8 patrol and anti-submarine warfare (ASW) aircraft has been commissioned and eventually a force of 35-40 such aircraft will be required to meet demands of surveillance.

The navy's current carrier-borne fighter is the Russian MiG-29(K), which operates from the *Vikramaditya* and may fly from its next carrier. The indigenous Tejas, having failed to meet the navy's requirement, a search has commenced for another aircraft to equip future carriers. Today, every sizable warship is equipped with one or more helicopters for anti-submarine warfare and other roles. The Service is currently in the process of selecting a medium-sized helicopter from the international market to replace its older machines and the navy's helicopter fleet is set to grow dramatically.

As a regional navy with limited aspirations of safeguarding national interests, the IN would probably aim for a stabilised strength of about 180-200 ships and submarines, and possibly 350-400 aircraft and helicopters.

India's Nuclear Submarines

Strategic nuclear deterrence is an important mission of the IN because in comparison with land-based missiles and aircraft, a submarine is invisible and hence invulnerable. Armed with nuclear-tipped ballistic missiles, such submarines—termed SSBNs—can take up operational patrols in the Bay of Bengal or even the Arabian Sea from where they could target cities and nuclear forces deep inside adversary nations with impunity. Thus the July 2009 launch of INS *Arihant*—India's first home-built nuclear submarine—was a significant event.

The weapon currently slated for fitment on the *Arihant* is understood to be the *Sagarika* K-15 missile of about 750-km range. While this range is quite inadequate, the *Arihant*-K-15 combination forms an essential stepping-stone for India to achieve true capability for a sub-launched nuclear deterrent. Work is under way on ballistic missiles of 5,000-8,000-km range and the *Arihant* will, therefore, be followed by at least two more submarines armed with intercontinental ballistic missiles, which will give us a full-fledged underwater nuclear deterrent.

A second type of nuclear-powered submarine, which does not carry ballistic missiles, is called an 'attack submarine' or SSN. In comparison with the slow and short-legged diesel submarines, the SSN not only has a far superior reach, endurance and speed but also carries a potent weapon outfit. A Russian nuclear-powered attack submarine, taken on lease, was inducted into the navy in 2012 and re-named INS *Chakra*. Equipped with torpedoes and cruise missiles, *Chakra's* roles include protecting carrier battle groups and hunting enemy submarines interdicting enemy shipping. There are plans to build several nuclear attack subs in Vishakhapatnam in the near future.

This review would remain incomplete without mention of three vital areas of concern in the domain of maritime security which call for urgent attention.

India's Neglected Maritime Sector

Unlike their Chinese counterparts, Indian decision-makers have failed to comprehend that the navy, by itself, constitutes just one component of the country's maritime capability. Without the remaining elements, India's maritime power will remain hollow. Despite exaggerated claims, India's ports and infrastructure remain backward, our ship-building industry is stagnating, the merchant fleet is static, we lack a viable fishing-industry, our inland waterways are neglected and seabed exploitation is yet to commence. Above all, we have not cared to train manpower for all these sectors.

India's failure to focus on maritime capacity-building represents not just a huge economic 'missed opportunity' but also undermines its maritime power. We need to emulate China, which, as I pointed out earlier, is already a world leader in shipbuilding, and has the world's largest merchant marine as well as fishing fleets. Its coast guard is the largest and in a few years, its navy will be the world's second most powerful in the world.

The Indian Navy's maritime doctrines and strategies, as well as initiatives like 'Sagar' abroad and 'Sagarmala' at home, will lack logic and coherence unless backed by a comprehensive National Strategy for Maritime Security. The faithful implementation of this strategy will create urgently-needed capacities that will not only benefit our economy but also reinforce maritime security.

Lack of Industrial Support

As a colony, India missed the intellectual renaissance as well as the industrial revolution that transformed Europe during the 17th and 18th centuries. Independent India has, thus, gone from the status of an 'agrarian economy' to become a 'service economy'; leapfrogging the industrial phase. Today, India is seen as a military and economic entity with great-power aspirations on the basis of its size, population, growing economy and nuclear arsenal. Thus, India finds itself in an anomalous situation wherein it possesses nuclear weapons and the world's third or fourth largest armed forces, but has to support their operational needs through massive imports.

The Government of India owns a vast complex, dedicated to defence R&D and industrial production, which would be the envy of many nations. Ironically, while a willing and capable private sector has been excluded from defence production, public sector undertakings have failed to deliver for many reasons;

being engaged, merely, in assembly of imported kits while claiming 'indigenisation'.

Neither liberalised FDI nor the 'make in India' campaign are likely to have a substantive impact on defence production unless we acknowledge the imperative need for re-structuring of our military-industrial complex. True self-reliance in defence production can be attained only if the vast resources of the DRDO and DPSUs are disaggregated and re-cast on the lines of successful models in the UK, Israel or Singapore. Integration of the private sector into the new defence-production paradigm will help eliminate the inefficiencies of the Public Sector.

Maritime Diplomacy

While Indian commentators frequently express loud concern about China's economic and military inroads into the Indian Ocean, the challenge lies in evolving creative and dynamic long-term alternatives to offer our neighbours. An attractive option is to employ the navy as an instrument of maritime diplomacy.

Countries in India's immediate neighbourhood, many of them island nations, seek maritime security; sometimes through direct naval presence, but more often through urgent requests for material aid, training assistance and advice. Responding to such requests in a reasonable timeframe requires close coordination between NHQ, MoD and Ministry of External Affairs. Unfortunately, such coordination is not always forthcoming and our lack of response has led to missed opportunities in Sri Lanka, Bangladesh and in the Maldives.

Against this backdrop, India's recent agreement with Oman, providing access, for 'military use and logistical support' in the new port of Duqm, has raised hopes that India is, belatedly, strengthening its maritime posture in the Indian Ocean Region (IOR). There have been other significant developments too; like President Kovind's visit to Djibouti; the conclusion of an Indo-Seychelles agreement for creation of air and naval facilities on Assumption Island; and the agreement with the UAE for joint naval exercises.

Accords on parallel lines could be in the offing with Mauritius and the Maldives. Similarly, membership of the emerging US-Japan-Australia-India 'Quadrilateral' is being recommended as a hedge against Chinese hegemony in the IOR. Whether all these measures herald a renewed impetus to India's maritime outreach will depend on whether they are random actions or components of a carefully thought-through, overarching national maritime strategy.

Conclusion

I had opened with a reminder of India's glorious maritime past and of the weaknesses that crept in subsequently resulting in domination by foreign powers. India's maritime security suffered neglect for generations because 'sea blindness' and a 'continental outlook' led our ancestors to believe that the mighty Himalayas would safeguard them.

Today's maritime environment is more hazardous and our dependence on it more critical than it has ever been in history. Recent developments on our northern borders as well as in the IOR have served to restore sharp focus on the maritime domain. However, if the navy is going to play the role of a 'game changer', India must accord due importance to the demands of maritime security; not only by acquiring all the attributes of maritime power, but also by enhancing the level of maritime consciousness amongst India's politico-bureaucratic elite.

3

India's Quest for a Regional Security Architecture

Christian Wagner

South Asia has often been described as a region of chronic instability. This infamous reputation is the result of a complex mix of security challenges. On the one hand, there are traditional security challenges like territorial disputes or regional rivalries, for instance the Kashmir issue between India and Pakistan, the border conflict between India and China, or the contentious Durand Line between Pakistan and Afghanistan. On the other hand, the region also faces a plethora of non-traditional security challenges. Those range from climate change and environmental degradation, which increases migration and rapid urbanisation, to different forms of militancy sparked by ethnic separatism, religious extremism and left-wing violence, as well as trafficking in drugs, arms and humans. It is widely accepted that non-traditional security challenges require more and closer collaboration between the affected states. But interestingly the literature on regional conflicts in South Asia mostly emphasises the contentious bilateral issues whereas the increasing cooperation between India and its neighbours on security issues is often overlooked.

The paper argues that India is slowly establishing a regional security architecture in order to cope with different forms of militancy. In order to elaborate the argument, the first part will lay out a conceptual framework. The second part will look at India's relations with its SAARC neighbours at the bi- and multilateral level. It is beyond the scope of this contribution to deal with the complexities of each aspect of the bilateral relationships. The focus will therefore primarily be on aspects of collaboration in the field of security and related matters as, for instance, in the judicial arena. The final part will put India's security cooperation in the context of its South Asia policy.

1. Security Architecture: A Conceptual Framework

Conceptual debates on security architecture start with the Conference on Security and Cooperation in Europe (CSCE). When the Helsinki Accords were signed in 1975, the CSCE included 35 countries from the Western and Eastern bloc which agreed to undertake permanent consultations and confidence-building measures (CBMs). They included first, military and security issues; second, economic, scientific, and technological cooperation; and third, human rights issues. The CSCE was regarded as a successful institution that helped overcome the antagonisms of the Cold War by diplomatic means. Its documents and agreements were not international treaties, but constituted a framework of norms, procedures and regulations. After the end of the Cold War, the CSCE was transformed into the Organisation for Security and Cooperation in Europe (OSCE).

The academic debate on security architecture was influenced by the seminal work of Tow and Taylor. They define security architecture as "an overarching, coherent and comprehensive security structure for a geographically-defined area, which facilitates the resolution of that region's policy concerns and achieves its security objectives."[1] Although the concept has been developed in the context of inter-state rivalries and conventional security challenges, i.e., Cold War antagonism, Tow and Taylor have pointed out that it can be used against non-conventional security threats as well.[2]

The definition of Tow/Taylor is also a useful tool to analyse the constellations in South Asia. First, the "geographically-defined area" can be equated with the member countries of the South Asian Association for Regional Cooperation (SAARC). Second, it is also possible to identify the "region's policy concerns" and "security objectives." Although the international attention is on the danger of a nuclear escalation between India and Pakistan, many South Asian countries have dealt with or still facing different forms of militancy and terrorism. There are also criteria that indicate a process towards an "overarching, coherent, and comprehensive security structure." "Overarching" signals that the efforts take place both on the bi- and multilateral level. "Coherence" refers to the political statements of governments, which emphasise the common security threat and the desire for closer collaboration. An example of a non-coherent policy would be, for instance, Pakistan's position on 'good' and 'bad' militant groups. "Comprehensive" implies that policies are not only confined to political statements, but would also include collaboration between the security forces including the police, and the creation of a legal framework, as for instance, through extradition treaties or mutual legal assistance treaties.

In recent years, the debate on security architecture has focussed on East and South East Asia.[3] In contrast, the debate in South Asia is still in a nascent stage. The attempts for closer security cooperation are focusing on India-Pakistan relations or the prospects of collaboration on non-traditional security challenges.[4] There have been various suggestions for a "cooperative security framework," a "strategic architecture" or a "regional security architecture" that should deal with the different security challenges in South Asia in a comprehensive way.[5]

Given the complex conflict constellations in South Asia, a comprehensive security architecture similar to the CSCE will not be possible. But the argument can be made that the various efforts in the field of security cooperation that India is pursuing with its neighbours since the 2000s may lead in the mid to long term to a unique security architecture against terrorism in South Asia. So this article continues the debate that was started by Pattanaik/Nayar who noted that, "Once non-traditional issues become the drivers of security cooperation they will open up new vistas in defence cooperation and the management of military security in the region."[6]

2. The Bilateral Level

India's approach to security in South Asia has seen several phases. Nehru secured India's interests vis-à-vis the Himalayan kingdoms by a system of friendship treaties. The approach of Indira and Rajiv Gandhi to pursue India's security interests by keeping great powers out of the region resulted in various interventions; for instance in Sri Lanka and the Maldives in the late 1980s. The economic liberalisation after 1991 also changed India's approach towards the region. The focus shifted towards economic cooperation with the "Gujral doctrine" emphasising the principle of non-reciprocity in India's bilateral relations, in 1996. The "Manmohan doctrine" highlighted the need for greater connectivity and economic collaboration in the 2000s. His remark that India should be a security provider for the region and the Indian Ocean was taken up by Prime Minister Modi and has led to new initiatives in the field of security cooperation.[7]

But India's regional ambitions have hardly been shared by its neighbours who have often regarded India as their main security concern. In reaction, all of them have played the 'China card' at some point of time, or have intensified their relations with other great powers in order to evade Indian pressure. Economically, China and other great powers have always been more attractive partners for India's neighbours. In the field of security, India was also only one and not necessarily the most important partner for its neighbours, for instance with regard to arms imports and training.

Hence, India has an ambivalent relationship with its South Asian neighbours. At the negative end of the spectrum are its relations with Pakistan. Four wars since 1947, three of which were over Kashmir and numerous bilateral incidents and tensions, illustrate the difficult relationship. On the positive side are relations with Afghanistan, Bhutan and the Maldives which have been smoother most of the time. Somewhere in between are relations with Bangladesh, Nepal and Sri Lanka which have been marked by periods of both cordiality and deep aversion. The overall context of these respective bilateral relationships has shaped—both positively and negatively—India's attempts for closer security cooperation with its neighbours.

Afghanistan

India and Afghanistan have traditionally had good bilateral relations, which are a result of their common rivalry with Pakistan. Afghanistan has laid territorial claims on the Pashtun areas of Pakistan and has still not recognised the Durand Line as the international border between the two countries. Afghanistan was also the only country that voted against Pakistan's accession to the United Nations (UN). Pakistan linked its disputes with India and Afghanistan, after the withdrawal of the Soviet Union from Afghanistan. In the 1990s, Pakistan supported the Taliban in Afghanistan in order to achieve "strategic depth" against India. After the attacks of 9/11 and the international intervention in Afghanistan, India has also stepped up its support for the government in Kabul. India is the biggest non-Western donor in Afghanistan and has invested more than two billion US dollars.

The Strategic Partnership agreement of 2011 laid the basis for the military cooperation. India has increased its logistical support and the training opportunities for the Afghan Security Forces.[8] With the partial withdrawal of international forces, India gave in to American requests and increased its training capacities for Afghan officers.[9] India has also started to train members of the Afghan Police Force.[10] In July 2013, India turned down the request of the Afghan government for the supply of "lethal" weaponry but continued its support for training, transport and logistics.[11]

In April 2015, India agreed to supply three Cheetal helicopters to Afghanistan.[12] India also gave four MI-25 attack helicopters to Afghanistan and will support the maintenance of the Afghan Air Force in collaboration with Russia.[13] In 2015-16, the Indian Air Force trained 193 pilots from Afghanistan.[14]

Moreover, both countries signed a Mutual Legal Assistance Treaty (MLAT) in order to strengthen intelligence cooperation and to improve collaboration in criminal matters.[15] Although India is among the largest donors in Afghanistan, it is thus far only a marginal player, compared to Western countries, with regard to the training of the Afghan National Army.[16]

Bangladesh

In 1971, India supported the Mukti Bahini in the civil war in East Pakistan and its military intervention in December led to the independence of Bangladesh. The leadership of the new government under the Awami League (AL) was initially close to India, but the Bangladesh Armed Forces always remained sceptical about India. The Peace and Friendship Treaty of 1972 which included a clause on security, was never fully implemented, because of the resentment within the Bangladeshi army.[17]

The bilateral relations have been marred by issues like the demarcation of the border and illegal migration. But the main bone of contention was camps of militant groups in Bangladesh and the infiltration of Islamic terrorists into India. In 2002, India handed over a list of 99 camps of different militant groups in Bangladesh.[18] But the BNP government of Prime Minister Khaleda Zia who collaborated with religious parties that presumably had links with militant groups did not take action against these camps.

The military relations with India improved during the military caretaker regime in Dhaka. The visit of army Chief Moeen Ahmad to India in 2008 paved the way for closer military cooperation. After the victory of the Awami

League in the 2008 elections, the security collaboration further improved. In February 2009, both countries held their first joint anti-terror exercise.[19] In 2010-11 similar exercises were held in Assam in India and Sylhet in Bangladesh, followed by naval exercises.[20] In 2010, agreements on Mutual Legal Assistance in Criminal Matters, on the Transfer of Sentenced Persons and on Combating International Terrorism, Organised Crime and Illicit Drug Trafficking were signed, improving the legal collaboration between the two countries. In 2011, a framework agreement for cooperation and development, that also included a clause for closer security cooperation, was signed.[21] In January 2013, both countries agreed on an extradition treaty in order to strengthen the fight against terrorism and cross-border crime.[22] During the visit of Prime Minister Sheikh Hasina to India in April 2017, a Memorandum of Understanding (MoU) for defence cooperation was signed, which will further expand the security cooperation. Moreover, India gave a line of credit of US $500 million to Bangladesh, which was especially for defence purchases. So far this was the largest line of credit for defence given to any country.[23]

India's security cooperation with Bangladesh, compared to all other South Asian countries, seems to have made the greatest progress since 2009. The number of military interactions has increased but also the institutional framework with a variety of new treaties, has improved the bilateral relationship.[24]

Bhutan

India has a long standing extensive military collaboration with Bhutan. The Friendship Treaty of August 1949, gave India substantial influence in the handling of the kingdom's international relations. The treaty also allowed India to protect its security interests in the Himalayan region vis-à-vis China. In reaction to the Chinese takeover of Tibet, India helped to set up a national militia in Bhutan in 1958, which developed into a standing army in 1963.[25] In the same year, the Indian Military Training Team (IMTRAT) was set up to support the training of the Bhutanese forces.[26] Starting in 1975, India was also instrumental in establishing the Royal Bhutan Police (RBP) by training the first instructors.[27]

In 2003, the military cooperation between both countries entered a new phase. Since the 1990s, militant groups from India's Northeast had been setting up camps in the southern part of Bhutan. In December 2003, the Bhutanese Army started a large-scale military operation and destroyed 30 such camps by January 2004.[28] The Indian Army did not take part in the fighting but supported the Bhutanese forces logistically and with medical services.[29]

Both countries have established the India-Bhutan Joint Group on Border Management and Security.[30] In 2013, the total strength of the Royal Bhutan Army (RBA) was 10,000.[31] In 2015-16 India reserved 575 places for Royal Bhutan Army and Royal Bhutan Guards personnel in its training institutions, which is more than five per cent of the total number of the RBA.[32]

The strong security cooperation between the two countries became visible in 2017 when India supported Bhutan against incursions from China which culminated in the Doklam crisis between the two Asian giants.[33]

Maldives

Security collaboration with the Maldives started in 1988, when India helped President Gayoom to put down a coup by dissidents who were supported by Tamil militants from Sri Lanka.[34] At that time, the small island state had neither a regular army nor a navy, but only a national security service of about 1,400 men.[35] In 2005, the Maldives sent a military attaché to its embassy in Delhi in order to strengthen military relations. In 2006, India donated a patrol boat to the Maldivian Navy. Since 2009, the Indian and Maldivian forces have held annual military exercises, and the navies undertake joint manoeuvres and patrols.[36] India has integrated the Maldives into the surveillance system of its own islands by setting up radar units in the Maldives and through surveillance flights undertaken by the Indian Air Force over the island state.[37] In summer 2016, India and the Maldives held their first Defence Cooperation Dialogue. India is also offering training to the members of the Maldivian National Defence Forces (MNDF). Moreover, in 2013, India, the Maldives, and Sri Lanka signed an agreement for closer cooperation in fighting piracy, terrorist networks and trafficking.[38]

Nepal

After Bhutan, India's most enduring military relations in South Asia have been with Nepal. The Peace and Friendship Treaty of 1950 regulated the bilateral relationship with the Himalayan kingdom and restricted the monarchy's international room for manoeuvre in favour of India.[39] Military collaboration started already in 1952 when King Tribhuvan sought the help of an Indian military support team for the reorganisation of the Royal Nepalese Army.

Nepal's open border creates special security challenges for India. First, during the Maoist rebellion in Nepal, India feared a closer cooperation with left-wing extremists groups in India. Hence, the government in New Delhi mediated between the monarchy, the democratic parties, and the Maoists which led to the peace agreement in 2006. Second, the open border has always been an entry point for Islamic militants from Pakistan. The hijacking of an Indian Airlines flight in December 1999, during which India had to release three high-ranking militant leaders, started in Kathmandu. In summer 2013, two leading terrorists—Abdul Karim Tunda who is regarded as one of the chief ideologues of the Lashkar-e-Taiba (LeT) in Pakistan, and Yasin Bhatkal who is perceived to be a co-founder of the Indian Mujahideen (IM)—were arrested at the Nepal border.[40]

In order to cope with the challenges, India and Nepal have established a series of new institutions. These include the Nepal-India Bilateral Consultative Group on Security Issues, the Joint Working Group on Border Management, and the Border District Coordination Committee.[41] India has also supported the training and equipment of the Nepali Police. Formal and informal networks have supported cross-border cooperation among the security agencies on both sides and have bolstered the fight against terrorism and counterfeit currencies.[42]

Pakistan

Despite the four wars and the various bilateral crises,[43] India and Pakistan have also developed some confidence-building measures in the nuclear, conventional, and non-conventional fields.[44]

In the conventional field, the first hotline between the Directors General of Military Operations (DGMOs) over the Line of Control in Kashmir was established after the war in 1971. Since 1991, both sides have agreed to announce military manoeuvres and large troop deployments.[45] In November 2003, both sides agreed on a ceasefire at the Line of Control. During the composite dialogue from 2004 to 2008 the Indian Coast Guard and the Pakistan Maritime Security Agency set up a hotline and agreed on a memorandum of understanding to avoid incidents at sea in 2005.[46] In 2006, both countries agreed to give pre-notification of test flights of ballistic missiles.[47] In the nuclear field, the Indian Prime Minister Rajiv Gandhi and the Pakistani Prime Minister Benazir Bhutto agreed to exchange lists of the nuclear installations that should not be attacked in case of war in 1988. In 2007, they signed an agreement to reduce the risk of accidents with nuclear weapons.[48] During the composite dialogue, India and Pakistan have even been able to establish a Joint Anti-Terror Mechanism (JATM) in 2006. Both sides shared information on terrorist attacks, for instance on the Samjhauta Express in 2007 and on the attack on the Indian embassy in Kabul in 2008.[49] The Mumbai attack in November 2008 put an abrupt end to the composite dialogue.

The hope that the new governments of Nawaz Sharif in 20013 and Narendra Modi in 2014 would bring a better bilateral relationship has not materialised. There have been some positive signs in the field of security, for instance in 2015, when the national security advisors met in Bangkok or in January 2016, when Pakistan could send a team to India to investigate the Pathankot attack.[50] In March 2016, India was warned by Pakistan about another attack by militants.[51] But after the terrorist attack in Uri in September 2016, which was followed by surgical strikes from India, the Modi government has refused any form of dialogue with Pakistan as long as terrorist groups are operating from Pakistani territory.

Sri Lanka

India had an ambivalent role in the ethnic conflict between the Singhalese and the Sri Lanka Tamils. In the early 1980s, India trained and supported various militant Tamil groups. In 1987, when India and Sri Lanka signed an accord, the Indian Peace Keeping Forces (IPKF) which was deployed in Sri Lanka became responsible for disarming the Liberation Tigers of Tamil Eelam (LTTE).[52] The operation turned into a military and political fiasco for India because the Sri Lankan government and the LTTE turned against New Delhi. In 1990, the IPKF had to leave Sri Lanka. In 1991, the LTTE assassinated Prime Minister Rajiv Gandhi during the election campaign in Tamil Nadu.

India did not have an official role in the peace process mediated by Norway that led to the ceasefire in 2002. In October 2004, India and Sri Lanka agreed to expand their military cooperation in the fight against the LTTE's shipping fleet and its supply lines.[53] India supported the training of the Sri Lankan police and the armed forces and provided military equipment.[54] The intelligence cooperation between the two countries contributed to the military defeat of the LTTE in May 2009.

Since then the two sides have further expanded their security cooperation. In 2011, New Delhi and Colombo agreed to hold an annual defence dialogue. India offered 1,400 places in its training institutions for Sri Lankan security forces, and the naval forces conducted joint military exercises in Sri Lankan waters for the first time.[55] In January 2013, both sides signed an Anti-Terror Agreement.[56] India's support for the training of the Sri Lankan forces seems to be substantial because nearly 80 per cent of their officers complete parts of their training in India.[57] The Sri Lankan Air Force personnel filled 367 of the vacancies of a total of 889, reserved by the Indian Air Force for Friendly Foreign Countries in 2015-16.[58] The Easter bombings in Sri Lanka in April 2019 have demonstrated that the Islamic State (IS) poses a common challenge although India has given information about the potential danger of an attack to the Sri Lankan authorities in advance. The transnational security threats emanating from terrorist groups like the IS underlines the necessity for more security cooperation between affected countries.

3. The Multilateral Level

Security considerations initially played an important role, when Bangladesh floated the concept of a regional organisation in South Asia in the late 1970s. The idea was that the smaller South Asian countries could use a regional institution as a bulwark against India's dominant role in the region. But when SAARC was established in 1985 contentious issues were excluded from its agenda. Nevertheless, the member states have often used SAARC summits to discuss informally bilateral conflicts, such as the tensions between India and Pakistan and the Tamil issue in Sri Lanka at the highest political level.

SAARC has only few instruments for security cooperation. Already in 1987, the SAARC members had agreed on a Regional Convention on Suppression of Terrorism. It underlined the shared concern against different forms of terrorism even if the convention was never implemented because India and Pakistan could not agree on a common definition of terrorism.[59] Following the UN declaration 1373 of September 28, 2001, SAARC passed the Additional Protocol to the SAARC Regional Convention on Terrorism.

In 1992, the interior ministers established the SAARC Drug Offences Monitoring Desk in Colombo in order to bundle information about the regional networks for drug trafficking. In 1995, the SAARC Terrorist Offences Monitoring Desk was set up in Colombo, in order to collect and exchange information on terrorist activities.[60] Since 1996 the heads of police of all SAARC members held annual meetings to discuss cross-border crimes like arms, drugs, human trafficking and money laundering.[61] Since 2006, the member states have been discussing the creation of SAARCPOL, a common regional police institution that would work on the lines of Interpol.[62] In 2008, all states agreed on the SAARC Convention on Mutual Assistance in Criminal Matters but it has not been ratified by all the members. The overall context of SAARC remains too weak to provide a fresh impetus for security cooperation.[63]

For India, BIMSTEC (the Bay of Bengal Initiative for Multi-Sectoral Technical and Economic Cooperation) seems to have become a more attractive regional platform to promote security cooperation. In reaction to the Uri attack in September 2016, India boycotted the SAARC summit in Islamabad. Other South Asian countries supported the Indian boycott so that the summit had to be postponed. The Indian government used the BIMSTEC summit in Goa, in November 2016, to forge a regional consensus against terrorism. First, it invited Afghanistan and the Maldives which were not members of BIMSTEC but of SAARC. Second, the outcome document of the BIMSTEC Goa Summit underlined the joint commitment against terrorism and emphasised India's efforts to foster security cooperation in the region.[64] In March 2017, the national security advisors of the BIMSTEC member states met for the first time to discuss common security challenges including cross-border terrorism.[65] Hence, India may foster BIMSTEC as an important regional institution not only for economic collaboration, but also for closer security cooperation.

4. India's Emerging Security Architecture in South Asia

India has intensified its security cooperation with most of its South Asian neighbours in recent years, on various levels. Although the process remains dependent on the overall bilateral relationship, the contours of India's security architecture are slowly becoming visible. First, the fight against terrorism has become the overarching topic in India's relations with its neighbours, both at the bi- and multilateral levels. The topic is highlighted in nearly all official documents and declarations. Moreover, India's efforts have also expanded to legal instruments like extradition treaties.

But India's approach also faces several challenges. First, the biggest problem is the overall nature of the bilateral relationships. New government constellation after elections can bring about changes on bilateral security issues like cross-border militancy as past experiences with Bangladesh or Sri Lanka have shown. Second, the implementation of bilateral security arrangements is often hampered by the lack of capacities in the police and the judiciary in most South Asian countries. Third, although India aspires to be a security provider it is not the only player in this field and often only of secondary importance for its neighbours, for instance on arms imports. India's main advantage is in "soft" security, i.e., its training capacities and sometimes "hard" security like joint operations. But training for security forces is also offered by other countries, and moreover, unlike China, India is not an arms exporter to its neighbours so far.

India's efforts to foster a more comprehensive regional security collaboration since the 2000s are a positive development. The rising cooperation among security forces and the increase in the numbers of legal instruments for countering militancy also indicate that the threat perception of the respective governments vis-à-vis non-state actors is converging. Today, security in South Asia is sought more and more through inter-state cooperation rather than by confrontation. This may be a small but nevertheless important achievement. It signals a major departure from the past and may open up new avenues for a more stable and peaceful South Asian region.

NOTES

1. William T. Tow Brendan Taylor, "What is Asian security architecture?" *Review of International Studies*, 36, 2010, p. 96.
2. William T. Tow, Brendan Taylor, *op cit.* p. 112.
3. Muthiah Alagappa (ed.), *Asian Security Order: Instrumental and Normative Features,* Stanford: Stanford University Press, 2003; Amitav Acharya, Evelyn Goh (eds.), *Reassessing Security Cooperation in the Asia-Pacific,* Cambridge: The MIT Press, 2007.
4. Alyson J. K. Bailes, "Regional Security Cooperation: A Challenge for South (and North-East) Asia", *Strategic Analysis,* 31 (4), 2007, pp. 665-674; Yang Xiaoping, *The Security Architecture of South Asia: Problems and Prospects,* New York: The New School, India China Institute, 2012, https://www.indiachinainstitute.org/resources/publications/workingpapers/ , (Accessed on May 3, 2017); Mahin Karim (ed.), *The future of South Asian Security. Prospects for a Nontraditional Regional Security Architecture,* Washington: The National Bureau of Asian Research, 2013.
5. S.D. Muni, "Strategic architecture in South Asia: Some Conceptual Parameters", in Nihar Nayak (ed.), *Cooperative Security Framework for South Asia,* New Delhi: Pentagon Press, 2013, pp. 3–11; Smruti S. Pattanaik, Nihar Nayak, "Does South Asia Need a Regional Security Architecture?" in: Nihar Nayak (ed.), *Cooperative Security Framework for South Asia,* New Delhi: Pentagon Press, 2013, pp. 52–68.
6. Smruti S. Pattanaik, Nihar Nayak, "Does South Asia Need a Regional Security Architecture?" in Nihar Nayak (ed.), *Cooperative Security Framework for South Asia,* New Delhi: Pentagon Press, 2013, p. 67.
7. Vinay Kumar, "India Well Positioned to Become a Net Provider of Security: Manmohan Singh," *The Hindu,* May 23, 2013, http://www.thehindu.com/news/national/india-wellpositioned-to-become-a-net-provider-of-security-manmohansingh/article4742337.ece (Accessed on May 23, 2013).
8. Nitin Gokhale, "India All Set to Train Afghan Army," *New Delhi Television,* November 17, 2011, http://www.ndtv.com/article/india/india-all-set-to-train-afghan-army-150491 (Accessed on November 17, 2011).
9. Chidanand Rajghatta, "America Persuades India to Expand Afghan Footprint," *Times of India,* June 14, 2012, http://articles.timesofindia.indiatimes.com/2012-06-14/us/32234576_1_afghanistan-and-pakistan-afghan-national-armyafghan-military-personnel

10. Government of India, *Ministry of Home Affairs, Annual Report 2009–2010*, New Delhi, 2010, p. 115.
11. "India Turns Down Afghanistan's Arms Plea," *The Hindu,* July 5, 2013, http://www.thehindu.com/news/international/south-asia/india-turns-down-afghanistans-armsplea/article4884695.ece
12. Ministry of External Affairs, Joint Statement during the State Visit of President of Islamic Republic of Afghanistan to India, April 28, 2015, http://mea.gov.in/bilateral-documents.htm?dtl/25137/Joint_Statement_during_the_State_Visit_of_President_of_Islamic_Republic_of_Afghanistan_to_India_April_28_2015 (Accessed April 30, 2015).
13. Dinakar Peri, "India to restore grounded aircraft in Afghanistan", *The Hindu*, November 27, 2016, http://www.thehindu.com/news/national/India-to-restore-grounded-aircraft-in-Afghanistan/article16711883.ece (Accessed November 27, 2016).
14. Government of India, *Ministry of Defence, Annual Report, 2015-16,* New Delhi 2016, p. 136.
15. Rahul Tripathi, "India set to sign treaty with Afghanistan to share intelligence, co-operation in dealing crimes", *Economic Times*, April 27, 2015, http://articles.economictimes.indiatimes.com/2015-04-27/news/61578046_1_legal-assistance-treaty-extradition-treaty-proceeds-and-instruments (Accessed on April 27, 2015).
16. Vishal Chandra, "Afghanistan's National Army: Expectations and Scepticism", in Vishal Chandra (ed.), *India's Neighbourhood: The Armies of South Asia,* New Delhi: Pentagon Press, 2013, pp. 8-10.
17. Smruti S. Pattanaik, "Bangladesh Army: Evolution, Structure, Threat Perception, and its Role", *op. cit.* p. 38.
18. Kanchan Lakshman, Sanjay K. Jha, "India-Bangladesh: Restoring Sovereignty on Neglected Borders," in K.P.S. Gill (Hg.), *Faultlines, Bd. XIV*, 2003, South Asia Terrorism Portal, http://www.satp.org/satporgtp/publication/faultlines/volume14/Article7.htm (Accessed on January 10, 2014).
19. Smruti S. Pattanaik, "Bangladesh Army: Evolution, Structure, Threat Perception, and its Role" *op. cit.*, p. 38.
20. "Indo-Bangla Military Cooperation Increasing," *The Times of India*, November 22, 2011, http://articles.timesofindia.indiatimes.com/2011-11-22/pune/30428193_1_military-exercise-bangladesh-army-bangladesh-military-academy (Accessed on January 10, 2014); "India-Bangladesh Border Guards Joint Border Patrol," *NorthEast Today,* August 8, 2012, http://www.northeasttoday.in/our-states/meghalaya/india-bangladesh-border-guards-joint-border-patrol/ (Accessed on April 9, 2013).
21. Smruti S. Pattanaik, "Bangladesh Army: Evolution, Structure, Threat Perception, and its Role", *op. cit.* p. 39.
22. See Binodkumar S. Singh, "India–Bangladesh: Continuous Consolidation," *South Asian Outlook,* March 2013, http://www.southasianoutlook.net/index.php/issue/2013/41-march/498-india-bangladesh-continuous-consolidation (Accessed on January 10, 2014).
23. Suhasini Haidar, "Teesta hangs fire as Sheikh Hasina arrives", *The Hindu,* April 06, 2017, http://www.thehindu.com/news/national/teesta-hangs-fire-as-bangladesh-pm-sheikh-hasina-arrives/article17855609.ece (Accessed on April 06, 2017); "Sheikh Hasina India visit: Transformative visit", *The Hindu,* April 11, 2017, http://www.thehindu.com/opinion/editorial/transformative-visit/article17913764.ece (Accessed on April 11, 2017).
24. Joyeeta Bhattacharjee, "Bangladesh: Strengthening defence cooperation with India", http://

orfonline.org/cms/sites/orfonline/modules/weeklyassessment/WeeklyAssessmentDetail.html?cmaid=91876&mmacmaid=91877&volumeno=VIII&issueno=49 (Accessed on December 11, 2015).

25. Anand Kumar, "The Royal Bhutan Army", in Vishal Chandra (ed.), *India's Neighbourhood: The Armies of South Asia,* New Delhi: Pentagon Press, 2013, p. 72.
26. Government of India, *Ministry of Defence, Annual Report 2011–2012,* New Delhi 2012, p. 190.
27. Anand Kumar, "The Royal Bhutan Army", *op. cit.* pp. 74-75.
28. "Bhutan's Army Launched First Attack in Its History to Help India," *Pakistan Defence,* September 6, 2010, http://www.defence.pk/forums/military-history-strategy/71854-bhutans-army-launched-first-attack-its-history-help-india.html#ixzz2PxI9yMQ5 (Accessed on April 9, 2013).
29. Dipankar Banerjee, Bidhan S. Laishram, "Bhutan's 'Operation All Clear': Implications for Insurgency and Security Cooperation", New Delhi: Institute of Peace and Conflict Studies, 2004 (*IPCS Issue Brief 18*), p. 1.
30. Government of India, *Ministry of Defence, Annual Report 2005–20*06, New Delhi 2006, p. 198.
31. Anand Kumar, "The Royal Bhutan Army", *op. cit.*, p. 75.
32. Government of India, *Ministry of Defence, Annual Report 2015-16,* New Delhi 2015, p. 19.
33. Suhasini Haidar, "The crossroads at the Doklam plateau", *The Hindu,* July 26. July, 2017, http://www.thehindu.com/opinion/lead/the-crossroads-at-the-doklam-plateau/article19359848.ece (Accessed on July 26, 2017).
34. Ravinatha Aryasinha, "Maldives, Sri Lanka and the 'India Factor,'" *Himâl Southasian,* March 1997, http://old.himalmag.com/component/content/article/2650-maldives-sri-lanka-and-the.html (Accessed on May 3, 2017).
35. Alok Bansal, "Maldives' Security Dilemma and its National Defence Force", in Vishal Chandra (ed.), *India's Neighbourhood: The Armies of South Asia,* New Delhi: Pentagon Press, 2013, p. 93.
36. Government of India, *Ministry of Defence, Annual Report 2015-16,* New Delhi 2015, p. 44.
37. Manu Pubby, "India Bringing Maldives into Its Security Net", *The Indian Express,* August 13, 2009, http://www.indianexpress.com/news/India-bringing-Maldives-into-its-security-net/501583 (Accessed on April 25, 2013); Rajat Pandit, "India to Further Bolster Defence Cooperation with Maldives," *The Times of India,* April 15, 2013, http://articles.timesofindia.indiatimes.com/2013-04-15/india/38555022_1_indian-ocean-region-india-and-maldives-maritime-patrol-and-surveillance; Vinay Kumar, "India, Maldives Holding Joint Military Training Exercises," *The Hindu,* November 12, 2012, http://www.thehindu.com/news/national/india-maldives-holding-joint-military-training-exercises/article4091069.ece (Both accessed on January 10, 2014). The Andamans and Nicobars in the Gulf of Bengal as well as the Lakshadweep Islands, which are north of the Maldives, belong to India.
38. Vijay Sakhuja, "Maritime Security and Piracy: Issues, Responses and Multilateral Cooperation in South Asia", Berlin: Konrad-Adenauer-Stiftung, 2013 (*EU-Asia Dialogue, Research Paper*); Government of India, *Ministry of Defence, Annual Report 2014-15,* New Delhi 2015, p. 49; Meera Srinivasan, "Indian Ocean Security Pact Signed," *The Hindu,* July 9, 2013, http://www.thehindu.com/news/international/south-asia/indian-ocean-security-pact-signed/article4898042.ece (Accessed on January 10, 2014).

39. S.D. Muni, *Foreign Policy of Nepal*, Delhi: Saraswati Printing Press, 1973, pp. 283–287.
40. Devesh K. Pandey, "'LeT Ideologue' Tunda in Police Custody," *The Hindu*, August 17, 2013, http://www.thehindu.com/news/national/let-ideologue-tunda-in-police-custody/article5031691.ece; Rahi Gaikwad, "Indian Mujahideen Co-founder Yasin Bhatkal Arrested," *The Hindu*, August 29, 2013, http://www.thehindu.com/news/national/indian-mujahideen-cofounder-yasin-bhatkal-arrested/article5070960.ece (Both accessed on January 10, 2014).
41. Akanshya Shah, "Nepal: Terrorist Arrests and Cooperation with India," *South Asia Weekly Report 6*, Observer Research Foundation, September 6, 2013, http://www.orfonline.org/research/nepal-terrorist-arrests-and-cooperation-with-india/ (Accessed on May 3, 2017).
42. B. Raman, "Rise of Maoists in Nepal. Implications for India," *Indian Defence Review* 23 (3), July–September 2008, p. 128.
43. Sumit Ganguly, *Conflict Unending: India-Pakistan Tensions since 1947*, Oxford: Oxford University Press, 2002.
44. For an overview on civilian and military confidence-building measures, see Stimson Center, South Asia Confidence Building Measures (CBM) Timeline, https://www.stimson.org/content/south-asia-confidence-building-measures-cbm-timeline-0 (Accessed on May 3, 2017).
45. "Confidence-Building and Nuclear Risk-Reduction Measures in South Asia," *Stimson Research Pages*, June 14, 2012, https://www.stimson.org/content/confidence-building-and-nuclear-risk-reduction-measures-south-asia (Accessed on May 3, 2017).
46. Government of India, *Ministry of Defence, Annual Report 2005–20*06, New Delhi, 2006, p. 198.
47. "Agreement between India and Pakistan on Pre-Notification of Flight Testing of Ballistic Missiles," *Stimson Research Pages*, October 24, 2012, https://www.stimson.org/agreement-between-india-and-pakistan-on-pre-notification-of-flight-tes (Accessed on May 3, 2017).
48. "Agreement on Reducing the Risk from Accidents Relating to Nuclear Weapons," *Stimson Research Pages*, February 21, 2007, https://www.stimson.org/agreement-on-reducing-the-risk-from-accidents-relating-to-nuclear-weap (Accessed on May 3, 2017).
49. See Shabana Fayyaz, Indo-Pak Joint Anti-Terrorism Mechanism. Perspectives from Pakistan, New Delhi: Institute of Peace and Conflict Studies, 2009 (*IPCS Issue Brief 126*), http://www.ipcs.org/pdf_file/issue/IB126-Ploughshares-Shabhana.pdf (Accessed on January 10, 2014).
50. Abdul Manan, "Pathankot attack: Pakistan to send special investigation team to India", *The Express Tribune*, January 13, 2016, http://tribune.com.pk/story/1026743/pathankot-attack-pakistan-to-send-special-investigation-team-to-india/ (Accessed on January 13, 2016).
51. Praveen Swami, "Pakistan NSA warned Ajit Doval of 26/11-type hit on Maha Shivratri", *The Indian Express*, March 7, 2016, http://indianexpress.com/article/india/india-news-india/delhi-gujarat-on-high-alert-following-terror-threat-security-beefed-up/ (Accessed on March 7, 2016).
52. S.D. Muni, *Pangs of Proximity. India and Sri Lanka's Ethnic Crisis*, New Delhi: Sage Publications, 1993.
53. "India's Naval Surveillance Big Help—FM," Ministry of Defence and Urban Development, Sri Lanka, December 30, 2010, http://www.defence.lk/new.asp?fname=20080605_01 (Accessed on January 10, 2014).
54. V.S. Sambandan, "Sri Lankan Police to Be Trained in India," *The Hindu*, September 29,

2005, http://www.hindu.com/2005/09/29/stories/2005092901211300.htm.

55. R.K. Radhakrishnan, "India Offers Training Slots for Sri Lankan Military Personnel," *The Hindu*, December 28, 2010, http://www.thehindu.com/news/international/india-offers-training-slots-for-sri-lankan-military-personnel/article1011469.ece (Accessed on January 10, 2014).
56. "India, Sri Lanka Sign Anti-terror, Tax Evasion Pacts," *The Hindu*, January 22, 2013, http://www.thehindu.com/news/national/india-sri-lanka-sign-antiterror-tax-evasion-pacts/article4332894.ece (Accessed on January 10, 2014).
57. Meera Srinivasan, "Navy Cadets of India, Sri Lanka Speak the Same Language," *The Hindu*, April 20, 2013, http://www.thehindu.com/news/international/south-asia/navy-cadets-of-india-sri-lanka-speak-the-same-language/article4636943.ece (Accessed on January 10, 2014).
58. Government of India, *Ministry of Defence, Annual Report, 2015-16*, New Delhi, 2016, p. 136.
59. P.R. Chari (ed.), *Perspectives on National Security in South Asia: In Search of a New Paradigm*, New Delhi: Manohar Publishers, 1999; Iftekherrazaman (ed.), *South Asia's Security: The Internal Dimension*, Dhaka: Academic Publishers, 1994.
60. SAARC Secretariat, "SAARC Terrorist Offences Monitoring Desk (STOMD)," http://saarc-sec.org/areaofcooperation/detail.php?activity_id=24 (Accessed on January 10, 2014).
61. SAARC Secretariat, "SAARC Conference on Cooperation in Police Matters," http://saarc-sec.org/areaofcooperation/detail.php?activity_id=20; "SAARC Home Ministers' Conference Concludes," *The Economic Times*, October 25, 2007, http://articles.economictimes.indiatimes.com/2007-10-25/news/27667901_1_saarc-home-ministers-islamabad-assistance-in-criminal-matters (Both accessed on January 10, 2014).
62. "Rare Blend. Regional Police Force, SAARCPOL, May Become a Reality Soon," *Force*, September 2012, http://www.forceindia.net/SepCoverstory14.aspx (Accessed on January 10, 2014).
63. Sumit Ganguly, Counterterrorism Cooperation in South Asia: History and Prospects, Seattle: National Bureau of Asian Research 2009 *(NBR Reports 21)*; Sandy Gordon, "Regionalism and Cross-Border Cooperation against Crime and Terrorism in the Asia-Pacific," *Security Challenges* 5 (4), Summer 2009, pp. 93–94.
64. "BIMSTEC Leaders' Retreat 2016 Outcome Document", Website of Narendra Modi, October 17, 2016, http://www.narendramodi.in/bimstec-leaders-retreat-2016-outcome-document-532768 (Accessed on November 25, 2016).
65. Dipanjan Roy Chaudhury, "BIMSTEC National Security Advisers strive to create common security space amid rising multiple threats," *The Economic Times*, March 22, 2017, http://economictimes.indiatimes.com/news/defence/bimstec-national-security-advisers-strive-to-create-common-security-space-amid-rising-multiple-threats/articleshow/57766714.cms (Accessed on March 31, 2017).

4

Emerging Trends in India's National Security

Maj Gen Dhruv C. Katoch (Retd.)

For nation-states, national security would mean securing the National Interest—but what constitutes the National Interest (NI) must first be determined and then clearly stated. Broadly, the NI could be seen in terms of the survival of the nation-state, wherein the minimum requirement would be the protection of its physical, political and cultural identity against encroachments by other nation-states.[1] These remain the primary and vital interests of a state, which cannot be compromised and which must be defended at all costs.

The above formulation, when placed in specifics for a nation-state, would encompass the preservation of, one, the territorial integrity of the state; two, the preservation of the existing politico-economic structure and three, the preservation of the nation-state's ethnic, religious, linguistic and historical norms and traditions. Post the First World War, American policy makers such as President Woodrow Wilson, while formulating their nation's foreign policy, drew upon the work of scholars and philosophers like Sir Alfred Zimmer, Nicholas Murray Butler and others who dedicated their efforts to promoting a more peaceful world and was essentially Utopian in concept. Post the Second World War, American foreign policy was driven by a sense of realism, promoted by the work of authors such as Hans J. Morgenthau, Hallet Carr, Reinhold

Niebuhr and others.[2] Indeed, Henry Kissinger credited Morgenthau with making the study of international relations into a major discipline.

In India, post-independence, the decision makers were not associated with an institutionalised doctrinal approach to foreign policy-making. Though attention to India's foreign policy making has attracted major intellectual inputs, it remains insulated from outside influence. India's national security policy-making process too has not yet been institutionalised, nor has it defined the incorporation of stakeholders and their role. The policy is personality driven and remains highly individualistic and hostage to those who are in key decision-making roles, with hardly any publicly accepted inputs from non-partisan strategic planners or experts belonging to think-tanks, the academia or public intellectuals.[3]

Shri Jaswant Singh, who in the Vajpayee-led government (1998-2004) held at various times the important portfolios of Defence, External Affairs and Finance, expounded on this aspect in 1995. He spoke of a document called the Operational Directive, which "seeks to bring out as clearly as possible, under the given circumstances, the threat situation which has been visualised in consultation not only with the three Services but the various agencies, the Ministry of External Affairs and, when necessary, with the Home Ministry in consultation with the Prime Minister's Office and, finally, it is approved by the Defence Minister".[4] He further went on to state that "the contents of this document required considerable change because of the enormous change that has taken place or is taking place not only in our immediate vicinity but all round....Now if you were to ask, is this the defence policy, I would not be able to say that the answer is in the affirmative because India's defence policy, to the extent that I can venture to make a statement on it, from 1947 onwards— more precisely from 1950 onwards—has been basically a policy to defend our territory, our sovereignty and our freedom, and no more than that".[5]

This very clearly brings out the fact that India at that time did not have a declared defence policy. The situation has not changed much until date in terms of a clear enunciation of a national security policy, which has led some Indian and foreign strategic thinkers to state that India lacks a strategic culture. Foremost amongst them, George Tanham came to the conclusion that Indian political elites showed little evidence of having thought coherently or systematically about national strategy, reasoning that the forces of history and culture had worked against the cultivation of a strategic mindset.[6] This however betrays a limited understanding of India and its civilisational construct of over five thousand years. We have the example of Kautilya's *Arthashastra*, which propounds the science of governance including the relationship with other powers, kingdoms and rulers. Hindu scriptures, the *Mahabharata* and the *Ramayana*, *Hitopadesa*, *Manu Smriti*, *Bhagavatam Purana* and others, all have large sections devoted to statecraft and external relations. So to state that India lacked strategic thought would not be accurate. India has a sense of history and is very clear of what it wants to be. It wants rapid domestic growth, abolition of poverty, national unity and equality. It is not looking to burning bridges, but will stand up for what is right and just, with a world view based on equality and non-discrimination.[7]

The objectives then of India's National Security, would be threefold: first, national stability and integrity; second, social political and economic progress; and third, peace and stability in terms of India's relationships with other countries across the globe. India's national security as an essential component to securitise its national interest must be seen in terms of these larger goals.[8] In effect, this would encompass ensuring a safe environment within the country, free from internal and external threats and a dynamic foreign policy to enable social, political and economic progress of the nation.

Changing Global Economic Scenario: The Rise of Asia

In the 17th century, Asia was the envy of Europe with India and China alone having nearly half the world's share of GDP. The Indian economy went into a state of decline at the beginning of the 18th century, though China continued to prosper for another hundred years before slipping into rapid decline at the turn of the 19th century, a period referred to by Chinese scholars as the century of humiliation, denoting the period between the First Opium War in 1839 and the end of the Chinese civil war in 1949.[9] A turnaround started towards the close of the 20th century as seen in Figure 1.[10] By 2000 CE, Asia accounted for just over a third of the world output. This is set to equal the output of the rest of the world in 2020, and thereafter surpass the economy of the rest of the world, marking the world's imminent entry into the Asian age. This is taking place, not just because of the growing economies of India and China, but also due to growth among smaller and midsize countries in Asia.[11] (See Figure 2)[12]

The reversal of the Asian decline has set in motion changes in the geopolitical landscape of the world, with nation-states coming to grips with an altered reality.

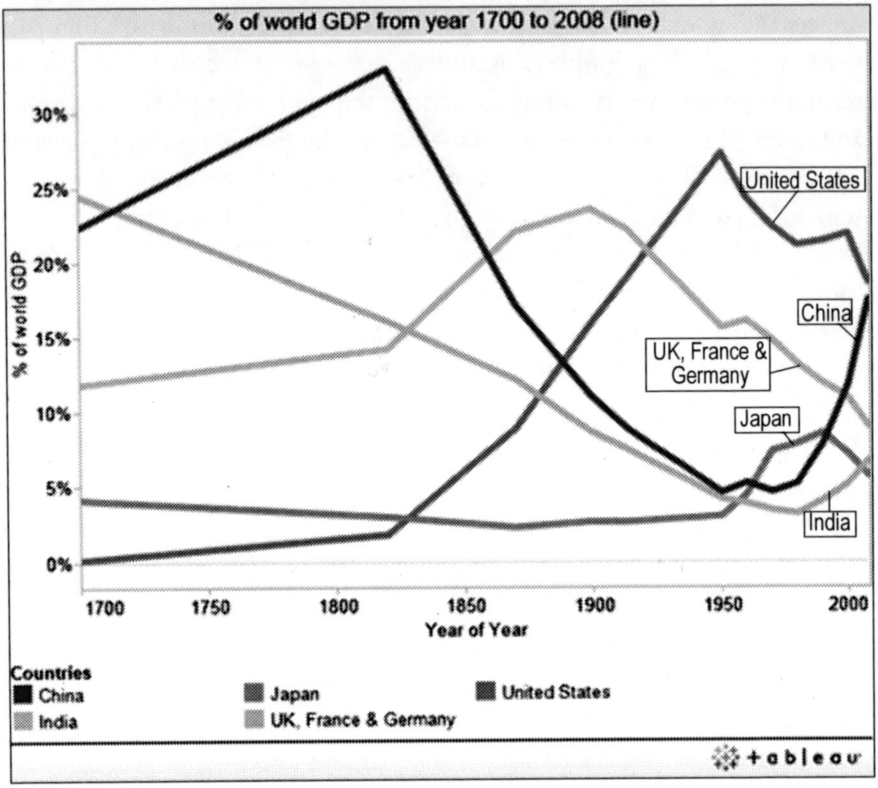
% of world GDP from year 1700 to 2008 (line)
30%
25%
20%
15%
10%
5%
0%
% of world GDP
1700
1750
1800
1850
1900
1950
2000
Year of Year
United States
China
UK, France &
Germany
Japan
India
Countries
China
India
Japan
UK, France & Germany
United States
+ableau

Fig. 1

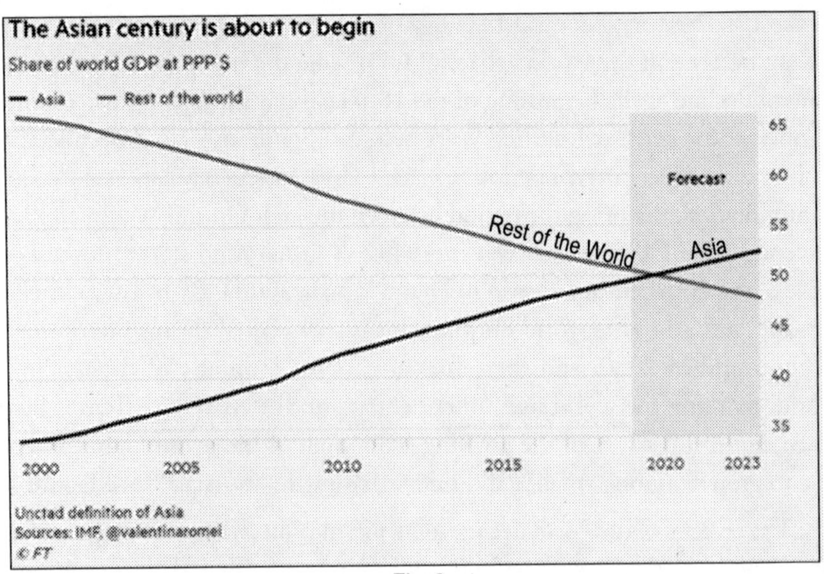
The Asian century is about to begin
Share of world GDP at PPP $
Asia
Rest of the world
Forecast
Rest of the World
Asia
65
60
55
50
45
40
35
2000
2005
2010
2015
2020
2023
Unctad definition of Asia
Sources: IMF, @valentinaromei
© FT

Fig. 2

The Chinese leadership is conscious of China's growing economic clout and has characterised the first two decades of the 21st century as a "period of strategic opportunity," to facilitate domestic development and the expansion of China's "comprehensive national power." China is leveraging its growing economic, diplomatic, and military clout to establish regional pre-eminence and expand the country's international influence.[13] In the 19th National Conference of the CPC, President Xi Jinping laid emphasis on a "great rejuvenation of the Chinese nation." He outlined China's ambition to emerge as a superpower by 2049, which will mark the centenary of the establishment of the People's Republic of China (PRC). Timelines to achieve those targets are the full modernisation of the PLA by 2020, emerging as a socialist modernised country by 2035 and having a world-class army and the eventual attainment of superpower status around the middle of the century.[14]

India's foreign policy too, under the Modi-led NDA government, has seen great transformational changes since 2014. Prime Minister Modi has led the transformation, which is clearly visible and is now seen to be more bold, proactive, innovative and ambitious—and also clearly showing an uncompromising firmness on issues relating to the nation's integrity and honour. While traditionally, India has been looked at as a notoriously reticent nation in international affairs, it is now being seen as proactive in its engagements with the international fora. There is a greater expectation of India's role in the world, as reflected by India emerging as a natural participant in several regional and global discourses. Another important transformation has been the rekindling and strengthening of India's linkages with its Diaspora, cooperation in the field of counter terrorism, emphasis on the neighbourhood with significant progress taking place in terms of physical and cultural connectivity and on a renewed economic vigour.[15]

China now views itself as the natural competitor to the USA, and seeks a bipolar world with China being the second pole. Within Asia, China views India as its only economic and geo-strategic rival. Regardless of any churning which may take place in the internal power dynamics in China's ruling Communist party, Beijing's policy towards Delhi will continue to be shaped by its desire to achieve pre-eminence in the region. There will thus be renewed competition between India and China, but there will also be cooperation.

The India-China Relationship

The driving force in the India-China relationship is political, with the governments of the two countries determining its shape and content. The people and the media have had little role to play in shaping this relationship; however, since the mid-Eighties, people-to-people interaction has enabled broadening and stabilising the relationship to some extent. Chinese perceptions of and policies regarding India have had greater continuity and focus than Indian perceptions of and policy towards China, largely due to the different nature of the polity of the two countries. Primarily, the focus of both has had a heavy security component. Since the mid-Eighties however, there is an increasing emphasis on development issues, helped in no small measure by a consensus that the 'development of one would in no way constitute a threat to the other'. History, however, imparts to both India and China the same need to restore a feeling of national pride, a need that each fulfils in parallel quests for greater international standing. In this paradigm, Beijing's policy towards Delhi will continue to be assertive, shaped by its desire to achieve pre-eminence, initially in the region and by 2050 in world affairs. Today, a combination of historical circumstances, cold war rivalry and a competition for resources is setting the agenda for the way the two nations perceive each other. While commonality of interests exists in some areas that widen the field for further cooperation, other factors are pushing the two countries towards the path of rivalry and confrontation in pursuance of each nation's perceived self-interest.

The India-China relationship remains strained, largely due to India's unsettled border with Tibet. Today, the relationship can be categorised as stable at the strategic level, but marked by political, diplomatic, and military instability at the tactical level.[16] The major irritant in the relationship is the unresolved border issue, which has the potential to lead the two countries to conflict. China illegally occupies the Aksai Chin plateau in Ladakh and also lays claim to the Indian state of Arunachal Pradesh. While the McMahon Line is the effective boundary between India and China, its legal status is disputed, as China does not accept the validity of the 1914 Simla Accord. India thus has both a territorial as well as a boundary dispute with China, which has the potential to lead to conflict in future. Massive upgradation of infrastructure in Tibet by China has a distinct military bias and is a cause of concern to India as it greatly enhances Chinese military capability across the Himalayas. When considered with growing military asymmetry including nuclear capability, the threat to India increases exponentially. It must be noted that China has moved away from its earlier theme of peace as the dominant trend, to stating that some conflicts may be inevitable. It is in this respect that India needs to be prepared to thwart any hostile activity by China across the Himalayas.

For many years, China has supported insurgencies in India's Northeastern states and continues with transgressions across the undemarcated Line of Actual Control (LAC). On the diplomatic front, China has been particularly assertive in recent years, continuously blocking Indian attempts to become a member of the Nuclear Suppliers Group and resisting India's attempt to seek a place on the high table as a permanent member of the UN Security Council. For long, it resisted India's efforts to list Masood Azhar, the founder of the Pakistan-based Jaish-e-Mohammad—a UN-designated terrorist group, to be labelled a terrorist by the 1267 Sanctions Committee of the United Nations Security Council (UNSC) and only relented on this on 1 May 2019, after China dropped its long-held objections to the move. Beijing had earlier put a "technical" hold on the 1267 UN resolution in March, the fourth time it had scuttled India's attempt to sanction the man it holds responsible for multiple terror attacks in India. China also needlessly objects every time an Indian political leader visits Arunachal Pradesh. But it is the collusive nuclear warhead-ballistic missile-military hardware nexus between China and Pakistan, described by both as an 'all-weather friendship,' which is of major concern to India.

Post the 1962 Sino-Indian conflict, the relations between India and China remained frozen for 26 years, thawing finally with the visit of the then Indian Prime Minister Rajiv Gandhi to Beijing in 1988. A slew of confidence-building measures started in September 1993, with the signing of the Agreement on the Maintenance of Peace and Tranquillity along the Line of Actual Control in the India-China border, which was followed up in 1996, 2005 and in 2012. However, to prevent border incidents from flaring up, the Border Defence Cooperation Agreement (BDCA) was signed by the two countries in October 2013. The BDCA reiterated the provisions of most of the earlier CBMs, but in addition, provided for additional mechanisms for the maintenance of peace in a situation involving a direct face-off between the soldiers of the two countries, such as Article VI which stipulates that the two sides shall not follow or tail patrols of the other side in areas where there is no common understanding of the LAC.[17] While the border has remained peaceful, with no incidents of firing since then, the possibility of a flare-up still exists as seen in the India-China border stand-off for 70 days in Doklam—a tri-junction between Bhutan, India and China. The statements issued by the Chinese government-controlled media during the course of the crisis including *Global Times*, *Xinhua* and others, as well as by spokespersons of the foreign and defence ministries of China went ballistic in condemning India. Offensive epithets were used to threaten India to withdraw or to face the consequences, which would be far worse than the defeat of 1962. India however stood its ground, and China was eventually forced to back off, marking a victory for the Indian stand,[18] and highlighting India's firmness and resolve, on issues relating to the nation's integrity and honour.

The Doklam face-off further strained relations between the two countries, but a reset took place with Prime Minister Modi meeting his Chinese counterpart, President Xi Jinxing, in Wuhan in April 2018.[19] The two leaders are set to meet again at an informal summit, this time in India, later in 2019.

Despite differing perceptions on many issues between India and China, India's approach in dealing with China has been one of pragmatism, wherein the focus has been on compartmentalising the problems and not letting the differences turn into disputes or disputes into conflict. Today, there is substantial economic engagement between the two countries as also an ever increasing people-to-people contact. There is also substantial cooperation on regional, multilateral and global issues, a prime example being on climate change. But despite the many positives, there is a need to reset the relationship in a new paradigm, as the relationship has entered a more challenging phase, though remaining as a mix of competition and cooperation.

There are growing concerns in India about China's increased assertiveness, and about China's regional and global ambitions. China is no longer seeking a multi-polar world, but seeks bipolarity and in the hierarchical order, aims eventually to replace the USA and occupy pole position. This is in strong contrast to India, which would like to see not only a multi-polar world, but also a multi-polar Asia. The India under Modi has a vision for the country that is distinct from the kind of approach taken earlier about India's role as a balancing power—a non-aligned power. That terminology fortunately lies buried now, and in its place is a new found assertion of Indian interests and what that means for India. This will lead to contestation, as India will not bow down to any foreign power. In the long term, the India-China relationship will hence be a difficult one to manage. India's core concerns will remain the economic upliftment of its people, technological advancement, military modernisation and gaining its rightful place under the sun. In this process, it would not like to be sidetracked by any distractions from China or any other power in the region.

China's Assertiveness in the Region

China's "One Belt, One Road," now renamed the "Belt and Road Initiative" (BRI), is intended to develop strong economic ties with other countries, shape their interests to align with China's, and deter confrontation or criticism of China's approach to sensitive issues. Countries participating in BRI could develop economic dependence on Chinese capital, which China could leverage to achieve its interests. For example, in July 2017, Sri Lanka and a Chinese state-owned enterprise (SOE) signed a 99-year lease for Hambantota Port, following similar deals in Piraeus, Greece, and Darwin, Australia.[20]

China seeks to secure its objectives without jeopardising the regional stability that remains critical to the economic development that has helped the CCP maintain its monopoly on power. However, China is also willing to employ coercive measures—both military and non-military—to advance its interests and mitigate opposition from other countries. For example, in 2017, China used economic and diplomatic pressure, unsuccessfully, in an attempt to urge South Korea to reconsider the deployment of the Terminal High-Altitude Area Defence (THAAD) system.[21]

In its regional territorial and maritime disputes, China continued construction of outposts in the Spratly Islands, but also continued its outreach to the South China Sea claimants to further its goal of effectively controlling disputed areas. China also maintained a consistent coast guard presence in the Senkakus.[22]

The Pakistan Factor

Chinese desire to contain India finds a willing ally in Pakistan. Here, the interests of both Beijing and Islamabad converge. The nuclear, missile and military hardware nexus between the two is well known and is a cause of serious concern for India. China is Pakistan's largest defence supplier and is widely perceived to be using Pakistan to fight its proxy war against India, to counter Indian power in the region and to divert Indian military force and strategic attention away from China. It also provides a bridge between Beijing and the Muslim world, a geographically convenient trading partner, and a channel into security and political relations in South Asia. For Pakistan, China is a high-value guarantor of security against India. Chinese officials also view a certain degree of India-Pakistan tension as advancing their own strategic interests as such friction bogs India down in South Asia and interferes with New Delhi's ability to assert its global ambitions and compete with China at the international level. China is also expanding its footprints in Nepal, Myanmar, Bangladesh and Sri Lanka, which leads to a perception within India of being hemmed in by the Chinese. When viewed with Chinese capability to support insurgent groups in Northeast India and to Left Wing Extremists, India's concerns deepen.

India is also concerned about China's Belt and Road Initiative (BRI), the crowning jewel of which is the China-Pakistan Economic Corridor (CPEC), connecting China's Xinjiang province to Gwadar in Balochistan, Pakistan. In April 2015, President Xi Jinping signed agreements with Pakistan over development projects worth USD 46 billion, focussed on building a 3,000-km (1,800 miles) CPEC. This corridor will connect Pakistan's deep-sea port Gwadar, located in the Arabian Sea, to China's western Xinjiang region. International analysts see this CPEC as President XI Jinping's biggest gambit in the One Belt One Road strategy. The projects under development are now assessed to be in the range of USD 62 billion.

Indian concerns over the CPEC pertain primarily to issues of sovereignty. In its annual report submitted to Parliament on 11 July 2018, the Union Defence Ministry bluntly stated, "The CPEC passing through Pakistan-occupied Kashmir challenges Indian sovereignty."[23] A large number of Chinese labour along with military personnel are also located in Gilgit-Baltistan, which has grave security implications for India.

Many in Pakistan, especially those in the military, see the completion of the CPEC as a possible game changer in the region, which could lift Pakistan out of poverty. That view is however now being contested as most of the economic benefits will go to Chinese hands. In the Gwadar port complex itself, where the expectation is that one million tons of cargo will be handled annually, 91 per cent share of the revenue from the operations of the port and the terminal and 85 per cent of the revenue generated by the free zone will go to Chinese companies. There is also the underlying fear that such a huge investment could result in a debt trap for Pakistan, much on the lines of the Hambantota port in Sri Lanka, which China has now taken over on a lease for 99 years. There are also fears that the CPEC may not reach fruition, primarily because it passes through territory which is increasingly being contested. In Balochistan, the ongoing freedom movement, which keeps cropping up off and on since 1947, is major source of concern for the Pakistani establishment. The current struggle of the Baloch people against Pakistani subjugation dates back to 2005. The ethnic Baloch feel marginalised at the plunder of their rich resources, and are waging a bitter freedom struggle against the government, targeting both the Pakistan security forces as well as the Chinese workers. The CPEC is also vulnerable to attacks emanating from Gilgit-Baltistan and from the TTP (Tehrik-e-Taliban Pakistan), which has forced it to upgrade security measures across the length of the project. Pakistan is now raising a Special Security Division comprising approximately 15,000 personnel to provide security for the CPEC against attacks.

Pakistan has also been waging an undeclared war on India since the last three decades, through what its leadership called for a 'war by a thousand cuts'.[24] The Indian response to Pakistani intransigence was reactive, and based on taking defensive measures to reduce the impact of terrorism which emanated from across the border. There was hence no punitive action taken against Pakistan, despite a series of highly provocative attacks such as the attack on India's Parliament in December 2001, Akshardham Temple in September 2002, Mumbai in September 2008, and Pathankot Air Base in January 2016 amongst others. But it was the attack on a forward military base in Uri in Kashmir which made the government rethink its strategy. It was Pakistan's analysis that India would not retaliate against a nuclear armed neighbour, and hence it continued these acts of terrorism on Indian soil under the nuclear umbrella. Indeed, when Indian forces raided a terrorist hideout in Myanmar, the Pakistan interior minister, Mr. Nisar Ali Khan, in response to a statement by Minister of State for Information & Broadcasting Rajyavardhan Singh Rathore that military action in Myanmar to hit back at rebels who killed 18 soldiers in Manipur was a message to other countries, said, "Pakistan is not like Myanmar". He further added that Pakistan will not be cowed down by threats from across the border.[25] That was an oblique reference to Pakistan's nuclear capability and response options. However, when the Indian forces carried out a retaliatory strike on terrorist hideouts within Pakistan-occupied Jammu & Kashmir, 11 days after the Uri attack, on 29 September 2016, it caught the Pakistani establishment off balance, especially because India's Director General of Military Operations, Lt Gen. Ranbir Singh, in a press conference, announced the details of the operation. Pakistan responded with a denial, saying that Indian troops had not entered Pakistani territory but had only fired at Pakistani positions which was for the most part ineffective. Denial by Pakistan was mainly to reassure its home constituency and enabled Pakistan to avoid confrontation and an escalation of hostilities. But on a more serious note, in a car bomb attack on an Indian police convoy on 14 February 2019 in Pulwama, J&K, which led to the death of 40 police personnel, the Indian Prime Minister made it clear that the attack would not go un-avenged. Pakistan's Prime Minister, in response, said that Pakistan would retaliate with all the means at their disposal if India were to attack Pakistan. Earlier, Pakistan officials had threatened to use nuclear weapons should India attack Pakistan.[26] The Indian response with an air strike against the base of Jaish-e-Mohammad in Khyber Pakhtunkhwa, deep inside Pakistani territory, shattered once and for all the nuclear myth and set in place a new normal in India-Pakistan relations. It gave a clear message to Pakistan and indeed the rest of the world that India will not be cowed down by the threat of nuclear weapons and would respond firmly to any attack on Indian soil, sponsored by Pakistan. The era of nuclear blackmail was over. To this end, it appears that India's policy towards Pakistan is veering from deterrence to compliance.

While the new Indian policy of taking the fight to the enemy in his own territory has set a new normal in India-Pakistan relations, it is yet to be seen whether this will impact Pakistan's support to terrorist groups based in its areas of control for operations against India. Pakistan views these groups as its strategic assets, and would be unwilling to disband them. The inter-se dynamic between the two countries will hence remain hostile, at least for the immediate future, and ties between the two countries will remain strained. While Pakistan is no longer a conventional military threat to India, its capacity to foment terrorism within India remains intact. That is a reality which India will have to live with. Peace can only come about if the costs to Pakistan for indulging in terror attacks are made unbearable and this will be the thrust of the Modi government in its second tenure after winning a handsome mandate in the elections in May 2019.

The Indian Ocean Region (IOR)

The Indian Ocean holds 16.8 per cent of the world's proven oil reserves and 27.9 per cent of proven natural gas reserves.[27] An abundance of natural resources in the Indian Ocean, among other factors, has facilitated trade-led growth within this region. Home to major sea routes connecting the Middle East, Africa and East Asia with Europe and the Americas, these vital sea routes facilitate maritime trade in the IOR, carry more than half of the world's sea-borne oil and host 23 of the world's top 100 container ports. Container traffic through the region's ports has increased fourfold from 46 million TEUs in 2000 to 166 million TEUs in 2017. Increased connectivity within the region has strengthened ties with external trading partners. China has emerged as the most important trading partner of the IOR, accounting for 16.1 per cent of its total goods trade in 2017, up from 4.8 per cent in 2000. On the other hand, between 2000 and 2017 the share of trade has declined with other major partners such as the EU (16.8 to 12.0 per cent), the US (13.9 to 7.9 per cent), and Japan (14.6 to 6.5 per cent). Intra-regional trade is even stronger, accounting for 27.2 per cent of total trade in 2017. Increasing share of trade to Asian players marks a shift to the Asian century.

Over 80 per cent of the world's seaborne trade in oil transits through the Indian Ocean (*Journal of the Indian Ocean*), making the sea lanes of vital strategic importance. This aspect gets magnified as the sea lanes pass through various choke points—the Strait of Hormuz (40 per cent), the Strait of Malacca (35 per cent) and the Bab el-Mandab Strait (8 per cent). Both India and China are dependent on their energy flows from these sea lanes. Over 70 per cent of China's oil imports come from the Middle East and Africa, which has to transit through these vulnerable choke points. While China is exploring other means of energy supply, the vulnerable sea transport from the Middle East and Africa will remain the primary mode of petroleum import for the foreseeable future. To secure its sea lines of Communication, China has embarked on what has been described as its "String of Pearls" geopolitical strategy. Stretching from Gwadar in Baluchistan province of Pakistan to the Hainan Islands, these strategic geopolitical 'pearls' have however been non-confrontational, with no evidence as yet of imperial or neo-colonial ambition. However, powerful and modernised armed forces provide China with military capabilities that could potentially alter the status quo in future. As of now, for both New Delhi and Beijing, trade and commercial activities will play the dominant role in their strategies for the IOR.

India's location in the Indian Ocean gives it a unique centrality and importance. While India's fixation since independence remained on its land borders, to deal with threats posed by China and Pakistan, this changed in the 1990s, when it started to look towards the Ocean to address severe economic problems at home. The Look East policy was initiated to boost trade and commercial ties to Southeast Asia and East Asia, while at the same time, ties were strengthened with the Gulf countries to secure energy supplies, to expand trade and to support the Indian Diaspora working in these regions. Thus, India's more militarised continental approach saw a shift towards an economically focussed strategy for the region.[28] This was given a much-needed push by the Modi government in 2015, with Prime Minister Modi enunciating a new vision for the IOR, called SAGAR (Security And Growth for All in the Region) and a strengthening of the Look East Policy which was called Act East. India's External Affairs Minister, Ms Sushma Swaraj, defined the region as extending from the Gulf of Aden in the West, through Chabahar Port in southwest Iran, and over to Myanmar and Thailand in the East. The emphasis is on commerce, infrastructure development and diplomatic engagement, all three drivers being critical to India's domestic economy and electoral politics.

China however treats the Indian Ocean as an extension of its Maritime Silk Road—the trade and infrastructure corridor linking coastal China to other Asian countries—which is a subset of its broader BRI, and seeks to expand China's links throughout Eurasia. For Beijing, the region has a wider sweep, extending from coastal China to the Saudi peninsula and African littoral. The land half of the BRI, the Silk Road Economic Belt, extends from western China through Central Asia to the Middle East, the Caucasus, and Russia, with both axes having endpoints in Europe. The aim of the BRI hence appears to be to dominate Eurasia, which leads Beijing to pursue an integrated set of trade, commercial, diplomatic, and military initiatives from the South China Sea to the African littoral.[29]

While the emphasis in the IOR is on trade, freedom of navigation and in keeping the Sea Lines of Communication secure, security considerations cannot be overlooked as presently, more than half the world's armed conflicts are located in the IOR. The waters too are home to continually evolving strategic developments including the competing rise of China and India, potential nuclear confrontation between India and Pakistan, the US interventions in Iraq and Afghanistan, Islamist terrorism, growing incidence of piracy in and around the Horn of Africa, and management of diminishing fishery resources. Consequently, there is a substantial deployment of military force in the IOR, with almost all the world's major powers have deploying substantial military forces in the Indian Ocean region.

Both India and China have genuine aspirations of developing blue water naval capabilities through the development and acquisition of aircraft carriers and an aggressive modernisation and expansion programme. As China increases its military presence in the Indian Ocean, the Indian Navy is increasingly focused on countering its Chinese counterpart. However, absent a direct confrontation, it seems likely that military factors will remain secondary drivers. In addition, the dominance of the army in Indian military planning, together with persistent problems in acquiring advanced naval and air equipment to operate in the Indian Ocean, will continue to undermine India's ability to be a strategic partner to the USA in the region.

The USA initiated a pivot or rebalance of its strategy towards Asia in 2011, marking a change in its perspective based on over seven decades of forward presence in East Asia. The Indo-Pacific strategy now enunciated ties the growing U.S.-India relationship to the wider Asia-Pacific region, reflecting the growing economic, trade, and diplomatic links between the littoral countries of the Indian Ocean and those in Southeast and East Asia. In terms of geographical reach, the Indo-Pacific strategy largely excludes Pakistan, the Arabian Peninsula, Iran, and the African littoral from its conception of the Indo-Pacific region. The USA has sought to de-hyphenate India from Pakistan, in order to improve its relations with India and views Pakistan as a part of its South Asia policy, which is focussed on counter terrorism. Iran, the Arabian Peninsula, and the African littoral are viewed as Middle Eastern or continental African issues, with U.S. strategy in the region being shaped by concerns relating to energy supplies, counter-terrorism, and other security matters. This fits in well with America's strategic interests in the Middle East, its ongoing troop commitment to Afghanistan, and its global role.[30]

While the USA will push for strengthening of ties with India, especially in the military domain, the Indian response will be more measured and cautious. The USA will continue to look at the region through a military lens, while the Indian concerns will predominantly be on increasing their economic footprints in the area. The region is likely to witness continued contestation and shifting coalitions between the USA, India and China with other countries in the IOR and outside powers like Russia and Japan.

China's aggressive soft power diplomacy has widely been seen as arguably the most important element in shaping the Indian Ocean strategic environment, transforming the entire region's dynamics. By providing large loans on generous repayment terms, investing in major infrastructure projects such as the building of roads, dams, ports, power plants, and railways, and offering military assistance and political support in the UN Security Council through its veto powers,

China has secured considerable goodwill and influence among countries in the Indian Ocean region.

India's centrality in the Indian Ocean region and its control over the air and sea lines of communication, provides it geographic domination. While India has increased its engagement with the region since the turn of the century, it faces challenges to its further expansion and cannot compete head-to-head with China which has much deeper pockets and is able to invest far more in trade and commercial investments. New Delhi will hence be forced to calibrate its resistance to Beijing. While increasingly aligning with the USA, New Delhi will seek to minimise the possibilities of a U.S.-China confrontation which could spill out of control.[31] As of now, the further escalation of such geopolitical tensions, as seen in the South China Sea, would threaten freedom of navigation which is vital for the smooth flow of Indian Ocean maritime trade and the openness of the region's sea routes, which would negatively impact on energy flows.

Neighbouring Countries

China's growing influence in Bangladesh, Myanmar and Nepal would need to be watched and countered both diplomatically and economically. Closer ties with China provide Bangladesh with a sense of security against India. China values Bangladesh for its immense natural gas reserves where Bangladesh's geographical proximity to Myanmar makes these reserves accessible to China through pipelines as also providing a strategic foothold to China in South Asia. During Chinese President Xi Jinping's visit to Dhaka in 2016, the two countries established a strategic partnership. Bangladesh has been an official partner of the China-led BRI since then. In terms of military cooperation, the Bangladesh armed forces are largely equipped with Chinese armaments. China also sold six surface ships to the Bangladesh Navy between 2009 and 2015 and two submarines in 2016. But it is the economic ties that form an important aspect of the bilateral relationship. China is Bangladesh's biggest trading partner with bilateral trade worth USD 10 billion, though the trade is skewed in China's favour. In terms of infrastructure development, China is building bridges, roads, railway tracks, airport, and power plants. In terms of economic cooperation, there is greater scope for Bangladesh trade with India. Relevant in this regard is a statement by the Bangladesh Additional Foreign Secretary, "We have nothing to sell to the Chinese. We could sell a great deal more to the Indians if they allowed us."[32] Bangladesh also shares three of its borders with India and none with China, thereby limiting Bangladesh's ability to distance itself from India.

While India considers Nepal a part of its sphere of influence, it is increasingly being challenged by China's inroads into Nepal with China providing assistance in exploiting Nepal's hydro electric potential and in construction of road and rail linkages. There has thus evolved a multi-layered engagement between China and Nepal which supports its wider South Asia policy. In Myanmar, China's strategic objective appears to be to gain direct access to the Bay of Bengal and Andaman Sea through Myanmar, bypassing the narrow Straits of Malacca. China has greater economic, political, and military clout than India and India is unlikely to replace China's position as the most influential country in Myanmar. However, both Chinese and Indian interests converge in Myanmar towards economic development and maintenance of peace. While there would be competition, there would also be cooperation.

Internal Armed Conflict and Terrorism

Internally, conflict in India's Northeast has reduced considerably, though Manipur still remains disturbed and getting peace to Nagaland is still a work in progress. Concerns remain in Assam about illegal immigration, wherein the influx of Bangladeshis has considerably altered the demography in certain areas. Left Wing Extremism (LWE) has been contained from the levels that existed in the period 2004-2014, but while the number of districts affected by LWE has reduced, the ability of the Maoists to cause casualties to the security forces remains. However, concerted efforts by the Centre and the states, both in enhancing security measures as well as in effective development, has reduced the reach of the Maoists and they are getting confined to increasingly smaller spaces.

The situation in J&K remains volatile. Conflict in the state is externally sponsored which is why it remains difficult to achieve conflict resolution. In Sri Lanka, the island-nation's military was able to defeat the LTTE because they were able to seal the battle space. The Soviet Union's inability to do so let to their exit from Afghanistan. The USA too, in its war against terror in Afghanistan, has not been able to defeat the Taliban as the latter have safe havens within Pakistan. Similarly, Pakistani support to terrorism in J&K has enabled the conflict to continue over the last three decades. However, the change in policy being adopted against Pakistan after calling out Pakistan's nuclear bluff, is likely to reduce Pakistan's overt support to the terrorist groups operating in the state. There is also a concerted effort by the Indian authorities to pursue the money trail and restrict the money flows to the coffers of terrorist groups. This, in conjunction with legal action being initiated against the Hurriyat and other groups supporting terrorists in the state is likely to have a positive impact and will likely lead to peace returning to the state.

A matter of concern is the Islamic State (IS) indicating its presence in India. IS's *Amaq News Agency*, in an announcement on 10 May 2019, named the new province, "Wilayah of Hind". The Easter Sunday bombings in Sri Lanka which killed over 250 people, had linkages with groups in southern India, which indicated that the ideological spread of the IS has made some inroads in certain parts of India. While the investigative agencies have made a number of arrests and while the IS has not carried out any terror attack in India, it would be advisable to err on the side of caution and presume the existence of sleeper cells which could get activated.

Assessment

As China and India rise politically and economically on the world stage, it is natural that they compete with one another for influence. Rivalry between the two nations will be fuelled especially by each country's efforts to reach into the other's traditional spheres of influence, for example, China in South Asia and India in Southeast Asia. China's willingness to overlook human rights and democracy concerns in its relations with the smaller South Asian states will at times leave India at a disadvantage in asserting its power in the region, as was seen recently in Nepal and Sri Lanka. India will need to significantly enlarge its economic footprint in the South Asian region to ensure it maintains an edge in its traditional spheres of influence.

Energy competition between India and China is also reflected in the two countries' assertions of naval power. As India reaches into the Malacca Strait, Beijing is developing facilities along the Indian Ocean littoral to protect sea lanes and ensure uninterrupted energy supplies. Militarily, there can be no let up in India's preparation to counter any Chinese misadventure. In the Himalayas, India will have to ensure air superiority at least in the areas south of the Tsang Po River. It will also have to upgrade its artillery capability in the mountains as well as develop infrastructure compatible to that which China has built up in Tibet. India will also have to ensure that its Navy maintains an edge in the

Indian Ocean region to protect national interests. To that extent, it is time that the country takes a de novo look on prioritising its defence expenditure to meet the challenges of the future. India also needs to change the way in which advice is tendered to the Government so that the Services concerns are adequately represented to ensure that the nation's defence is not compromised.

Pakistan is unlikely to cease support to terrorist groups which it uses as its strategic assets against India. However, it will lay greater stress on promoting and using indigenous groups within the state of J&K to target the security forces or to carry out suicide attacks, so that the blowback against Pakistan can be avoided. India will, however continue to put diplomatic, economic and political pressure against Pakistan, to compel it mend its ways. In case of Pakistani intransigence, a military response by India remains a high possibility.

The downward trend in terrorist-related activity in areas impacted by LWE is likely to continue. However, resolving the problem is unlikely at least in the immediate future. We are likely to see sporadic attacks by the Maoists in the coming years, thought the intensity and the frequency will see a decrease.

The coming decade will see a further decrease in violence levels in the Northeast. A political solution to the problem in Nagaland is possible and would greatly alter the security scenario in the entire region. However, the problem of illegal infiltration, which has altered the demographic balance is likely to create social tension in the region which would require strong governance to keep the situation under control. However, much of the angst will be reduced if the Act East policy of the Centre creates huge economic opportunities for the states

The state of J&K is likely to limp back to normalcy, provided the Centre continues with the firm policy which it has adopted, which constitutes firm action against the terrorists by the Army, restricting financial flows to terrorist groups, and investigating and prosecuting all those involved in fraudulent financial dealings and in providing support to terrorist groups. Certain legislations, like repeal of Article 35A and the abrogation of Article 370 may throw up temporary instability, but will in the long run lead to the emotional integration of the state with the rest of the Union.

Overall, India can look forward to a more safe and secure security environment in the coming decade.

NOTES

1. Hans J. Morgenthau, *Dilemmas of Politics,* University Of Chicago Press, 1958, p. 65.
2. M. Benjamin Mollov, *Power and Transcendence: Hans J. Morgenthau and the Jewish Experience,* Lexington, 2002, pp. 5-15.
3. Gautama Sen, "Institutionalising National Security Policy-Making in India," *Issue Brief,* No. 81, Centre for Land Warfare Studies, July 2016.
4. Jaswant Singh, "What Constitutes National Security in a Changing World Order: India's Strategic Thought," Issue 6 of *CASI Occasional Paper,* June 06, 1998.
5. Ibid.
6. Tanham, G. (1992). Indian Strategic Culture, *The Washington Quarterly,* pp. 129-142.
7. Shakti Sinha, Indian Strategic Thought, in Dhruv Katoch (ed.), India's Foreign Policy: Towards Resurgence, Pentagon, 2019.
8. G. Sen, "India's National Security Policy-Making Prism," *CLAWS Journal,* Winter 2016.
9. Alison Kaufman, "The 'Century of Humiliation,' Then and Now: Changing Chinese Perceptions of the International Order," available at https://papers.ssrn.com/sol3/papers.cfm?abstract_id=1449346
10. Line chart taken from https://infogram.com/share-of-world-gdp-throughout-history-1gjk92e6yjwqm16, accessed on 13 June 2019.
11. Valentina Romel and John Reed, "The Asian century is set to begin," available at https://www.ft.com/content/520cb6f6-2958-11e9-a5ab-ff8ef2b976c7
12. Ibid.
13. US Department of Defence, Annual Report to Congress 2018: Military and Security Developments Involving the People's Republic of China, available at https://media.defense.gov/2018/Aug/16/2001955282/-1/-1/1/2018-CHINA-MILITARY-POWER-REPORT.PDF
14. Xi Jinping, "Secure Decisive Victory in Building a Moderately Prosperous Society in All Respects and Strive for the Great Success of Socialism with Chinese Characteristics for a New Era", Speech delivered at the 19th National Congress of the Communist Party of China, October 18, 2017, at http://www.xinhuanet.com/english/download/Xi_Jinping's_report_at_19th_CPC_National_Congress.pdf (Accessed June 14, 2019).
15. Ram Madhav, "Panch Amrit: The Five Pillars of Indian Foreign Policy," in Dhruv Katoch (ed), *India's Foreign Policy: Towards Resurgence,* Pentagon, 2019.
16. Gurmeet Kanwal, "Can India fight China and Pakistan simultaneously?" available at https://www.rediff.com/news/column/can-india-fight-china-and-pakistan-simultaneously/20171010.htm
17. P Stobdan, "BDCA with China and its Implications for India," available at https://idsa.in/idsacomments/BDCAwithChinaanditsImplicationsforIndia_pstobdan_291013
18. Ashok Sajjanhar, "The Diplomatic Crisis ends: A Diplomatic Victory for India," available at https://www.orfonline.org/expert-speak/the-doklam-crisis-ends-a-diplomatic-victory-for-india/
19. "Wisdom at Wuhan: on the Modi-Xi meeting," *The Hindu,* 30 April 2018.
20. US Department of Defence, Annual Report to Congress 2018.
21. Ibid.
22. Ibid.

23. https://economictimes.indiatimes.com/news/defence/india-expresses-strong-opposition-to-china-pakistan-economic-corridor-says-challenges-indian-sovereignty/articleshow/57664537.cms?from=mdr
24. Husain Haqqani, Pakistan: Between Mosque and Military, Carnegie Endowment for International Peace, 2010, p. 67.
25. *India Today*, June 10, 2015.
26. Pakistan vows retaliation if India attacks, *Financial Times*, 19 January 2019.
27. British Petroleum (2017), *BP Statistical Review of World Energy 2017*, pp.12-34, available at: https://calculators.io/statistical-review-of-world-energy/
28. Harri I. Hannah, "The Great Game Moves to Sea: Tripolar Competition in the Indian Ocean Region," available at https://warontherocks.com/2019/04/the-great-game-moves-to-sea-tripolar-competition-in-the-indian-ocean-region/
29. Ibid.
30. Ibid.
31. Ibid.
32. Noor Mohammad Sarker, "Bangladesh-China Relationship at the Dawn of the Twenty-first Century," *Peace and Security Review*, Vol. 6, No. 11, First Quarter, 2014, pp. 72-96.

5

From Strategic Lethargy to Strategic Stability: The Long Road to 2030

M.J. Akbar

A security doctrine is shaped by a fixed imperative at one side, and flexibility at the other. The necessity of keeping our borders impregnable from all forms of aggression, encroachment or any kind of upheaval is a constant. The flexibility lies in an evolutionary dynamic, driven by a nation's changing dimensions as its international framework, economic aspirations and security capabilities expand to accommodate new internal and external challenges.

India's borders have been volatile since 1947. Within the first 15 years, independent India paid an extremely heavy price for either miscalculation or complacence. Our primary problem was a direct consequence of partition, after Congress accepted vivisection of a great subcontinent on communal parameters, engineered by the Muslim League and sponsored by British colonial interests. It was a brutal division that went against both our civilisational inheritance and the logic of practical commonsense. This triggered a reinvention of strategic compulsions, even as it set off seismic demographic tremors that generated conflicts which bedevil us until today.

In late October 1947, or within six weeks of freedom, Pakistan tried to change the emerging map of free India with terrorist aggression, when it sought to seize Jammu and Kashmir through war, rather than permit a peaceful resolution through mechanisms created for the transition of power from Britain to sovereign India. Pakistan tried to camouflage its aggression by calling it an insurrection, but that fudge collapsed immediately. Even the British refused to accept Pakistan's deceit. Both India and Pakistan were Dominions until they adopted their own Constitutions, which was why Lord Mountbatten, the last viceroy, could be appointed the first governor-general of India. Mountbatten endorsed the legal accession of Jammu and Kashmir to India and authorised British officers commanding the Indian Army to send Indian troops to Srinagar to reverse Pakistan's aggression.

By 1948, both the legal case and the military situation were in India's favour. However, for reasons that have never been adequately explained, let alone justified, Prime Minister Jawaharlal Nehru accepted a ceasefire in Kashmir that left Pakistan in occupation of a western chunk of the province, against the advice of Indian generals who believed that they were on the verge of pushing Pakistani troops completely out of Kashmir. Instead of victory, we settled for a strategic non-sequitur, a stalemate that continues to bleed the subcontinent.

As if one blunder was insufficient, Nehru embarked upon an inexplicable decade of strategic lethargy during the 1950s. This led to a catastrophe on the disputed border with China. Nehru left India's defence in limbo on the bizarre assumption that China would never opt for aggression because he believed in peace. In 1962, China took advantage of India's myopia, attacked across the Himalayas and imposed a line of control after a war for which we were politically, psychologically and militarily unprepared.

20th century China had never accepted Tibet as an independent nation. This was as true of Chiang Kai Sheik's 'Nationalists' as it was of Mao Zigong's communists. The British Raj, conversely, dealt with Tibet as an independent entity, kept a legation in Lhasa, signed a trade treaty and demarcated a border with India [which China refused to recognise].

Lord Wavell, the penultimate Viceroy, ignored China's protests when hosting Tibetan delegations, despite the fact that this was a rebuff to a crucial ally in the critical war against Japan. Tibet was the buffer against any potential confrontation with China. Even from their departure lounge, all that the British would express, as they did on 8 April 1947, that they would remain a "benevolent spectator" while Tibet and China as independent nations worked out a mutually satisfactory agreement.

Less than a fortnight earlier, Jawaharlal Nehru, then head of an Interim Government during the transition to freedom, had made his first significant foray into foreign policy. In the last week of March 1947, he was host to the Asian Relations Conference at the picturesque Old Fort in Delhi. British rule, however, was not over. Tibet was among the 30-plus delegations invited. The four Tibetans, led by Shampoo Heidi, walked for 21 days across the mountains to claim their separate credentials. China was also present.

After independence, a creeping ambiguity began to shadow Nehru's policy towards Tibet, which strengthened after Mao Zedong won the civil war against Chiang Kai Shek. Nehru blandly accepted China's note, sent in August 1950, that Beijing would pursue the "liberation" of Tibet by "peaceful and friendly" means. Nehru assumed that the qualification was a safeguard. Indeed, he was under the delusion that China would seek his advice. There was a touch of self-congratulation in his letter to Vijaylakshmi Pandit, his sister and India's then ambassador to Washington, in September 1948, claiming that the "Chinese listen to us". That was something that he yearned for; to be the leadership voice of Afro-Asia. The only potential competition was from China.

Mao Zedong did not waste time when he wanted to strip illusions. In October 1948, Beijing announced military operations to seize Tibet, which was neither peaceful nor friendly. Nehru's response was hapless, to put it politely. Delhi sent an unofficial and unsigned note to the Chinese foreign office expressing regret and surprise through India's ambassador in Beijing, K.M. Panikkar, who had a direct line with Nehru often leaving the foreign secretary, Girija Shankar Bajpai, frothing with frustration. China's response was a cool snub. Beijing accused Nehru of being under the influence of foreign powers which were hostile to China.

Nehru reacted with even more conciliation. He wrote to Pannikar on 25 October 1950 that friendly relations with China remained the cornerstone of his policy. On 30 October, Nehru echoed the Beijing line, asking the world to appreciate Chinese and Russian fears, "however unfounded", of intrigue against Communist China from Tibet, although his most senior colleagues, like Sadder Patel and the venerable C. Rajagopalachari, were openly critical of what they described as Chinese aggression. By 4 November, China had swallowed Tibet. On 7 November 1948, Patel wrote to Nehru, bitterly critical of Chinese "perfidy," lamenting the betrayal of Tibet, and warning that "For the first time after centuries, India's defence has to concentrate itself on two fronts simultaneously", Pakistan and China. Nehru did not answer this letter.

On 18 November 1950, Nehru put his own assessment on paper. India could not save Tibet, but would try to help through moderation and diplomacy. As for the security threat from China, Nehru was categorical: "I think it is extremely unlikely that we have to face any real military invasion from the Chinese side." He ruled out any major attack by China since "It is inconceivable that China should divert its forces and its strength across the inhospitable terrain of Tibet and undertake a wild adventure across the Himalayas."

Very few strategic miscalculations have been as Himalayan as that.

Over the next decade, Nehru bent backwards to shepherd an amused, or sometimes bemused, China on the world stage. Astonishingly, he even subverted Indian interests in the process. Twice Nehru was offered permanent membership of the UN Security Council [UNSC], and twice he refused to push the idea forward in deference to Chinese interests. In 1950, America suggested that India take the seat. In August 1950, Nehru wrote to Mrs. Pandit that India would not become a member at the cost of Communist China's claims. In 1955, Premier Bulganin of the Soviet Union received a similar response. Nehru kept this decision secret, fully conscious of its negative impact on Indian public opinion.

Today, China leads the opposition to India's campaign for permanent membership of the UNSC.

Nehru was victim of a fallacy which he promoted into a policy. He was convinced that a desire for peace was equivalent to peace. From such confusion emerged "non-alignment" as the panacea for the "third world," terms heard at the Asian Relations Conference. A direct consequence was neglect of India's security needs, even as his blustery defence minister V.K. Krishna Menon consciously downgraded defence production and capability.

As father of the proposition, Nehru turned non-alignment, or equidistance from the two superpowers of the Cold War and attendant demilitarisation, into the foundation of Indian foreign policy, without recognising its fundamental weakness. Nehru mistook an idea for an ideology.

> The high point of "goodwill-ism" was reached at Bandung in 1955, where 29 nations, including China, signed a *mantra* called Panchshila. Its five points—territorial integrity, non-aggression, non-interference, peaceful co-existence and equality—apart from being repetitive, had little resonance in

> a rapidly changing world where conflict frequently found new reasons. Nehru, as mentor-star, with Egypt's Nasser and Yugoslovakia's Tito by his side, helped raise non-alignment to the status of an international movement at Belgrade in 1961.

Precisely one year later, in October 1962, China, a signatory to Bandung, took full advantage of India's strategic timidity, and did precisely what Nehru believed would never happen. India's troops, under-clothed, under-armed and under-resourced, were pushed back. China advanced, and, on a day of its choosing, withdrew to a line drawn by its guns. A visibly shattered Nehru had to hastily abandon a basic tenet of non-alignment and ask America for military aid. That was too little and too late.

No "non-aligned" nation rushed to India's help in its terrible hour of need. Nor did any come to India's assistance when Pakistan tried a second time to seize Kashmir, in 1965. Conversely, a number of them offered to send military supplies to Pakistan at the height of the war. Non-alignment left India lonely rather than aligned.

India learnt the very hard way that solidarity is impotent without substance, and picked up some savvy from experience. In 1970, NAM members resolved at Lusaka to abstain from big power alliances; in 1971, India signed a treaty with the Soviet Union. NAM was effectively over but its busy ghost continued to occupy a prominent office in India's External Affairs Ministry until it was quietly interred in the second decade of the 21st century. Half a century after it was born, non-alignment had become a baby with a beard; it had never grown up.

Today, India's policy is focused on multi-alignment: a series of parallel relationships that strengthen bilateral partnerships which reinforce the search for a common approach towards regional and international security, economic equity and the elimination of existential dangers like terrorism. India believes in friendship and cooperation in the common cause of stability, dialogue and equitable prosperity as fundamentals of the 21st century world order. Dividing the world into parcels of "big powers" and "dependent" powers is a recipe for polarisation. The world is a family of sovereign nations. All nations do not have the same capacities, but they have the same rights, duties and obligations. Stability rests on multi-polar support systems that promote economic aspirations and regional security.

The five pillars of Prime Minister Narendra Modi's foreign policy are rooted in India's national interest, civilisational philosophy and the republican, democratic ethos of modernity. They are *Sammaan*: respect for every nation's sovereignty; *Samvaad:* greater engagement with all countries; *Suraksha:* security; *Samriddhi*: shared prosperity; *Sanskriti* and *Sabhyata*: the persuasive reach of cultural values anchored in a philosophy which believes that the world is a family. These principles enable India to maintain friendships across binaries. Observers and analysts are sometimes surprised to learn that Prime Minister Modi can welcome Prime Minister Binyamin Netanyahu of Israel in Delhi as an honoured guest, and within three weeks become the first Indian PM to visit Palestine and receive its highest civilian award. But no Indian is surprised. Indeed, Indians would consider it remiss if both did not happen.

Friendships have graduated from phrase-laden fluff to brick-and-mortar bridge-building sustained by diplomacy, even as Prime Minister Modi expands the architecture of multilateral relations through personal chemistry and a patient exposition of a mutually beneficial way forward. The route map to 2030 is being laid out with clarity, focus, balanced vision, and creative energy incubated by fresh ideas.

The most dynamic of them has been a redefinition of the meaning of "neighbour." For too long our thinking has been trapped by geography, famously encapsulated in the adage that you can change your friends but you cannot change your neighbour. Proximity has been replaced by reach. Reach, to give a relevant example, has made the Gulf a far closer neighbour than Pakistan.

Prime Minister Modi did not effect this without giving geography a chance. His very first foreign policy decision, upon winning the elections in 2014, was to invite SAARC heads of government to his oath-taking ceremony. It was an effort at new beginnings. There had been, quite shockingly, no bilateral visit to Nepal for nearly two decades, or to UAE for over three decades. The repair work was immediate and intense.

Prime Minister Modi transformed the Gulf into India's neighbour connected by human, economic and strategic routes, carefully underlined by the fact that nothing walks on a one-way street. Simultaneously, he strengthened relations with ASEAN; in 2018, in a remarkable display of new bonds, all ASEAN heads of government came to Delhi as honoured guests for the Republic Day celebrations. Slowly but surely, India is becoming the pivotal nation within the southern half of Asia. This merges seamlessly with the initiative across the Indo-

Pacific. India's arc of neighbourhood has been expanded to sweep between the Red Sea and the Indian Ocean.

No security doctrine can be based on the best-case scenario; it has to prepare adequately for the worst. India does not believe in aggression; it never has. On the other hand, every inch of India's territory is sacrosanct, and if any Indian is a victim of foreign terrorism there will be accountability. Prime Minister Modi has raised the level of response to cross-border terrorism with cross-border accountability. The message is simple. The rewards of peace far outweigh the pitiful dividend of hostility.

The nature of conflict is constantly evolving. We conventionally assume that there have been only two world wars in the last hundred years; I can think of at least five. The end of the first world war in 1919 was followed by the worldwide wars for liberation from colonialism, with Mahatma Gandhi among the pantheon of heroes seeking change through non-violence. But there was enough violence elsewhere. The Cold War, which continued for more than four decades, was very warm in Asia, Africa and Latin America, with Vietnam become the iconic intersection point of anti-colonial determination and cold war politics. We are currently in the midst of a fifth world conflict, the war against terrorism. It is a dangerous, barbaric, immoral and viral epidemic that remains to fully crushed.

Another form of war has begun to loom on the charred landscape: the Long Warm War. It has many commas, but no full stop. Its embers glow and singe and kill, but it stops short of becoming a conflagration. Its battlefields are rife with false flags. Fought in the cause of faith-supremacy, it aims at destabilisation of multi-faith societies, and the spread of that dangerous epidemic, fear.

While the Fifth Column does the bulk of the fighting, its four supporting columns operate from the background, at denial distance, helping with intelligence, finance, training, weapons and arms-length propaganda. The fighting is sporadic, the objective is to do damage that leaves psychological as well as real scars. Its tactical and operational impetus lies in the power of uncertainty and arbitrary choice of targets, with great emphasis on civilian havoc. This terrorism, honed in the last century, continues to acquire sophistication in the hands of new perpetrators, using high-grade technology. We will have to manage and seek a careful response to different kinds of war in the coming decades. The ideological war is not behind us; it continues to be ahead of us, with religion stoking the fire this time.

There is nothing as unpredictable as the future, as even an astrologer knows. Who in 1910 could have foreseen that in just four years a war would begin that would take 20 million lives and leave another 21 million wounded; or the implosion of three great empires, Tsarist, Ottoman and Austro-Hungarian? Or that by 1919-1920, Mahatma Gandhi would launch a mass movement that would end the age of colonisation? Who could have imagined, on the edge of the third decade of the 20th century, that a great depression would bring capitalism to its knees? How many Germans thought in 1930 that Hitler would be the all-powerful dictator in four years, or begin a blitzkrieg offensive by 1939 that would leave 70 million dead by the time it ended? Did anyone in 1940 envisage a Hiroshima in their worst nightmares? To come closer to our age, which pundit in 2000 thought that 9/11 was only a year and would be followed by wars in Afghanistan and Iraq wars that would leave vast regions devastated, and instigate a new tornado-rise of terrorism? A future war is often beyond the scope of imagination.

Civilised nations must seek to crush the seeds of poison before it becomes viral. That is the challenge today. And if that poison cannot be neutralised then we must have the resources to minimise its awful cost when it finds momentum. That is the challenge of tomorrow. India will have to play an elemental role in both phases.

6

India's Internal Security: Threats and Solutions

M.L. Kumawat

Since Independence, India has faced several grave internal security threats, including communal holocausts, secessionist movements, militancy, violent farmer and student agitations, caste-conflicts, pro- and anti-reservation movements, and left-wing extremist movement. Over 33,000 policemen have martyred to protect the integrity of the nation and to maintain public order. Incidentally, the term 'internal security', which is an element of 'national security', has not been defined in any official document of the Government of India. As it happens, neither has the term 'national security'. Conventionally, national security implied physical or geographic protection and was thus largely equated with 'national defence'. However, the definition of national security has expanded over time from territorial defence to protection and preservation of the core values and vital interests critical to the nation state from external and internal challenges and threats.

Internal security, a sub-set of national security, is therefore concerned with threats and challenges emanating from within a country having the potential to adversely affect public order and security of the nation. Currently, India faces an array of grave internal security threats: insurgency in Kashmir and the Northeast, Naxalism, terrorism, including cross-border terrorism, illegal migration, communalism, organised crime, etc. Then there are emerging internal security threats such as cyber crime, environment, including water-related conflicts, unemployment and internal migration related conflicts, and mob violence in the form of lynching.

AN OVERVIEW OF INTERNAL SECURITY CHALLENGES

Kashmir

No state of India has suffered from internal turmoil as well as attacks from across the frontier than the state of Jammu and Kashmir. Before India's independence, the state remained free from communal violence and other large-scale conflict. However, taking advantage of widespread organised conflict in Poonch, a tribal invasion, aided and abetted by Pakistan, was launched in the first half of October 1947, which escalated into the first Indo-Pak war (1947-48). Yet again, Pakistan waged full-fledged war in 1965 and a battle in 1999 to wrest Kashmir from India. However, it failed in its mission every time.

The militancy in the 1990s was the worst period in the history of Kashmir when terrorists from across the frontier—supported by the Pakistani army—indiscriminately targeted not only security forces but also opinion makers, ideologues, social activists, politically affiliated people and religious minorities which resulted in the deaths of over 40,000 people, including over 13,000 civilians and 4,000 Security Force personnel. Security operations contained militants' violence significantly around 2006 when the UPA government initiated a number of measures for restoring normalcy and economic development of the state. Confidence Building Measures (CBMs) included commencing of bus service in the Srinagar-Muzaffarabad and Poonch-Rawalkot routes; and cross Line of Control (LoC) trade between J&K and Pakistan-Occupied Kashmir (PoK). However, the period of comparative peace was short lived.

Violence gripped the Valley in the wake of the Amarnath land issue in 2008 and large-scale protests and police firings in 2010 which led to the death of over 120 people, mostly youth. The killing of Burhan Wani, a young militant, in July 2016 revived militancy in a big way.

There are new worrying trends, namely, people's demand for 'Azadi', local youth joining militancy in larger numbers, a sea of mourners in the funeral processions of militants, people obstructing security forces operations, stone pelting by youth including girl students, etc. It is widely believed that militancy in the Valley has evolved into insurgency which poses a formidable challenge to the state. After the abrogation of Article 370 of the Indian Constitution and conversion of the state of Jammu and Kashmir into a Union Territory, the security forces have increased counter-insurgency operations. Will this strategy help? Argues security expert David Kilcullan,

> "At the start of a conventional engagement if we are facing one hundred of the enemy and we kill twenty, we can assume that eighty are left. In counter-insurgency, this logic does not hold: the 20 killed may have 40 relatives who are new in blood feud with and are obligated to take revenge on the security forces who killed the 20, so the new number is 120."

So what then is the resolution to the Kashmir conundrum? One argument is to increase security forces stationed in Kashmir, which is already one of the most militarised areas in the world. Security forces may well bring down violence but is not likely to resolve the tangled problem. In such a scenario, besides continuing security operations, the state needs to work for winning the hearts and minds of the people of Kashmir through development at greater pace and good governance.

Insurgency in the North-East

The Northeastern region comprising eight states is of great strategic importance. Except Sikkim, all the other states have witnessed intense insurgencies and violence at one point of time or the other. In fact, the situation in North-Eastern states, especially in Nagaland, Mizoram, Assam and Manipur had been grave and threatened the integrity of India. Presently, Mizoram, Tripura and Sikkim are free from insurgency but the remaining states, namely, Assam, Arunachal Pradesh, Manipur, Meghalaya and Nagaland are still affected by criminal activities of insurgent groups albeit much less than at any time in the past. This became possible due to security operations against insurgent groups coupled with the policy of negotiations with them resulting in Suspension of Operations (SoO), Memorandum of Settlements (MoS) and ceasefire agreements.

Notwithstanding significant improvement in the security situation, acts of kidnappings, extortions, killings of security personnel and of the cadres of rival groups continue to beset the region. More important, the demand for Greater Nagalim—a very sensitive and complex issue—is yet to be resolved. It is not clear how the present regime intends to settle it. Whether the solution will be acceptable to Nagaland, Manipur and Arunachal Pradesh is to be seen.

What is needed is to deal with the armed cadres of different banned groups engaged in criminal activities like extortions, kidnappings, killings, etc., effectively and explore political solutions to the vexed problems of the region. Rapid development coupled with emotional integration of the people of the Northeast with mainland India will be a lasting solution.

Left-wing Extremism

India has a long history of extremism emerging from the far left ideologies. Soon after the launching of the Communist Party of India (CPI) in 1925, an armed struggle was put into practice in the Telangana region (then a part of the Hyderabad kingdom) in 1946. After the merger of Hyderabad into India in 1948, more than 50,000 armed personnel were deployed by the Government of India to deal with the movement. It is estimated that 4,000 communists and peasant militants were killed. The movement continued until October 1951.

The second left extremist movement in India, known as the Naxalite movement, originated in the Naxalbari area of West Bengal in 1967 and it continues. In its over half-a-century long existence, the movement has shown tremendous grit and resilience. At its peak in the last decade after the merger of Peoples' War Group (PWG) and Maoist Communist Centre (MCC) in 2004 (the united outfit called the Communist Party of India, Maoist) its influence spanned 223 districts across 20 states, although of course, the degree of activity varied vastly. The CPI (Maoist) carried out big attacks on police armouries, jails, police camps and caused heavy loss of life and property. Jehanabad (Bihar) jail break (November 2005), attack on Nayagarh police armoury, police station (February, 2008) and Sukma, Chhattisgarh (April 2010 in which 76 CRPF men were killed) are among the worst attacks.

Owing to a slew of concerted measures taken by the Central and State governments especially after the creation of the Naxal Management Division in the Ministry of Home Affairs (MHA) like raising of a new force—Commando Battalion for Resolute Action (COBRA) on the pattern of Greyhound, an acclaimed commando force of Andhra Pradesh—and providing over 120 battalions of Central Armed Police Forces (CAPFs) to the Naxal-affected states, financial assistance to states to raise India Reserve Battalions and development in the Naxal-affected states, there is a significant improvement in the situation.

Though the Naxalite movement once described by Manmohan Singh, former Prime Minister, as 'the worst internal security threat that India ever faced' has been considerably contained, the fact remains that it is still a menace in 35 districts of seven states, namely, Chhattisgarh, Jharkhand, Odisha, Maharashtra, Bihar, Andhra Pradesh and Telangana.

What is the prognosis of the Naxal movement? So long as severe disparities in level of living, heavy incidence of unemployment, lack of economic opportunities, continued exploitation of disadvantageous segments of society and atrocities on the weaker sections persist, the Naxalite problem is not likely to totally eradicated. The problem, therefore, will have to be tackled by adopting a multi-pronged integrated strategy. While coordinated and stringent security operations are necessary, simultaneous imaginative and radical administrative, political and developmental measures are imperative to remove the socio-economic malaise which has sustained the movement.

Terrorism

The scourge of terrorism has affected nations across the world and India has been among the worst hit. The Ministry of Home Affairs has banned 39 terrorist organisations. Some of the worst terror strikes which shocked the world are: Mumbai (March 1993, 257 deaths, 717 injured); Coimbatore (1998, 58 deaths, 200 injured); Attack on Parliament (2001, 9 killed); Akshardham, Gandhinagar (2002, 30 deaths); Delhi (October 2005, 62 deaths); Varanasi (2006, 21 deaths); Mumbai (2006, 209 deaths), Malegaon (2006, 40 deaths); Panipat (Samjhauta Express, 66 killed); Hyderabad (August 25, 2007, 42 killed); Ahmedabad (July 2008, 29 deaths, 110 injured); Delhi (September 13, 2008, 33 deaths, 110 injured); Guwahati (October 2008, 81 deaths, 470 injured).

But the terror attack on Mumbai on 26 November, 2008 by sea-borne terrorists of the Lashkar-e-Taiba from Pakistan, which claimed 163 lives and injured 239, shocked the world like never before as the victims were from across the world—USA, UK, Japan, Israel, Canada, etc.

The 26/11 Mumbai attack forced the Central and State governments to revamp Intelligence agencies and create the 'National Investigation Agency'. Private business establishments like shopping malls, hotels, etc., also improved their security. All these measures have yielded good results. But cross-border terrorism sponsored by the Pakistan Army and ISI continues to bleed India in Kashmir and elsewhere. The Islamic State is also striving to make its presence in India. The need, therefore, is to establish a 'National Counter Terrorism Centre' (NCTC) to prevent terror attacks as the mandate of the NIA is only to investigate terror attacks once they have taken place. In this regard, the recent statement of

National Security Advisor (NSA) Ajit Doval is very important. During his address before the chiefs of state anti-terror squads (ATS) in New Delhi in October 2019, Doval underlined the absence of a central nodal agency as a big hurdle to combat terrorism since the Intelligence Bureau, the Army, RAW and NIA were not able to work in tandem.

Communalism

If there is one single cause that has played havoc in the life our nation, it is the bane of communalism. The communal seeds sown and nurtured by the British caused the vivisection of the Indian subcontinent. Partition unleashed a human tragedy hitherto unseen, in world history. It is estimated that two million people were killed and 15 million people migrated in both directions under great hardship. The Father of the Nation was also assassinated by a communal bigot.

Sadly, the virus of communalism did not die down in free India. Quite a large number of communal riots have rocked different parts of India in the past seven decades, the worst being—Moradabad (1980, 1500 deaths); Nellie, Assam (1983, 1819 deaths); Delhi (1984, 2733 deaths); Bhagalpur (1989, 1161 deaths); Gujarat (2002, 1267 deaths). Incidents of communal violence continue to bleed India as the following chart shows:

Table 1: Number of Persons Killed and Injured in Communal Violence

Year	*Number of persons killed*	*Number of persons injured*
2014	95	1921
2015	97	2264
2016	86	2321
2017 (up to May)	44	892

Source: Reply to the Lok Sabha on 8 August, 2017.

Not surprisingly, India was ranked fourth in the world in 2015—after Syria, Nigeria and Iraq—for the highest social hostilities involving religion (*Huffington Post*, 14 April, 2017).

Being acutely aware of India's widening communal fault line, former US President Barack Obama during his visit to India in 2015 cautioned, 'India will succeed so long as it is not splintered along the lines of religious faith...and is unified as one nation.'

Communal harmony in India has been mainly vitiated by political leaders to garner votes. Fundamentalists have also contributed to this malaise by their impassioned rhetoric. After the Supreme Court's recent verdict in the Ayodhya

Ram Mandir-Babri Masjid case, the government will have to remain vigilant and ensure communal harmony in society.

The police, being a part of the society it operates in, has also been affected by the virus of communalism. Even in the aftermath of Partition when communal violence was at its peak, many policemen affected with this malaise did not try to avert riots; rather, they too participated in it. A number of commissions which were appointed to enquire into the communal riots have lamented about this creeping threat. Khushwant Singh in his book, '*The End of India*' quotes the observations of Justice Madon who enquired into the riots in Bhiwandi and Jalgaon in 1970 about the nefarious role of politicians and policemen in perpetrating as well as dealing with the communal violence:

> "It was a lonely, arduous and weary journey through a land of hatred and violence, of prejudice and perjury. The encounters on the way were with men without compassion, lusting for the blood of their fellow men, with politicians who trafficked in communal hatred and religious fanaticism, with local leaders who sought power by sowing disunity and bitterness, with police officers and policemen who were unworthy of their uniform, with investigating officers without honour and without scruples, with men committed to falsehood and wedded to fraud and with dealers in mayhem and murder."

Many years later, the Srikrishna Commission which inquired into riots in Mumbai in December 1992-93 had also, inter-alia, brought out the factors which had contributed to the lack of effectiveness of police. These included, among many others, Communalisation of Police. Madhav Godbole in his well-researched work '*The Holocaust of Indian Partition: An inquest*' quotes the relevant part of the report of the Srikrishna Commission:

> "The evidence before the Commission suggests that in some measure at least there has been polarisation in the police force on communal lines....It is true that the policeman is a constituent of society and cannot avoid being impressed (sic) by the communal influences in the society in which he lives. While communal thinking in an ordinary citizen, however objectionable, may not produce immediately visible pernicious results, communalisation of a policeman has that effect."

To overcome the malaise of communalisation in police, Madhav Godbole writes, the Central Government constituted on 7 October 1992 a new wing of the Central Reserve Police called Rapid Action Force (RAF) to render assistance to the states.

Organised Crime

The menace of organised crime has emerged as a grave internal security threat. Back in 1993, the N.N. Vohra Committee made the startling revelation that 'the network of Mafia is virtually running a parallel government'. Elaborating on the nexus between mafias, bureaucrats, politicians and judiciary, it mentions:

> "The big smuggling syndicates, having international linkages, have spread into and infected the various economic and financial activities including Hawala transactions, circulation of Black Money and operations of a vicious parallel economy causing serious damage to the economic fibre of the country. These syndicates have acquired substantial financial and muscle power and social respectability and have successfully corrupted the government machinery at all levels and wield enough influence to make the talk of investigating and prosecution agencies extremely difficult; even the members of judicial system have not escaped the embrace of the Mafia."

In the past quarter century, the multi-headed monster has gripped almost every aspect of national life. For instance, now there are mineral mafia, sand mafia, water mafia, examination mafia, etc.

Strangely, only two states (Maharashtra and Delhi) have a specific law to combat organised crime. The National Investigating Agency (NIA) created in 2008 has not been mandated to investigate organised crime. Nor is there any national agency collecting information about a variety of criminal syndicates operating in more than one state and to advising states for co-ordinated preventive action.

The most sinister development in recent times is that the mafia who hitherto provided only financial and muscle support to politicians are now themselves joining politics and many of them have entered into state legislative assemblies and Parliament.

Illegal Migration

Speaking in Parliament, former Deputy Prime Minister L. K. Advani described illegal migration from Bangladesh as the most dangerous and creeping internal security threat. It is estimated that India has around 20 million illegal migrants from Bangladesh who have settled in different parts of India.

However, the impact of illegal migration has been most marked in Assam and Tripura. While it has changed the electoral balance in many districts of Assam, the majority of the tribal population of Tripura at the time of independence has been turned into a minority. Lt. General Sinha, then Governor of Assam, described illegal migration from Bangladesh as 'demographic invasion' of Assam. No wonder on this issue Assam faced a bloody insurgency (1979-1985) which seriously threatened the integrity of India. The question of four million people excluded from the National Register of Citizens (NRC) in Assam recently has the potential to turn into yet another internal security challenge. The updated NRC which was published on August 31, has left 19 lakh people stateless and exposed to the prospect of being lodged in detention camps after exhausting appeals against their exclusion from the Register. An editorial in the *Indian Express*, published on November 22, 2019, sums up the implications"

> "By all accounts, the NRC in Assam has been a failure: It did not satisfy any section of the society, reopened faultlines of religion, language and ethnicity, and left millions of people on the edge... The past few years have seen Assam emerge from this morass of violence and rebuild its economy. But the NRC, and its by-product, the Citizenship Amendment Bill, have threatened a regression into a past that saw one section of society pitted against the other.

The Government of India has also taken a series of measures which inter alia include: a dedicated border guarding force, the BSF, to guard 4,096 km of the Indo-Bangladesh border, creation of over 2,000 km long fence along the border, construction of border road and Border Area Development Program (BADP), etc. However, despite these measures, illegal migration has not fully abated on account of the porous border (more than a thousand kilometres being riverine and due to other reasons are still unfenced).

It is, therefore, imperative that the border-guarding mechanism be further strengthened by speeding up the construction/erection of the fence, resettlement of the people residing in about 100 villages right on the border and at least five hundred metres inside Indian territory and stop diversion of the BSF for other internal security duties, etc.

Environmental Security

> "*Conflict between states is not the most pressing threat to human security, safety and survival. There are far greater catastrophes awaiting humanity. Alleviating poverty, ensuring access to water, health and education in order to fulfil basic human needs is priority.*"
>
> **Sunjoy Joshi**, Director, Observer Research Foundation

> *"Water may become a more significant source of contention than energy or minerals out to 2030 at both the intra-state and inter-state levels."*
>
> **'Global Trends 2030: Alternative Worlds'**,
> A publication of the National Intelligence Council, USA, 2013

Water has been the *raison d'être* for the rise and fall of human civilisations. It is said that the next world war will be fought on water issues. India has water disputes with most of its neighbours—Pakistan, China, Nepal and Bangladesh. Within India, the inter-state river water disputes are among the most contentious and emotive issues. Karnataka and Tamil Nadu have often been rocked by violent agitations over the Cauvery water dispute.

Daily brawls over water are a common occurrence/sight in slums of cities and towns all over the country. Road blockades and protests for supply of water are also common in the summer months. A few years ago, the police had to resort to firing on farmers agitating for water resulting in the death of four farmers in Sriganganagar district (2004) and five farmers in Tonk district (2015).

Against this backdrop, NITI Aayog reports that "India is facing its worst water crisis in history and that demand for potable water will outstrip supply by 2030" portends an ominous situation. In such a scenario, water crisis emerging as one of the foremost internal security threats is a distinct possibility. Therefore, Central and State governments must take all possible measures to save India from plunging into water related civil wars.

Youth Unemployment and Internal Migration

India has almost added 1,000 million people to its population since independence in 1947. According to the United Nations Population Fund's (UNFPA) 'State of the World Population 2018' report, India's population grew at 1.2 per cent a year between 2010 and 2019, which is slightly higher than the global average of 1.1 per cent a year in this period. Today, it has the largest number of youth (356 million in the age group of 10-24 as per a 2014 UN report). What does it signify? In this regard, a research finding of Harvard Kennedy School is instructive:

> "When 15-24 year olds made up more than 35 per cent of the population as is common in developing countries, the risk of conflict was 150% higher than with a rich country age profile."

Sadly, a majority of our youth lack employable skills. This vast reservoir of youth is always available for agitations—be they be on the reservation issue or for the ban of a film like *Padmavati.*

A large number of unemployed youth migrate north to south since the socio-economic development of the southern states is considerably higher and that attracts people. As per the 2011 Census, 46.4 million people migrated from economically less developed states to more developed ones between 2001-2011, and mostly to southern states. Internal migrations have been a cause of conflict in the 1960s. Assam witnessed a violent agitation against 'Marwaris'. In Maharashtra, the Shiv Sena spearheaded a movement against people coming to Mumbai in search of jobs from other states. In August, 2007, 29 Hindi-speaking workers were killed in Karbi Anglong district of Assam and recently Shillong, the capital of Meghalaya, witnessed a violent agitation against the Sikhs who had migrated there long ago.

According to the World Youth Report 2018, released by the United Nations Department of Economic and Social Affairs, "In India, the unemployment rate for youth remains at about 10 per cent, but there are concerns that this will increase if India's high economic growth rate of 7 per cent per year fails to boost employment at the rates needed to generate sufficient work for the country's growing youth population." Therefore, the unskilled youth bulge—mostly unemployable—has many facets impinging on internal security which call for imaginative solutions at the national level.

Cyber Security

The advent of Computers and the Internet has profoundly affected every aspect of life. In fact, it is all pervading. The 21st century is rightly called the cyber-century. The technological revolution has fundamentally altered the way we live, work and relate to one another. In scale, scope and complexity, the transformation is unprecedented in human history. Indians are among the top users of smartphones and Internet. The number of smartphone users is estimated to hit 317 million by the end of 2018.

While it has positively affected every walk of life, there are attendant threats looming large on the horizon initially in the form of cyber crime and finally cyber war. Articulating the dangers posed to cyber security, Prime Minister Narendra Modi says, "Clouds of a bloodless war are hovering over the world."

As far as the impact of IT on internal security challenges is concerned, it has added to the complexity of every issue, be it organised crime, terrorism, insurgency, communalism, public agitation, etc. For instance in Kashmir, the present upsurge in insurgency owes a great deal to the use of social media like WhatsApp and Facebook by militants and the local people. In no time, everyone in the Valley learns about security operations and killings of militants which bring instant protests and stone pelting on security forces. Burhan Wani's joining militancy and his killing in 2016 gave a great impetus to insurgency, mainly due to the use of the cyber media. No wonder there are frequent stoppage/ curtailment of Internet services in the Valley to maintain public order. In Rajasthan recently, Internet services were stopped for two days to ensure the smooth conduct of an examination.

Organised criminal syndicates, especially the drug mafia, have opened 'Internet-Pharmacies' to sell drugs online. ATM and credit card frauds are rising. Hate videos are going viral. As per the 'Crime in India Report for the year 2017', released by the National Crime Records Bureau on October 21, 2019, a 77 per cent rise in the number of cyber crime cases was observed in 2017 compared to 2016.

Cyber crime is a new phenomenon and the preparedness of the police forces of the states is uneven. While the southern states and metro cities have taken some measures, most police stations in India lack the expertise to tackle this growing challenge. The Central and State governments must invest in human resources and infrastructure to improve the investigative skills of policemen across the country.

THE ROAD AHEAD

In the past seven decades, the Indian Police has faced a number of grave internal security challenges. Measures were taken by the Central and State governments to improve the functioning of internal security systems comprising the Central and State police forces, infrastructure and laws to tackle the ever-increasing internal security challenges. Specialised forces have been raised to combat specific challenges: Border Security Force (BSF), Central Industrial Security Force (CISF), National Security Guard (NSG), Indo-Tibetan Border Police (ITBP), Rapid Action Force (RAF), Commando Battalions for Resolute Action (COBRA), National Investigation Agency (NIA), Greyhounds—an anti-Naxal force of Andhra Pradesh, etc. The enactment of specific laws like the National Security Act, Unlawful Activities (Prevention) Act, The National Investigation Agency Act, Information Technology Act, etc., are some of the measures in this direction.

In the aftermath of the 26/11 Mumbai attack, coastal security received greater impetus. Notwithstanding the above measures taken by the MHA and the State governments from time to time, the fact remains that these were piecemeal and after crises and not as part of an Internal Security Doctrine and concomitant strategy. The following suggestions will go a long way in improving the internal security system as well as in making Indian police SMART.

SMART is an acronym coined by Prime Minister Modi for police which means Strict and Sensitive, Modern and Mobile, Alert and Accountable, Reliable and Responsive, Techno savvy and Trained.

Re-organisation of Ministry of Home Affairs (MHA)

India is perhaps the only country in the world where the key sovereign function—maintenance of internal security—is one of the many functions of a ministry (Ministry of Home Affairs) burdened with a large number of subjects unconnected with internal security. There is no justification to have matters such as official language, warrants of precedence, appointment of Governors, creation of new states, inter-state boundary disputes, pension to erstwhile rulers, rehabilitation of people affected by disasters, natural calamities and man-made disasters, Padma Awards, etc., in the charter of the MHA.

It is imperative to have an exclusive ministry—Ministry of Interior or Internal Security, to deal with a range of complex and burning issues relating to internal security. Further, there is a need for specialists to be given senior positions in the ministry at the level of joint secretaries and above.

Need for Police Reforms

Successive surveys on the police reveal the general dissatisfaction of people and complaints against the Indian Police of unprofessionalism, high-handedness, corruption, backing of crime, custodial torture, etc. This is not surprising since the police that the British created was 'to rule' rather than 'to serve' the people. Evidently, there are many areas which call for urgent reforms. Unfortunately, very little has been done in this regard. Prakash Singh, a former Director-General of Police, BSF and a crusader for police reforms expressed his anguish thus:

> "There have been any number of commissions, both at the state and central levels—State Police Commissions, National Police Commissions, Gore Committee, Ribeiro Committee, Padmanabhaiah Committee, Malimath Committee, to name only a few—which made recommendations for reforms,

> but these received no more than cosmetic treatment at the hands of the government with the result that there has been hardly any change in the colonial policing which we inherited from the British."

On quite a few occasions, the Supreme Court of India has expressed dismay and dissatisfaction over the indifference to the issue of police reforms. In fact, the directions of the Supreme Court have consistently been stonewalled. It is, therefore, imperative in the national interest that the Government of India passes a Central legislation on the lines of the Model Police Act drafted by the Soli Sorabjee committee incorporating therein the directions of the Supreme Court. The State governments should also comply with the directions of the Supreme Court and establish 'State Security Commissions', 'the Police Establishment Board' and 'the Police Complaints Authority' among others which will go a long way in making Indian Police people friendly, accountable and a professional service.

(a) The Number Crunch

Indian Police, both Central and States, is 3.61 million strong. However, the police-population ratio (192 policemen per one hundred thousand of population as on 1 January, 2017) is one of the lowest in the world. The United nations recommended 230 policemen per 100,000 people. Coupled with this, the vacancy position is enormous (21.8 per cent as on 01.01.2017). Therefore, the actual strength available for general policing (maintenance of law and order and crime investigation) and internal security duties is grossly inadequate.

Table 2: Indian Police

	State Police Forces	*Central Police Forces*	*Total*
Sanctioned Strength	2.464 million	1.154 million	3.618 million
Actual Strength	1.926 million	0.987 million	2.913 million
Vacancy	0.538 million	0.167 million	0.705 million

Source: Bureau of Police Research and Development.

Despite huge vacancies, the recruitment process is highly irregular. Thus, in 2016, only 71,711 policemen were recruited as against the total vacancies exceeding 0.7 million! States generally fill up vacancies in an election year with an eye on votes rather than on actual requirement.

Irregular and large scale recruitment in one go affects the quality of personnel recruited, training, promotions and therefore morale, and more importantly, policing itself that includes maintenance of internal security. It is, therefore, imperative that the governments of both the Centre and the States conduct police recruitments annually taking into account the vacancies that would arise after three years as the process of recruitment and training takes at least three years. Incidentally, the importance of annual and planned police recruitment was stressed upon the Chief Ministers by former Prime Minister Manmohan Singh in the Internal Security Conference in 2007, but only to be ignored by most of the states.

(b) Training

Though training is of great significance for imparting necessary skills and knowledge, it is the most neglected aspect, especially in the State police forces. The 'Status of Policing in India Report 2019', released recently has highlighted several inadequacies and the dismal conditions of the police force in India. The report is based on a survey of about 12,000 police personnel and 10,595 members of their families from 21 states. During the last five years, only 6.4 per cent of the police could be given in-service training.

Similarly, a quality audit carried out by BPR&D-2016 revealed a number of serious deficiencies, namely, inadequate number of trainees, lack of motivation and suitable qualification of trainers, inadequate infrastructure, etc. Irregular and large-scale recruitment in a particular year adds to the existing problems of the training institutes which in turn affects quality of the basic training. Ill-trained policemen cannot be expected to cope with the challenges they are required to face.

In the fast-changing world, it is important that the policemen are given in-service training from time to time. However, at the cutting edge level, i.e., constables who constitute over 90 per cent of the force, in-service training is imparted after 15-20 years and then too, the emphasis is on physical training. The need of the hour in a democratic republic is to lay greater emphasis on the constitutional ethos, human rights and scientific aids to investigation, both during the basic as well as in-service training of policemen.

(c) Modernisation of Police Forces

The modernisation of police forces including police stations is crucial for meeting the current and emerging internal security challenges. The scheme for Modernisation of Police Forces (MPF) initiated by the MHA in 2000 is a significant initiative towards capacity building and improving infrastructure.

However, the allocation of amount has been reduced considerably (chart below) over the years.

Table 3: Funds Allocation under Police Modernisation by MHA

S. No.	*Financial Year*	*Annual released funds (in billion Rs.)*
1.	2013-14	13.38
2.	2014-15	13.97
3.	2015-16	6.61
4.	2016-17	5.92
5.	2017-18	1.32

Source: MHA Annual Reports 2013-18.

The State police forces are always short of funds for improving infrastructure, mobility and training. The reduction of funds by the MHA is likely to affect their modernisation programmes. The Union Government, therefore, must enhance the amount under this scheme.

NEED TO STRENGTHEN COORDINATION

The 26/11 Mumbai attack clearly brought out the lack of co-ordination between different agencies of the Central and State governments. Neither the Intelligence input given by the Intelligence Bureau to the Maharashtra Government was acted upon nor did the Intelligence Bureau follow it up with the state after conveying the Intelligence input. The Coast Guard authorities who had earlier detained and later released the sea-borne terrorists, did not inform the State police or Central Intelligence agencies about it. The result: ten terrorists could wreak havoc and cause mayhem in the financial capital of India.

It is for the political and bureaucratic leadership of the nation to ensure effective coordination between different agencies and SFs concerned with national security.

Legal Reform and Internal Security Doctrine

It is an irony that in India, which aspires to be a super power, its criminal justice system of which the police is a part and the first responder to tackle internal security challenges, continues to function within the legal framework provided by the British in the nineteenth century. No wonder that it takes decades for courts to decide even simple cases. People therefore lose faith in the criminal justice system and take the law into their own hands. Lynching and mob violence are visible symptoms of the fast-eroding faith of the people in the rule of law.

The Indian Police Act 1861 has remained unchanged despite demands from police professionals and directions from the apex court. There is no central law to deal with organised crime which is a serious internal security challenge. The Private Detective Agencies (Regulation) Bill is pending in Parliament for the last 11 years. Drones are likely to be misused by terrorists and anti-social elements but there is no law on the horizon to deal with the challenge.

Lack of a national security doctrine includes an internal security doctrine that allows the political leadership to buckle under pressure and take decisions which erode the rule of law. The withdrawal of criminal cases against supporters of the party in power by State governments has become a new normal.

CONCLUSION

How robust is our internal security system? Have we taken adequate measures to revamp police and security forces? Are we addressing the root causes of internal security challenges? The answers may not be flattering. There are several weaknesses in India's internal security setup, as described in this essay.

India has lacked comprehensive security reviews of its preparedness and responses to internal security threats. A case in point is the 26/11 attack in Mumbai. While the USA appointed a commission to look into what went wrong during the 9/11 attacks, there has been no such body appointed by the Government of India. Where there have been other commissions and committees to inquire into various communal riots, violent public agitations and police reforms, not enough cognizance has been given to the recommendations made by them. India needs comprehensive internal security reforms instead of the usual piecemeal reactionary measures in the wake of every crisis.

REFERENCES

Annual Report 2017-18, Ministry of Home Affairs, Government of India.

Ayaz Memon, Ronzone Banerji, *India 50: The Making of Nation*, Book Quest Publishers, Bombay, 1997.

Balraj Puri, *Kashmir: Insurgency and After*, Orient Longman, 2008.

Crime in India 2016, National Crime Records Bureau, MHA.

Data on Police Organizations, BPR&D, MHA.

David Kilcullen, *Counter-Insurgency*, Oxford University Press, 2010.

Global Trends 2030: Alternative World, National Intelligence Council, USA, 2012.

India Vision 2020, National Planning Commission, Govt. of India, 2004.

Initiatives for Peace and Development in Jammu and Kashmir, MHA, Government of India, 2006.

Khushwant Singh, *The End of India*, Penguin, 2017.

Madhav Godbole, *The Holocaust of Indian Partition: An Inquest*, Rupa & Co, 2006.

Neil Padukone, *Security in a Complex Era: Emerging Challenges Facing India*, Observer Research Foundation, 2016.

Public Order, Fifth Report, Second Administrative Reforms Commission, Govt. of India, 2007.

The 9/11 Commission Report, WE Norton & Company, New York.

World Youth Report, "Youth and the 2030 Agenda for Sustainable Development," United Nations Department of Economic and Social Affairs, 2018.

7

Comprehensive Border Security: Foundations to Secure the Nation

R.K. Arora

Modern border security has gained indisputable importance in matters of national security as the forces of globalisation have unleashed a phenomenon of highly integrated nation-states with its extreme vulnerability and consequent porous borders magnifying the risk posed to the internal and external security of a geographically diverse nation like ours. The security of our land borders presents a daunting challenge, as it requires coordinated and concerted action by the administrative, diplomatic, security, intelligence, legal, regulatory and economic apparatus of the country to secure our frontiers and maximise the state's interests.

Border security cannot be viewed through a narrow national security prism as it has a much broader scope and outlook where cross-border relations with our immediate neighbours play an unmistakable role in the augmentation of infrastructural and economic development. Paving the way for pragmatism and exposing the futility of engaging in any covert or overt military tactics, border security thus becomes an essential byproduct of cordial cross-border terms and a necessity for continuous economic engagement.

The role of border guarding forces in the formulation of any effective border security strategy assumes critical significance, especially when there are conflict-ridden historical legacy, frequent border skirmishes, and lack of strong trade and investment ties as repeatedly seen in case of our intractable western neighbour. The border guarding forces also face the insurmountable challenge of cross-border infiltration, illegal migration, smuggling and other forms of trans-border crimes. Border management, besides guarding, defending and managing the borders, includes maintaining, developing and fostering of a conducive economic and cultural zone where there is a joint effort of border guarding forces of respective countries thus also highlighting the 'strategic deterrent' role played by the forces.

The current era of high interdependence and economic rationale has redefined the concept of border security and border management with one term often being interchanged for the other. Such recalibration and reorientation of this concept have gained widespread acceptance due to the foray of border guarding forces into the non-traditional peace and security realm. Earlier, there was a sharp delineation where border guarding was a policing task and border defence, as the name indicates, was a security-related task; all these have been subsumed under a broad aegis of border management with a comprehensive and an all-encompassing overview.

In India, the issue of border management was given its belated nomenclature and a clear enunciated role when the Department of Border Management was created in the Ministry of Home Affairs (MHA) in January 2004. The department was created to pay focused attention to the targeted issues in relation to the management of the international land and coastal borders, strengthening of border policing and guarding infrastructure creation such as roads, fencing and floodlighting of the borders and implementation of the Border Area Development Program (BADP). Moreover, a Border Management Division under the Department of Border Management was created which dealt with matters pertaining to coordination of the Department of Border Management, including issues related to Empowered Committee on Border Infrastructure (ECBI), issues related to Border Area Development Program (BADP), Integrated Check Posts (ICPs), Land Ports Authority of India (LPAI), Management of Indo-Bangladesh Border, Indo-Pakistan Border, Indo-Nepal Border, Indo-China Border, Indo-Bhutan Border and finally management of Indo-Myanmar Border.[1]

A country such as ours with difficult geographical terrain and high border porosity makes the adoption of upgraded technology and constant innovations in a technological realm an unavoidable option to not only survive but to pre-empt any impending threat. There has been a steady rise of various new and evolving security threats. Thus, there has been growing emphasis on allocation of funds and deployment of a suitable mix and class of different types of hi-tech electronic surveillance equipment like Night Vision Devices (NVDs), Hand-Held Thermal Imagers (HHTIs), Battle Field Surveillance Radars (BFSRs), Direction Finders (DFs), Unattended Ground Sensors (UGS), high powered telescopes, etc., on the international borders (IB) of the country, to act as a force multiplier for effective 'border governance & border management'.[2]

India has shared land borders of 15,106.7 km with seven neighbouring countries. This border area consists of 111 districts, spread over 15 states and two Union Territories. Guarding an unmarked border coupled with a highly difficult terrain makes it an enormous task for the border guarding forces to completely secure the entire stretch of the border with minimum intrusions and infiltrations. Thus, the role of better infrastructure, trained and motivated manpower, improved, and state-of the-art surveillance technology, modernisation of border guarding forces and joint coordination among all the stakeholders is highly imperative.[3]

Global Best Practices in Border Security

The September 11, 2001 terror attacks on the USA transformed the conceptions of border security globally. Internationally, many countries took steps to rethink approaches to border security in the post-9/11 environment. Some countries moved to emphasise border control as part of a larger and emerging "homeland security enterprise" that dealt with how internal, external, and trans-boundary threats affect domestic security. This chapter has briefly analysed the best practices adopted by the USA, Israel and China in the context of topography, surveillance technology and infrastructure and manpower integration with technology.

The primary reason for studying the border management of these countries is not difficult to understand. The USA had one of the busiest borders and modern border management practices with Mexico in terms of illegal crossing and with the use of technology and active confluence between various departments at the policy level, which led to control of the situation. Israel is a long-standing partner of India in defence technologies and facing severe problems of illegal border crossing and hostilities in the Israel-Palestinian border. China is an emerging power internationally and developing its border management by using new approaches effectively. More importantly, China is India's most important neighbour with whom India has long-standing border disputes; therefore, whatever China does on its border has direct national security implications on India.

United States of America

The United States of America (USA), a global superpower and far ahead of developing countries like India in the field of surveillance technology, had traditionally viewed border management as mostly a Customs and immigration based challenge. But after 9/11, policymakers and officials increasingly viewed borders as potential points of entry for would-be terrorists. The USA shares 11,200 km of land borders with Canada and Mexico as well as rivers, lakes and coastal waters around the country. The border of the USA with Canada is quite peaceful with hardly any major issue of smuggling, infiltration or terrorist activity. However, the USA-Mexico border is the busiest land crossing in the world and one of the most heavily fortified.

The Department of Home Land Security (DHS) in the USA works to secure borders through the deployment of personnel, technology and infrastructure. The department works closely with neighbours in Canada and Mexico and many other federal, state, local, tribal and territorial partners.[4] Customs and Border Protection (CBP) Border Patrol agents and officers guard America's front lines. Their major responsibility is to prevent terrorists and their weapons from entering the USA while continuing their mission of seizing contraband and apprehending criminals and others who illegally attempt to enter the USA. Patrols in the Southwest border of the USA have substantially increased the amount of drugs, guns, and cash being seized.

Topography: The USA-Mexico border is 3,200-km-long stretching from San Diego on the Pacific coast to Brownsville on the Gulf of Mexico. It runs through four US and six Mexican states, areas of forbidding desert and urban sprawl. The border traverses a variety of terrains, ranging from major metropolitan areas to uninhabitable deserts. The region is characterised by deserts, rugged hills and two major rivers—the Colorado and the Rio Grande which provide waters to the largely arid but fertile lands along the rivers in both countries.

Surveillance Technology: The CBP is responsible for securing the borders of the USA and employs various technologies to enforce laws and regulations at the border, including immigration and narcotics enforcement laws. One of the premier technologies is the Border Surveillance System (BSS) which is a combination of surveillance technologies designed to assist the CBP in detecting, identifying, apprehending, and removing persons illegally entering the USA at and between ports of entry and enforcing US laws.[5] The BSS monitors a particular individual or location as part of its law enforcement investigation and criminal proceedings. It is located across urban, rural, and remote areas along the US border and includes tethered aerial video, radars, mobile and fixed ground video with day and night thermal capabilities, ground sensors, radio frequency sensors, ultra-light aircraft, detection and acoustic sensing devices. Each surveillance system is deployed taking into account the surrounding terrain and population. The BSS may capture persons in urban, rural, and remote areas along the US. border through video cameras, laser range finders, radar, radio frequency sensors and acoustic devices, or some combination thereof.

Infrastructure: *Mobile Border Surveillance Systems:* Mobile border surveillance systems are capable of collecting surveillance data from various locations because the surveillance platform and can physically be moved to meet the ever-changing mission and its needs. A description of each of the mobile border surveillance systems is as follows: Mobile Video Surveillance System (MVSS) uses mobile video recording units on platforms that can be moved to provide the best visual range for surveillance of several miles. MVSS provides day and night surveillance images that allow the user or operator to determine if there are items of interest or suspicious criminal activities occurring within the area of coverage and to provide situational awareness to the interdicting Border Patrol Agent.

Mobile Surveillance Capability (MSC) uses truck-mounted mobile video recording units with cameras and radar mounted to extended masts that allow on-board monitoring of surveillance images by an attending user. MSC covers a range of several miles under optimal conditions. It is deployed primarily in remote rural areas or other areas where no fixed surveillance technologies are deployed. Agent Portable Surveillance System (APSS) is a surveillance suite that includes cameras with a visual range for surveillance of several miles and ground radar that can be carried and used by Border Patrol Agents in areas where fixed and vehicle-mounted solutions are not feasible or appropriate.

Ultra-Light Aircraft Detection (ULAD) is a mobile radar system that is being tested to detect and track small, low, or slow flying aircraft with a small radar cross section, known as ultra-light aircraft, in remote areas along US borders. The ULAD system increases and enhances the operators' ability to identify suspicious small aircraft so that the CBP can monitor possible smuggling routes and make an interdiction. The ULAD system tracks aircraft from entry to either landing or exiting the USA when aerial assets are not within response range.

Fixed Border Surveillance Systems: Fixed border surveillance systems are capable of collecting surveillance data from a dedicated location. A description of each of the fixed border surveillance systems follows:[6]

- Tethered Aerostat Radar System (TARS) uses the aerostat (a large unmanned blimp or balloon) as a stationary airborne platform for surveillance radar. TARS detects and monitors low-altitude aircraft and vessels along the USA-Mexico border, the Straits of Florida, and a portion of the Caribbean in support of the Counter-Narcotics Program with the Department of Defence (DOD). The program's primary mission is to provide persistent, long-range, detection and monitoring of low-level air, maritime and surface narcotics traffickers using radar detection. There are currently eight operational sites in continental USA and Puerto Rico. Some TARS are equipped with a video camera capable of assisting CBP users in detecting and tracking pedestrian and vehicular traffic; other sites monitor maritime traffic and relay CBP communications to facilitate interagency operations.
- Integrated Fixed Tower (IFT) sensor suites include towers with mounted day and night cameras and radar that can be monitored from a local CBP Border Patrol sector facility.
- Remote Video Surveillance System (RVSS) provides automated day and night wide-area surveillance along the USA border using multiple colour cameras and thermal infrared detection video cameras. CBP uses RVSS to detect and track illegal entries. The sensor images are transmitted via a dedicated communications system to a CBP facility where the information is processed and displayed.
- Law Enforcement Technical Collection (LETC) intercepts radio communications on HF, VHF, and UHF frequencies. LETC operators only collect radio communications in compliance with applicable laws,

directives, and policies. CBP officials make notes of suspicious radio chatter including frequency used, location of transmission, code names, and code words to log suspicions. LETC supports the prevention of unauthorised entry by persons; interdiction of smuggled, hazardous material and contraband; and it assists investigative efforts using a risk-based strategy.

Manpower Integration with Technology: The combination of fixed and mobile surveillance systems supports CBP's persistent and situational surveillance of the US border at and between ports of entry. Sensor information may be relayed to a Border Patrol sector station, Headquarters, port of entry or users at a fusion centre to coordinate a response when available and where necessary to respond. Sensor information is displayed to authorised users at these locations based on their assigned duties and the need to know. CBP is better able to respond to and coordinate its interdictions and law enforcement responses to events at or near the border using sensor technologies.

Although the US government has spent a lot of resources, including technological solutions for US-Mexico border security, in recent times, there is a paradigm shift in the border security strategy and policy on the US-Mexico border. As border security has acquired political dimension in US domestic politics the Trump Administration has approved construction of a wall along the US-Mexico border. However, there is uncertainty about the actual cost of the wall as different stakeholders are projecting the costs according to their estimates which vary from $12 billion to $70 billion. However, there are some question marks about the policy continuity regarding the border wall by the incoming Presidential election in the USA.

Israel

Israel's border management is quite similar to our border management requirements as highly hostile neighbours surround both countries. Israeli technology, developed to safeguard Israel's national security, is both sophisticated and innovative and among the best in the world.

Topography: Israel topography is very diverse, with desert conditions in the south and snow-capped mountains in the north. It is bounded to the north by Lebanon, the northeast by Syria, the east by Jordan and the West Bank, and the southwest by Egypt. The West Bank mountain ridge contributes to Israeli security in significant ways. Israel's military control of the Jordan Valley allows it to prevent the smuggling of advanced weapons to Palestinian terrorist groups. The West Bank mainly comprises a north-south mountain ridge that dominates vital Israeli infrastructure along the coast, including Israel's international airport, high-tech companies, and most of the major highways connecting Haifa, Tel Aviv, and Jerusalem.

Surveillance Technology: Israel's border management responsibility lies with Israel defence force (IDF). IDF is using the latest surveillance technology for border management and for critical crossing-point protection. Since the IDF has operational needs for controlling the borders and must be prepared for a variety of combat scenarios, therefore, they put in a lot of efforts and resources in the testing of advanced technologies that will help control and manage the borders. Presently, the latest surveillance technology being used by Israel for border protection has two main configurations. The first is a fence configuration that gives a detection strip all along the fence. The second is for critical crossing-points which have monitoring systems for short ranges in the sensitive crossing line. Aerostat-based sensors and unmanned patrol units employing autonomous, unmanned vehicles can also be integrated into the system. A wide variety of access controls, tampering sensors and sophisticated cyber guards are also used to extend this protection to cyberspace.[7]

Infrastructure: The border Infrastructure available for the IDF is a wide range of capabilities which include perimeter protection by physical obstacles (fences) and virtual obstacles (electro-optical, radar, seismic or magnetic sensors), triggering alarms when an intrusion is detected, blacktop/concrete road for smooth movement of troops, fully-equipped high watchtowers along the perimeter fence and repair and maintenance facility near the border for immediate repair and maintenance of sophisticated surveillance technologies and arrangement of Quick Reaction Teams (QRT) at suitable distances.

Manpower Integration with Technology: Integration of manpower with the advanced technology is essential to achieve the desired outcome. Israel defence force personnel are well trained to handle these sophisticated technologies like electronic fencing and modern covert technologies, backed by video motion detection capabilities, radar and electro-optical-based surveillance sensors, and autonomous, unmanned aerial, ground sensors. Manpower integration with the latest surveillance technologies offers sophisticated tracking and screening of people, vehicles and cargo, ensuring effective border domination and border protection. The availability of nearby manufacturing units and repair facilities for the surveillance technology has resulted in quick repair and replacement of defective equipment/technology, thus making the Israeli defence forces among the best in the world in the field of border security.

China

China has solved its border disputes with all her neighbouring countries except India. Because of heightened infiltration activities in the Xinjiang region, it has lately garnered international attention with the increasing radicalisation of the Muslim Uyghur community post 9/11, thus posing a massive challenge to border security. In addition, the remoteness of the India-China border, the inhospitable terrain and its distance from major consumption centres have generally acted as a disincentive to trans-border crimes like large-scale smuggling. In China, the border check authorities are known as *"the frontline"* for short and their main task is to manage people, to check passports and visas of people entering or leaving the Chinese border; to monitor and protect transportation tools and to check luggage, if necessary. Different border check stations manage specific work. Customs officers of the General Administration of Customs in each opened-up port and officers of border police stations operate together in the same ports. If there is a border check station, then there is a Customs office and vice versa.[8]

Topography: The topography of China is diverse with snow-capped mountains, deep river valleys, and broad basins, high plateaus, plains, hills and sandy dunes. In general, the land is high in the west and descends to the east coast. China's borders have more than 20,000 km of land frontier shared with nearly all the nations of mainland East Asia and have been disputed at several points. In the western sector, China claimed portions of the 41,000-sq-km Pamir Mountains area where the borders of Afghanistan, Pakistan, the former Soviet Union and China meet in Central Asia. The 6,542-kilometre frontier with the former USSR has been a source of continual friction. Eastward from Bhutan and north of the Brahmaputra River, the area was demarcated by the British as the McMahon Line, drawn along the Himalayas in 1914 as the Sino-Indian border. India accepts, but China rejects this boundary. Most of the mountainous and militarised boundary with India is still in dispute.

Surveillance Technology: China has evolved an advanced border surveillance technological system. Under this integrated round-the-clock frontier monitoring system, China had deployed advanced radars and drones in Tibetan areas bordering India as well as in Xinjiang and Yunnan regions to curb illegal border crossings and drug trafficking. The Border Surveillance system has integrated electro-optical devices, radars, communications equipment, command-and-control instruments and tools for image analysis. The system gave border patrol teams the capability to perform round-the-clock, all-weather surveillance of illegal cross-border movements. When people try to cross the border, they are detected by the system, which then automatically notifies soldiers. Compared with traditional border monitoring networks that mainly depend on video surveillance, the Chinese border surveillance system has a broader coverage and more deterrence due to the use of drones and acoustic weapons.[9]

Infrastructure: *China has built up massive support along the Sino-Indian border, integrating the border region to the Chinese mainland with accessibility to the Line of Actual Control (LAC) and strengthening counter offensive capabilities.* The Chinese, thus, retains a clear advantage in military mobilisation and capabilities vis-a-vis their Indian counterparts. China has been developing infrastructure along the border to integrate its front-lying region with the Chinese mainland, a strategy most visible in China's infrastructure projects in the Tibet Autonomous Region (TAR), which was occupied in 1949. A defence build-up for quick mobilisation supported by a robust air defence system and an uncomplicated administrative framework is the second objective of this strategy. And thirdly, the strategy is all about extending China's accessibility to the LAC through rail networks and in many cases using some of the bordering countries like Nepal and Pakistan to strengthen its strategic hold in the border areas. Expanding its communication network is yet another important feature of integrating the border region with the Chinese mainland. As many as 665 townships of the TAR have been connected with optic fibre cable (OFC).[10]

Manpower Integration with Technology: Chinese defence force personnel are well trained to handle these sophisticated technologies like video motion detection capabilities, radar and electro-optical-based surveillance sensors and autonomous, unmanned aerial and ground sensors. Manpower integration with the latest surveillance technologies offers sophisticated tracking and screening of people, vehicles, and cargo, ensuring effective border domination and border protection. China is also developing a repair facility near its borders to provide timely repair and maintenance of arms and equipment, including surveillance equipment.

We have discussed various border security models of the USA, Israel and China to understand the global perspective and how, with technological advancement, new technologies are emerging and how many countries are making use of these technologies for effective management of their borders. Every day, a new dimension is being added to border management and these dimensions shape the practices being used worldwide.

Border Security in Indian Perspective

Border security becomes more critical for India as it is like an island of democracy between the seas of anarchical or unstable states. There is cross-border smuggling of drugs, cattle, humans, artefacts and fake currency notes. Unfortunately, in this scenario, our border guarding forces like the BSF, SSB, ITBP and AR appear to be severely understaffed and under-equipped which is taking a heavy toll on the economic, social and political stability of our country.

The 2001 Group of Ministers (GoM) review of border management gave many important recommendations regarding the security of our borders. One of the significant recommendations was the setting up of a separate department of border management within the Ministry of Home Affairs. This has been done. Yet other major recommendations like early settlement of our maritime borders and the demarcation of land boundaries have not yet been fully implemented. The GoM had strongly recommended the principle of *"one border one force"* for better accountability and specialisation. It emphasised the imperative of not deploying the border guarding forces for law and order duties and counter-insurgency operations. It made some recommendations specific to better management of the India-Pakistan, India-Nepal and other borders. As a result of these recommendations, border security has received more attention but the recent attacks in Pathankot, Uri, Nagrota and Pulwama have again shown that a lot more needs to be done to improve India's border security.

India's most hostile Indo-Pak border guarded by the Border Security Force (BSF) also has the mandate to guard the border with Bangladesh in the east. The boundary between India and Pakistan, the most sensitive of India's frontiers, spans 3,323 kilometres stretching from NJ 9842 in Jammu and Kashmir to the Rann of Kutch in Gujarat. In the 1990s, India began to fence this massive border of which 550 km in J&K were completed in 2004. By 2011, almost all of the border fencing along J&K, Punjab, Rajasthan and Gujarat was completed. The entire border is also lit with strong floodlights installed on more than 50,000 poles. As a result, the Indo-Pak border can actually be seen from space at night.

The Government of India has initiated various steps to ensure the security of Indian borders. Border security in India poses a peculiar challenge for the security agencies due to varied topography, climatic conditions, extreme weather variations and relations with neighbouring countries.

In the western theatre, the Indo-Pak border is very active and one of the most hostile borders of the world along which the Border Security Force and the Indian Army are deployed. The eastern border of India has different challenges and working conditions. The Nepal, Bhutan and Myanmar borders face different varieties of challenges for the government; the border with Bangladesh poses a new dimension of border security.

The Indo-China border is very complex and challenging for border security. The government is working on these issues and has deployed many resources in the form of fencing, floodlights, construction of roads, improvement of border outposts, improving border security infrastructure and also giving priority to enhancing border security and the living conditions of the border population.

However, in the present scenario, border guarding forces together are a highly manpower-intensive force. There should be greater infusion of technology into our border guarding force, taking into account the peculiarities of each border segment, and the perceived threat, terrain and local population sensitivities. At the same time, developing a suitable infrastructure as per the requirement of the latest surveillance technology is as essential as the latest technology.

Topography: The Indian border terrain poses a big challenge to border surveillance and security. In the western theatre, the India-Pakistan boundary does not follow any geographical barrier. It is easy to infiltrate from this stretch as compared to the heavily-mined and guarded Line of Control as well as the international border in J&K. Dense fog in winters makes border surveillance an added challenge. As the border terrain is broken and forested, the rivulet beds provide an ideal cover for terrorists who can sneak in and reach the busy highways that snake along the border. This enables terrorists to hijack vehicles and mount rapid strikes. In almost all the terror attacks, militants used snatched cars to attack the intended targets, mostly catching security forces off-guard. The porosity of this border has facilitated various illegal activities such as smuggling, drugs and arms trafficking, and infiltration. Heroin and fake Indian currency are the two predominant items of smuggling along this border. Other items include saffron, textiles and mercury, which are smuggled from Pakistan. The villagers adjacent to the border are alleged to be involved in the smuggling in a big way. Money laundering is also quite rampant along the border. A large-scale hawala network is flourishing in Punjab, especially in Ludhiana. Besides, the border population has also been subjected to hostile propaganda by Pakistan, designed to mislead and sway their loyalties.

In the eastern theatre, riverine, mountains and thick forested area are the key challenges to border security. In future, India's eastern border will be more hostile and needs hefty resources to secure them.

Surveillance Technology: The extreme weather conditions and hostile environment along Indian borders make surveillance a challenging task. The BGFs (border guarding forces) have been instrumental in the introduction of latest surveillance technology for taking on the challenges of border security along the Pakistan borders and in some patches of the eastern borders. Presently, surveillance is carried out by conducting regular OP/patrolling duties day and night by BSF personnel. In addition, several electronic surveillance equipment like Passive Night Vision Devices (PNVDs), Hand Held Thermal Imagers (HHTIs), Battle Field Surveillance Radars (BFSRs), Long Range Finders (LRFs), Unattended Ground Sensors (UGS), High Powered Telescope, Long Range Reconnaissance and Observation System (LORROS) are used by the BSF along the Punjab border as force multipliers for greater surveillance. Apart from the above, at some places, especially in riverine areas, IR sensors and PTZ cameras are also employed on a trial basis. The camera provides observation capabilities in full darkness as well as under harsh battlefield and degraded visibility conditions.

Infrastructure: The government has carried out several infrastructure development work like border fencing and floodlighting projects.

Fencing: The entire western and mostly Bangladesh border has been fenced with only the riverine areas left unfenced. In Rajasthan, fencing and floodlighting have also been completed, except for shifting sand dune areas that cannot be fenced. Fencing in Kashmir is complete, although floodlighting remains to be finished. A portion of the LOC has also been fenced. Gujarat is the last state to complete the fencing process. However, the infrastructure required for the deployment of sophisticated and costly surveillance equipment is still a farfetched dream. These surveillance equipment without proper infrastructure like large watchtowers with platforms for placing the equipment and adequate facility for power source results in improper/underutilisation and frequent breakdowns.

Manpower Integration with Technology: The end-users in BGFs are still looking at the latest surveillance technology as a burden on them instead of taking them as a force multiplier because it is adding to the inventory without providing any relief or ease in performing border guarding duty. One of the primary reasons is the lack of knowledge about the equipment as there is no proper training policy on this matter. Moreover, surveillance equipment, which is critical and sophisticated, requires specialised training and regular refresher courses to update requisite skills. The BSF also requires the integration of human resources with surveillance technology.

The repair and maintenance aspect of the force is also a major point of concern. The channelised procedure of reporting the defect in the equipment and then sending the stuff for repair through the same channel is an extremely time-consuming process in most cases, and is more than a month. During the period of repair, there is no substitute equipment available as replacement. The long time taken in repairs is because of non-availability of major repair facility near the border. Further, due to continuing with old/obsolete equipment also results in frequent defects in the system. Moreover, lack of proper infrastructure and training of troops in the handling of surveillance equipment are a big reason for numerous defects in them.

Smart Solutions for Border Security

Surveillance Technology: The gap in surveillance technology between India and other countries like the USA and Israel is enormous. The equipment that we have today has been in use in the USA and Israel for many decades. When we were using second-generation Image Intensifier Tube (IITubes) based PNVDs, the USA and Israel were using fourth-generation IITube based PNVDs. The present infrastructure at the border is not sufficient even for the existing surveillance equipment.

Training: Training has always been the strength of BGFs in comparison to other police organisations, but the same cannot be claimed regarding training on surveillance equipment. BGFs still do not have any proper training policy for surveillance equipment. Presently, some training modules on surveillance equipment are being imparted for a few selected persons for one or two weeks' duration at different levels and this too is not a regular feature. This does not suffice the considerable need for trained manpower required for border surveillance. Since these surveillance equipments are now present with all field formations of BGFs, though not as per actual requirement, it becomes more pertinent to have all BGF persons who are involved in border duties to get regular proper training on surveillance equipment with the continuous support of refresher courses. Particular focus should be given for technically sophisticated equipment like BFSRs, LORROS and HHTI.

Weather Condition and Topography: The weather conditions in India are extreme with a varied topography which offers challenges to BGF personnel as well as to the surveillance equipment used by them. Challenges involve dealing with temperatures varying from minus 30 degrees in the snow-clad mountains of the Himalayas to 55 degrees in the desert of Thar, extreme humidity in the north-east to the salty Rann of Kutch. The varying climate from sweltering summers to rainy and foggy conditions also limits the role of surveillance equipment. Such trying weather conditions reduce the efficiency of surveillance equipment.

Reaction Time: The reaction time on detection of trans-border crime activity depends on the logistic support and available infrastructure. The present available logistics and infrastructure does not fill the purpose. If we see the best practices in the world, we are lagging far behind. The reason may also be because of the long length of the border and varying terrain apart from lack of logistic support and infrastructure.

Recommendations

Comprehensive border security is the need of the hour when threats our borders have multiplied with the changing pattern of crimes on the borders. During the past few years, terrorist attacks in Pathankot, Uri and Pulwama and other incidents sponsored from across the border have challenged India's border security in different ways.

Maritime security concerns in the South China Sea are increasing for several reasons such as higher volumes of shipping traffic, protection of exclusive economic zone resources, piracy, terrorist threats, greater international scrutiny of ports, and the modernisation of regional coast guard forces. This is bound to affect India's border security, both directly and indirectly. As the government strengthens security for the maritime and coastal borders, criminal syndicates and terrorists are likely to find gaps in the land borders. There will be more pressure on the border guarding forces to safeguard the land borders.

In this complex scenario, traditional practices of border security are not able to mitigate the threats. Hence, we need innovative and introduce new border security solutions.

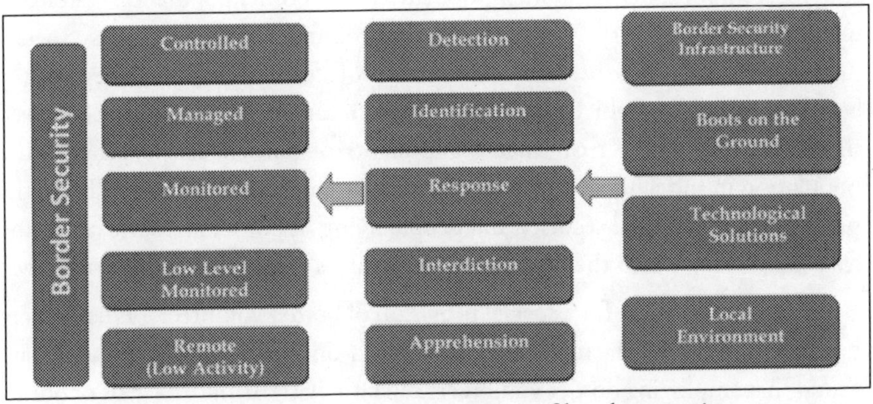

Basically, there are four major components of border security:

- Border security infrastructure
- Border guarding forces
- Technological solutions
- Local environment (Border population + state agencies + other security organisations + civil society)

In addition to the above, different borders need different types of commitment and policies to mitigate operational threats to the borders of any country. As per the degree of security requirements, there are (i) **controlled** borders, (ii) **managed** borders, (iii) **monitored** borders, (iv) **low level monitored**, and (v) **remote** borders. However, border security infrastructure along each of these borders cannot be the same, as the response mechanism in terms of (i) **detection**, (ii) **identification**, and (iii) **reaction** depends on the degree of threat. For instance, the Indo-Pak border would need an extremely high degree of preparedness from the perspective of all four components. In contrast, the same cannot be the case with the Indo-Bangladesh borders and Indo-Nepal borders.

Keeping in view the significance of these components, India has taken several steps to develop necessary infrastructure on borders, to promote the capacity of border guarding forces, to promote the use of state-of-the-art technology and to address the local environment in terms of improving the living conditions of the border population.

Therefore, it is important to understand that there should be a healthy local environment which includes state government, sister agencies, civil society and, most importantly, the border population. The border population is strategic property of any country. Most of the secure countries of the world give special importance to their border population to protect their borders. They are the best force multipliers which no other component can replace. It has been observed that compared to the first three components of border security, the border population in India has not received as much attention as is necessary. From the perspective of national security, the people living in border areas must develop friendly relations with the border guarding forces engaged in border security.

I would also argue for a special provision of border volunteers. This concept has been developed during my long research on border security, and I have found that employing border volunteers can be a masterstroke in terms of border security. They can be a valuable source of information and intelligence about cross-border infiltration and other illegal activities; they can reduce the administrative work burden, and implementation of this scheme can also reduce the involvement of border people in multiple crimes.

The MHA should look into the allocation of a greater share of funds/resources to the BSF to develop the requisite physical infrastructure, authorisation of workforce and surveillance equipment in the BSF. There is a need for diversification for transfer of technologies, collaborations and technological partnership with countries that have such state-of-the-art technologies. Over-dependence on a few countries (Israel and the USA) creates impediments for technical upgradation. We need to develop indigenous capabilities according to the peculiarities of each border.

Border guarding forces should look into the framing of a proper training policy to incorporate the handling and operation of surveillance equipment in the training and promotional courses at all levels. And a separate specialised training institute should be established at the force level to develop trained manpower for operation, handling, repair and maintenance.

Border guarding practitioners should emphasise on field requirements/ topography/climatic conditions for an official authorisation of specialised surveillance equipment.

The present fencing system is antiquated, which needs a complete replacement with SMART solutions which are cost-effective embedment of Intelligence with existing resources. Due to the latest sophistication in the nature of security threats, it is recommended to use UAVs and drones to gain increased traction of infiltration as well as to keep our cross-border counterparts under surveillance.

Last, but not least, we need smart users for smart solutions.

NOTES

1. Gautam Das "Securing India's Borders: Challenges and Policy Options", Delhi: Centre for Land Warfare Studies, 2011.
2. Annual Report 2008-09, "Chapter III: Border Management", Ministry of Home Affairs, Government of India, pp. 24-38.
3. Pushpita Das, "India's Border Management: Select Documents", New Delhi: Institute for Defence Studies and Analyses, 2010.
4. For further information, https://www.dhs.gov/border-security-overview.
5. Privacy Impact Assessment for the Border Surveillance Systems (BSS) DHS/CBP/PIA-022, August 29, 2014. https://www.dhs.gov/sites/default/files/publications/privacy_pia_CBP_BSS_August2014.pdf
6. Thomas M. Manson, "Border security technology", *Public Safety IT, Nov/Dec 2006*, http://www.hendonpub.com/resources/article_archive/results/details?id=3478
7. For further information, http://mops.gov.il/english/researchanddevelopmenteng/pages/hls_technology
8. For further information, https://www.wired.com/images_blogs/threatlevel/files/cisco_presentation.pdf
9. "China deploys radars, drones to enhance border surveillance", 9 November 2015, http://www.tibetanreview.net/china-deploys-radars-drones-to-enhance-border-surveillance.
10. Jhinuk Chowdhury, "Expanding Chinese Infrastructure on the Indian border", 11 March 2016, http://mantraya.org/expanding-chinese-infrastructure-at-the-indian-border

8

India and the Global Order in Reset: The Effects of Uncertain Dynamism

Lt Gen Syed Ata Hasnain (Retd.)

The last time the world entered transition in search of a new world order was in 1989-90. Glasnost and Perestroika, initiated by Mikhail Gorbachev in the mid-Eighties, triggered and to an extent even enabled the onset. However, while the two super powers themselves maintained a balanced relationship with receding threats of conflict between them the period yet was turbulent. The former Soviet Union was dismantling its structure with the creation of 15 new republics, Warsaw Pact nations were no longer remaining bound to the former Soviet club and former Yugoslavia was imploding into civil war with creation of six nations. Away from Europe and Eurasia, the latent but suppressed forces of ethno-nationalism were getting released. In Africa and in Central Asia these forces were manifesting in violence. The United Nations (UN) had suddenly found a new voice with an enlarged role in attempting to stabilise the internal, proxy and other conflicts with peace enforcement, peacemaking or peacekeeping operations. Human rights and globalisation became bywords. With the USA as the only remaining superpower and Europe yet fresh and strong from the victory in the Cold War, the partnership was strong. For a new world order to emerge there was no necessity of an imposed international system or even a Westphalian kind of treaty. Geopolitics shaped the progression and that happened through the last 30 years with the interests of nations being sought and fought over, alternative ideologies attempting to muscle their way and emerging technologies playing their role.

To understand why two decades into the new millennium suddenly the world is taking note of another emerging change in the world order it is necessary to briefly examine what the major factors were which shaped the current world order through the last 30 years. It is important to take note of the fact that this time it is being termed a 'Reset' and not a new world order. The broad implication of that understanding is the fact that unlike 1989-90, this time the transition is in place much quieter and without a preceding jolt, unless you wish to term the arrival of the Trump presidency a jolt.

The major trends of the last 30 years which shaped the new world order, in no order of priority, were as follows:

- Domination of the USA and unsuccessful attempts to refocus on the Asia Pacific after 50 years of the core areas of conflict being Europe and the Middle East. As much as it tried to neutralise the potential rise of China the USA remained mired in conflicts in the Middle East and the Af-Pak region; China was important but yet secondary. US core interests continued to be dictated by the energy resources of the Middle East until the shale gas revolution diluted its dependency leading to relative receding interest by 2012 or so.
- Areas which had remained stable due to the balance of power which the Cold War brought with it emerged into internal sub-national conflicts. Africa, the Balkans, Central Asia and Russia's other near abroad regions were among these. Progressive stabilisation occurred as new nations emerged in Europe and older ones changed their political outlook with the purge of the ghosts of the communist era. The EU and NATO's eastward march promised them greater opportunities.
- Terror and its linkages with elements within Islam threatened to subsume the world. Progressively it divided the world on the basis of faith; faith becoming a political term. The main strain of Islam which attempted to hijack the faith was the Saudi version—Wahabi Sunni, which primarily aimed at the return of Islam to its original moorings. The interventions in Afghanistan and Iraq gave a spurt to greater divisiveness among faiths and greater resort to the hybrid nature of conflicts. This

led organisations such as the Al-Qaeda to initially gain ground in less charted areas and from that came the rise of the Islamic State (IS) as a potential Caliphate based upon the employment of extreme, unbridled violence.

- The information technology boom led to migrations of working populations, outsourcing and a general flattening of the world with far greater international travel and tourism becoming a major economy booster. Nations such as India benefitted from the software boom emerging as giants in that field and becoming the core centres of outsourcing giving a fillip to their economies.
- Terror was enabled by the progress in technology; it provided ease of financing, command and control, training and coordination of terror acts. Later, the IS revolutionised online motivation towards radical extremist violence.
- 9/11 came like a half-way mark triggering the launch of the global war on terror (GWOT). It led to conventional expeditionary intervention with no positive results. GWOT remains in place, much lesser in intensity but a temporary halt in international terror activities may lead to a dilution of interest in the transnational structures against terror and efforts towards counter-terrorism which could potentially lead to resurgence at a later stage.
- Even as all the above was in progress, Islam itself was threatened by sectarian divide. The Shia-Sunni conflict overflowed into proxy conflicts fought in different parts of the Middle East. Iran's isolation from the Western world and the rest of the Middle East gave it inspirational progression towards achieving nuclear weapon status. The attempts at prevention of this dictated much of the time and energy spent by international diplomats culminating in an agreement in 2015—the Joint Comprehensive Plan of Action (JCPOA), now abrogated by unilateral US decision under President Trump.
- The emergence of China and India as fast developing economies influenced the international economic order. The term Middle Powers came into existence and by the later years in this millennium, their clubbing attempted a breakout from the stranglehold of the West and of the traditional advanced economies. The formation of BRICS gave rise to more economic blocs with ASEAN, although older, becoming among the most successful ones. The EU model flattened Europe with

common controls on borders, migration and economies.

- The economic progress of the world was largely based on globalisation which triggered expansion of free trade.
- Climate change became a greater threat even as the world struggled with protocols culminating in the Paris Accord in 2015.
- Without doubt the one supremely dominant factor through this period remained the rise of China and its voracious appetite for development which could only be fuelled through expanding trade and investment and assured energy imports. It led to the ambitious infrastructure projects connecting China to areas of potential economic growth. The Belt and Road Initiative (BRI) followed its New Silk Route initiatives. Yet doubts persist whether China's intent behind BRI is economic or strategic.
- The rise of China which was relatively peaceful through the Nineties and the early millennium changed course as the three modernisations of Deng Xiao Ping were progressively achieved—agriculture, industry and technical education. The fourth modernisation—the People's Liberation Army (PLA), last in priority, received an impetus in the early part of the millennium and with its progress China's experiments with coercion and actions against the rule-based order commenced.
- The one nation with whom the triggers of the new world order were linked was Russia. Its relative importance receded even though it remained a member of the UN Security Council and retained its nuclear arsenal. Two other fields helped it to retain influence; first, its abundant availability of gas with which it fed Europe and made it inextricably dependent and second, its arms industry which became much more commercial. As Russia hurtled downwards in political power, it latched on to China and the partnership helped it to avert further decline. Threatened by the eastward march of NATO and the potential of Central Asia going the Islamic way Russia's response towards retention and recovery of its power was messaged through its intervention in Ukraine, the annexation of Crimea and the active involvement in the Syrian Civil War. It was a way of communicating the re-emergence of Russia and its true aspirations.

The World in Reset Mode

Awkwardly it was the second quarter of 2018 when talk of reset in the world order began. A trail of events through 2015-18, a relatively short period, probably hastened change. The tilt of the world towards right-wing political thinking and ideological make up started to take shape. It did not succeed everywhere. In France and in Germany there was sufficient resistance by old world liberalism. However, right of centre as a philosophy gained primacy as much as authoritarianism, even within old democratic structures.

Obviously, the first assumption on which any current change is based is the perception of regression of US comprehensive power and the rise of alternative power centres. This always remains a highly debatable issue. In 1989-90, it was the USA alone supported by the larger Atlantic community of NATO which facilitated the change.

The arrival of a non-career politician at the helm of the US leadership ceased further change in the traditionally progressing new world order which was still in the making. Trump's disruptive style of leadership did not trigger the reset, it only hastened it. Obama had been aware of US limitations but was pragmatic to continue pushing for US primacy even as partnerships became more equal. Trump's strategic orientation, dictated largely by his many advisers remains in the shade of grey. The perception that the USA was bearing too much cost for the leadership of the world and that others needed to share the same is creating a backlash. The USA under Trump wishes to spend less, be less responsible for the management of international security and yet retain primacy of position in the pecking order. Trump's 'America First' is out of sync with attempts to retain power and influence. Without assuming responsibility, without readiness to shoulder greater financial burden and without more adjustment and willingness to compromise, the USA cannot hope to retain the kind of power and influence it held in the immediate post-Cold War period.

The greyness in perceptions across the world has forced a reset because nations are holding on to the few gains and unsure where these will take them in the complex 21st century strategic environment. If there were more transparency and clarity perhaps the process of change towards another world order would have been more perceptive. At present it is not. Trump's achievements such as the efforts towards stabilisation of the Korean Peninsula are noteworthy no doubt but the post event management of the dynamics remains in doubt due to unpredictability and lack of consistency.

In contrast, China's aggressive selling of its Belt and Road Initiative (BRI) to pump its version of reset may appear more appropriate but the expenses for it too are not being undertaken with free lunches but rather through coercive debt trap diplomacy. Its decision to ignore and virtually mock the judgment of the UN's International Tribunal for arbitration on the South China Sea issue, calling it "a piece of paper that is destined to come to naught", was a major trigger for the world to take note of its intent as more assertiveness and unwillingness to adhere to a rule-based order.

The real trigger for the ongoing reset was not recent and simply blaming the arrival of President Trump would be an unfair assumption. In fact this was in the making for some time once it was progressively realised that the liberal democratic order being sought by the USA and less energetically by the US allies could not adjust to China or Russia's political ideologies; a reset based upon only confrontation would spell a return to a new cold war. The decline of Russia post the end of the Cold War was mistakenly taken as a trend in perpetuity. The return of Russia's emphatic international role came with its decision to contest the Western march on Ukraine. The failed Arab Spring also gave the USA enough indicators of its inability to take forward the liberal democratic agenda contributing to its cooling and comparatively lower assertiveness in the Middle East.

Russia's return to active big power politics was challenged by the USA and Europe without sufficient muscle and unity. The expansion of NATO to Russia's doorstep was a challenge the latter had to resist. Yet Europe's dependence on Russian gas prevents unified sanctions on Russia and enhances the latter's ability to resist. For example in the European Union, as Germany expelled Russian diplomats, it quietly approved the construction of the Nord Stream 2 pipeline on its territory.

Not the least of triggers is the ongoing trade war seriously diluting 25 years of effective globalisation and interdependency. The reset is giving direction to new regional trade blocs such as the Regional Comprehensive Economic Partnership which includes ASEAN nations with China, Japan, South Korea, New Zealand and Australia; a reality within 2019 and much against US interests, it has also found India reluctant to come on board due to concerns about getting swamped by imports under the agreement—putting its domestic industry and agriculture at risk. Most countries yet do not want to give up the liberal approach in trade without control regimes. In fact, the USA withdrew from the Trans-Pacific Partnership (TPP) it initiated several years ago but other countries are trying to recreate it without US presence. The new protectionism the USA is attempting to foist, the politicisation of economic relations and attempts to foil positive economic interdependence in Europe, based on Russian natural gas supplies in exchange for European goods, as also China's unwillingness to be intimidated by trade wars may witness a path towards a new economic order which will form the basis of the reset underway.

It may seem apparently far-fetched but the US decision to withdraw from the JCPOA on Iran's nuclear efforts has been a clear trigger. The cleavage in the USA and European perceptions on management of international security came out into the open. The progressive attempts to isolate and coerce Iran with a potential regime change as the main intent are likely to be resisted in greater measure than the USA may have perceived.

The Middle East which had been the focus of the world through 2011-2017 due to the Syrian civil war, the rise and eventual defeat of the ISIS, the migrations to Europe and the entry of Russia, has apparently cooled. Yet, the sectarian divide in Islam has manifested in direct potential conflict between Saudi Arabia and Iran with the latter's continuing expansion of influence in the Levant. Not the least among the trends is the apparent change in Saudi Arabia sought by Prince Mohammad bin Salman (MbS), diluting its radical approach to faith and preparing the nation for the future. It is facilitating a more acceptable Saudi Arabia with stronger relationships with the USA and Israel. The Saudis remain deeply entrenched in an unwinnable war in Yemen against alleged Iranian proxies thus affecting both its economy and flexibility within the Middle East cauldron. It is perceptibly clear that the USA can ill afford to coerce Iran militarily any more than it has economically with sanctions. What is relevant is that there are limits to US military power in the Middle East, alone or in conjunction with its main allies, Saudi Arabia and Israel. Iran's anticipated response to military action against it is likely to be the launch of a series of irregular attacks using proxies, all over the Gulf region. That is a situation close to apocalypse and deeply against Indian interests too.

India's Role

Of interest to us is the fact that Obama perceived India as an important potential strategic partner; the geostrategic location in the Indian Ocean, its emerging power status, fast growing economy, hunger for technology and young population gave India a status of huge strategic importance for the USA. India as a foil and to balance the rise of China was the underlying theme. Trump appears to have shifted focus from that without a clear understanding of the potential of India and taking mutual interests into focus.

While India's role in this emerging reset may yet be unclear there are some indicators that a quiet diplomacy to retrace some steps and prevent being strait jacketed in relationships, is also underway, the symptoms of which are quite obvious to keen observers. The enthusiastic indicators of an emerging Indo-US strategic partnership which appeared evident in 2014-16 and perhaps even a little later have given way to an ominous reconsideration with a realisation that the world will neither be unipolar nor bipolar in the future. It was realised that the larger role envisaged for India in the Indo Pacific by the USA would emerge in clash with the interests of other power centres. China's support to Pakistan and its aggressive posturing in India's neighbourhood were messages in response to the increasing Indian propensity to be seen to be in league with the USA.

Doklam momentarily upset Indian perceptions even though it was being drawn into multilateral arrangements such as the US-Japan-India equation and the Quad of Nations without a full think through on the future implications. The signals emanating from Moscow were also none too positive and a potential Russia-China-Pakistan equation was likely to militate against Indian interests. At the beginning of 2018, a reset in India's relationships was already on the cards; Wuhan, Sochi and Qingdao followed in quick succession. President Xi Jinping's visit to India for the second Sino-India informal summit in October 2019 has opened avenues for further informal consultation between the two countries. In 2019 also some aggressive Indian diplomacy has seen India establish itself a little more strongly, especially after the recent decisions on Jammu & Kashmir. In later years, any examination of the progressive international reset will recall these meets as important waypoints but none of this has anything permanent or lasting in nature; they are all emerging situations at best.

There is no closure to a process such as an international reset, as witnessed in the past. There are already enough issues that are on the cards which will dictate which way the progression will go. Not the least is the handling of Iran by the international community with regard to the sanctions regime; India has had to acquiesce under pressure response to US pressure to abide by sanctions. Russia's ability to wade through the sanctions against it, retain its European interests against US pressure and continue safeguarding the core joint interests with China with strengthened mutual trust will decide the order that will emerge. The progress of Shanghai Cooperation Organisation's (SCO) 'eastern NATO' status will also be under test.

For India, it is almost back to non-alignment and issue and interest based cooperation because polarity in the international order will be far more diffused. For India, straddling will become the order of the day rather than cosying with any of the strategic dispensations. Yet, it cannot afford complete obfuscation of its foreign policy. The NDA Government displayed a fine understanding of its interests in the beginning of 2018 and followed it with some deft handling of emerging threats to its interests. The virtual ASEAN summit on India's Republic Day, visits by the Prime Minister to the Middle East in February 2018 and return visits by the Israeli Prime Minister and the Iranian President and that of the King of Jordan signified a straddling effort. The efforts to set aside emerging conflict of interests with China and Russia and a slowdown in the move towards the Quadrilateral of Nations were significant decisions towards a reset. However, the speed of reset is as yet slow. As it picks up pace India may have to display even more deftness in its relationships. The Iran sanctions issue and the decision to remain firm on the commitment to purchase arms and equipment from Russia will remain among the major challenges. The renegotiation with RCEP to allow India entry will also dictate how India is viewed on the all-important issue of free trade. For India to realise its dream of a 5 trillion USD economy by 2012-4 it would be essential to load positives in its favour. It already has political stability at the centre but needs calming of border tension with Pakistan, stability of its international multilateral equations and good internal management of politics, to allow it to concentrate on its avowed path to greater growth and its eventual place at the high table of international politics.

(This is a revised and updated version of the essay first published in South Asia Defence & Strategic Review in mid-2018)

9

Security Challenges from the Neighbourhood

S.D. Muni

India's neighbourhood poses two sets of security challenges, namely conventional and non-traditional. Conventional challenges include war, as India has already experienced in 1947, 1962, 1965, 1971 and 1999. The Kargil war in 1999 was initiated by Pakistan even under the situation where both India and Pakistan had demonstrated and declared their nuclear capabilities. Traditional and unconventional threats from the neighbourhood include terrorism, spillover of internal turbulence and conflicts and the imperatives of the presence of an adversarial power in the neighbourhood. It may be difficult to precisely predict the nature of these challenges unfolding after a decade in 2030, but some plausible directions may be identified.

Conventional Threats: Remote but not Impossible

As already noted, India has been subjected to wars and aggression in the past by its two neighbours, Pakistan and China. The largest number of them, four, was initiated by Pakistan in 1947, 1965, 1971 and 1999. China accounts for totally unprovoked aggression in 1962 on the disputed Himalayan border, and there have been a number of cases of intrusions and encroachments from China subsequently, since 1967, along that border. The latest example of intrusion and encroachment has been in the Doklam region which is disputed between

China and Bhutan. This intrusion led to a military faceoff between China and India not only because the Chinese presence in Doklam poses a direct threat to India's territorial integrity in the Northeast corridor, but also because Bhutan has close security ties with India and India is obliged to support Bhutan in defence of its territorial sovereignty.

Threat of a direct military confrontation with Pakistan does not look imminent but this possibility cannot be ruled out for ever. Pakistan is economically weak and socially highly turbulent. After the Kargil war and changing Indian responses to Pakistan's cross-border terrorism like in the Balakot destruction of terrorist camps through precision air strikes in February 2019, direct military confrontation is not a viable option for it against India. With the peace process in Afghanistan being thrown into chaos by the USA breaking its negotiations with the Taliban, Pakistan is also concerned about peace and stability on its western front. There is not much international support for any military adventure on the part of Pakistan as all its so-called supporters are asking it to have a dialogue and bilateral negotiation with India on the contentious issue of Kashmir. Even China did so during the visit of its Foreign Minister, Wang Yi, in September 2019. He asked for a negotiated resolution of the Kashmir dispute on the basis of UN Resolutions and bilateral agreements.[1]

Yet, the Pakistan front will have to be watched carefully. More so after the removal of Kashmir's special constitutional status under Art. 370. This has knocked down the most important issue for Pakistan's military and its political/strategic establishments in dealing with India. It is hoped that India will move faster on the consolidation of Kashmir's integration, which may not be an easy task. But India's Minister of External Affairs, Dr. S. Jaishankar, has stated in categorical terms on September 17, that India will one day have physical possession of Pakistan Occupied Kashmir (POK) as well.[2] Prime Minister Modi and other senior ministers of India have also been underlining this point, saying that the only issue that remains to be discussed with Pakistan is the transfer of POK. Pakistan will try its best to frustrate India's efforts in this respect. However, as India advances its moves to firmly integrate Kashmir, and as Pakistan's cross-border terrorism fails in deterring India, Pakistan's nervousness will increase, tempting it to undertake military adventure in desperation, though not on the basis of rational assessment.

As noted earlier, Pakistan's economic weakness and its social turbulence, such as in Baluchistan, Sindh and Pakistan-occupied Kashmir, including Gilgit-

Baltistan, if left unmanaged for a long time may also turn from a deterrent to a trigger for military adventure against India. Any serious rupture of civil-military equation, as well as increased tensions between the civilian regime and radicalised Jihadi forces, may also look for diversion such as a military conflict with India. The combination of these factors with Pakistan's frustration on Kashmir makes a really volatile cocktail for military adventure. Prime Minister Imran Khan in his interview to *Al Jazeera* news channel on September 14, 2019, clearly said that developments in Kashmir may precipitate conflict between India and Pakistan.

Pakistan has a tendency of nuclear bragging on any escalation of dispute with India. Pakistan's many times defence minister Khwaja Muhammad Asif has repeatedly threatened that if need be Pakistan would not hesitate to use nuclear weapons in war against India.[3] In view of strong reactions against such statements, Prime Minister Imran Khan however said, "*We're two nuclear-armed neighbours. If going ahead, tensions rise, then the whole world is threatened. So this is why I'm telling you that our side will never be the one to start things.*" But on September 14, 2019, in an interview, he again said that any conventional conflict with India may lead to a nuclear clash. In that interview, he admitted that Pakistan will lose the conventional war with India and for keeping its honour and existence, may resort to nuclear weapons.[4] For years, Pakistan has been claiming to have miniaturised its nuclear arsenal for tactical use against India in an unforeseen situation, since its conventional capabilities are no match to that of India's.[5] It may be clearly understood that the repeated threats of nuclear conflict with India by Pakistan is a tactical ploy of deterring any conventional conflict and also dragging the international community into the bilateral India-Pakistan dispute.

There is no dependable assessment of Pakistan's nuclear threshold. Will it use nuclear weapons when it fails to deter India from launching an aggression? In a conventional war with India, will the nuclear trigger be used when it loses its occupied Kashmir or when more of its territory in Punjab is lost creating a prospect of a humiliating defeat? Will the destruction of its major city centres or large sections of its population trigger its nuclear arsenals? A Carnegie study by a Pakistani scholar on its nuclear threshold concluded:

> "The discourse in Pakistan reveals a widely held belief that a large-scale war between India and Pakistan is unlikely, as is the use of nuclear weapons. However, several contingencies that may lead Pakistan to contemplate the

> use of nuclear weapons cannot be entirely ruled out. These include a failure of Pakistan's conventional deterrence, India's growing military capabilities and the likelihood of pre-emption, a failure of command and control, and the possibility of inadvertent war. However, there has been no serious debate about escalation control and war termination. It is often said that in such an eventuality, the logic of war will take over. This is alarming. Serious thinking needs to be invested in reducing the risk of war and also in developing strategies for escalation control and war termination, particularly if a crisis inadvertently escalates."[6]

India will have to remain on guard against the areas of uncertainty and ambiguity in Pakistan's nuclear doctrine. But this, however, does not lead to any justification for India to revisit its nuclear doctrine and give up or even dilute the commitment to "No first use" as is being periodically debated in some of the strategic circles, including those patronised by the ruling establishment in NDA-II. India has enough resilience in its nuclear posture as defined, to take care of all possible contingencies. Presenting India's draft nuclear doctrine document on August 17, 1999, the then National Security Adviser Brijesh Mishra had said: "From this, flows the decision to adopt a no-first-use posture. We have therefore given *unconditional guarantees to States that do not have nuclear weapons, or are not aligned with nuclear weapon powers.*" (italics added).

The qualification underlined in Mishra's statement excludes Pakistan and China for both being nuclear weapon states.

A big question before India's strategic planners has been, would China join or help in any substantial manner a Pakistani military adventure against India? In general, the answer to this question has been 'No,' on the basis of past experience and the well-known dictum that no country fights another country's war. Moreover, China also has huge economic stakes in India so as not to vitiate them and hurt its own long-term interests. It has built a number of mutual confidence measures and made several bilateral commitments that it will resolve all its problems with India peacefully, through negotiations and without resorting to conflict. But there are two factors that may belie these assumptions.

One is China's art of deception.[7] This was evident in 1962. Nehru's India also had a firm understanding that China would never resort to military aggression against India on the question of the disputed border. But Mao tse Tung moved its forces against India in a surprise decision after concurring with a close coterie around him. Secondly, China is very sensitive to the developments in Tibet and also closely monitors India's relations with great powers like the

USA. The situation in Tibet can take any turn following the death of the present Dalai Lama and the choosing of his successor. If the turn in the Tibetan situation appears to be getting out of control for China, the possibility of a military move against India as a diversionary tactic, cannot be ruled out. This possibility gets strengthened also as strategic proximity between India and the USA in the emerging context of the Indo-Pacific dynamics and the emergence of QUAD increases and gets consolidated. India is conscious of China's sensitivities in this respect and is keeping a balance in its relations with China and the USA.

India is keeping an eye on the possibility of facing a two-front war if the military coalition between Pakistan and China assumes a violent form against India. After assuming his duties as India's Army Chief, Gen. Bipin Rawat said on December 31, 2017: "The two-front is a real scenario. Much has changed from before in terms of our capabilities.... The Army, Navy and IAF are now jointly very much prepared for such an eventuality."[8] While it is legitimate for India to build its capabilities for such an eventuality, let us hope that India does not have to face a two-front war. That will not only be catastrophic for India but the whole of Asia and the world would be shaken by such a conflict.

Non-Conventional Threats: China's Push into Neighbourhood

More than direct conflict, India's main concern from China is regarding the latter's push into India's immediate neighbourhood. China's interest in the Indian subcontinent is not new. It has traditional roots and China has always tried to keep them alive. However, the difference between China's traditional interests and recent initiatives is rather stark and worrisome. Until the end of the last century, China offered itself as a counter-balance against India to India's neighbours whenever they sought China's involvement to deal with their moments of discomfort in relations with India. Since the beginning of this century, China is driven to India's neighbourhood by its own interests and is therefore, more assertive.

China's current push into South Asia is taking place under the cover of its Belt and Road Initiative (BRI) launched by President Xi Jinping in 2013. Under this initiative, China has promised and is investing billions of dollars in infrastructure projects such as ports, roads, rail line connectivity, power stations, communication connectivity and the like, in these countries. Three specific fronts have been identified in this respect; the China-Pakistan Economic Corridor (CPEC), Trans-Himalayan Economic Corridor and BCIM (Bangladesh, China,

India and Myanmar) Economic Corridor. Besides these Corridors is the Maritime Silk Road that aims at accessing the Bay of Bengal and Indian Ocean ports in Myanmar, Bangladesh, Sri Lanka, Maldives, Pakistan, Iran and the west coast of Africa. The highest investments have so far been promised to Pakistan under CPEC going to the extent of 80 billion US dollars. China's stakes in Bangladesh have also been raised recently to nearly 40 billion US dollars.[9]

Five major drivers of China's BRI that specifically cover India's neighbourhood may be identified.[10] One is China's concerns for stability and development in its fragile periphery constituted by Yunnan, Xinjiang and Tibet. All these Chinese regions border South Asian countries making it imperative for China to befriend them and enhance its strategic presence in these countries. It is widely known that China is guarding its Pakistan-Xinjiang border in collaboration with Pakistani security forces[11] and putting pressure on Nepal not to allow Tibetan refugees to seek shelter and/or transit to other countries through Nepal.[12] The second driver is the pressure on Chinese economy of its excess infrastructure building capacity and declining economic growth. BRI projects are opening opportunities for such surplus capacities to be employed and they also open prospects of Chinese trade and resource extraction in South Asia. This is a region of 1.6 billion people growing at an average rate of 5-6 per cent which no aspiring economy can neglect. Thirdly, for alleviating its Malacca dilemma, of securing the smooth transition of more than 80 per cent of its trade, including energy trade, China needs to strengthen its presence in the Indian Ocean and seek access to the sea through ports and transit links in countries like Bangladesh, Myanmar, Sri Lanka and Pakistan. Fourthly, through its greater economic and strategic presence in India's neighbourhood, China seeks to deter them from joining any of its adversarial mobilisations led by the USA and its allies. China has not forgotten that from 1960 to 1975, the USA had supported through resources and intelligence back-up, a war by the Khampa tribal groups of Nepal in Tibet. It may be kept in mind that countries like the USA and Japan have become active in India's neighbourhood to dent the impact of China's BRI. And lastly, China would also like to see India pinned down within the region to ensure that it does not challenge China in Asia either by joining the USA and its allies or by itself.

A detailed discussion about China's BRI is out of the scope of this paper. It may, however, be kept in mind that the BRI projects are being carefully scrutinised in the recipient countries and by the strategic community the world over. The projects are being questioned for their economic non-viability, their debt trap, lack of transparency, dependency relationship generated by them and so on. China is constantly responding to these criticisms and redefining the BRI goals and processes in order to meet the criticism. There seems to be little doubt that the BRI would be strongly pursued by China and its real implications would be far more clearer by 2030. India will have to prepare itself to cope with the adverse implications of the BRI in its neighbourhood.

What are these adverse implications and how do they impinge on India's security? China is getting deeply engaged with South Asian countries not only economically as a result of the BRI projects but also politically (including in the game of regime change), socio-culturally (Buddhism, Chinese language, Confucius institutions) and strategically (newer security relationships). This is denting and reducing India's economic and strategic space in its immediate and sensitive neighbourhood. India may still have an advantage but if the trend continues, it will be a big loser in the long run. It is increasingly becoming evident that some of the BRI projects have strong security underpinnings. India has already taken exception to the BRI projects in the POK, which is a breach of its sovereignty and deterrence to re-integration of that part into the Indian Union. The Gadara port in Pakistan, that was started as a commercial project, is no longer so. China can use it for security purposes and access it by its warships. In Sri Lanka, China managed to dock submarines raising objections from affected countries like India. Most of these ports will be ready for use by 2030. They will be used for China's naval presence and consolidation in the Indian Ocean, including the Bay of Bengal. As and when road and rail links are established between Lhasa and Kathmandu, no one will be able to stop the Chinese from ferrying PLA troops as and when they like, through these connectivity projects. Nepal is repeatedly asserting that China is no threat to its security and that it is prepared to forge a new security equation with its rising northern neighbour. That knocks down the very rationale of the mutual security component in the Indo-Nepal Friendship Treaty of 1950. There is a strong possibility that with the increase in China's influence in Nepal through the BRI the former would like the latter to ensure that the Nepali Gurkha troops in the Indian Army are not deployed and used along the Sino-Indian border in the Himalayas.

Internal Political and Social Turbulence in the Neighbourhood

India's neighbourhood is full of sharp and stressful social and political fault-lines that erupt into serious conflicts periodically. Politically, there is lack of constitutional consensus in India's neighbouring countries. Nepal has adopted a Republican, Federal Constitution but the power-sharing with the Madhes and Janjati communities has not been resolved fully. Sri Lanka is struggling to have a new and more democratic Constitution. Myanmar is uneasy with the continuing share of decisive power with the military both constitutionally and in the composition of the Parliament. Political parties, media and judiciary continue to remain weak and vulnerable in these countries and the struggle for power is intense and has seeped into political corruption in almost the entire region. This is reflected in the frequent changes of governments and ruling coalitions as well as mal-governance and a growing role of illegal and disruptive social groups that operate across the border with India, affecting the latter's stability and economy.

There are multiple social fault-lines of religion, region, caste and class in India as well as in India's neighbourhood. These fault-lines have a tendency to precipitate serious internal conflicts in these countries. Examples of Sri Lanka's Tamil insurgency, Bhutan's problems with its Nepali population settled in the southern belt, the Maoists' revolt in Nepal, and the Rohingya problem in Myanmar may be recalled in this respect. In Pakistan, Sindhis and Baluchis have never felt comfortable in the company of the Punjabis. These internal conflicts spill over into India in terms of refugees, flow of arms and anti-social elements, and interference of extra-regional powers. India is dragged into these conflicts resulting in instability and turbulence in its own bordering areas with the country affected. This spill over also results in vitiating its bilateral relations with the country affected.

There is no way in which India can insulate itself from the disrupting spil-overs of the internal conflicts in neighbouring countries by 2030. It will have to sharpen its diplomatic resilience to cope with these spillovers both through political engagements and economic and development support to meet the post-conflict contingencies. It is easier said than done as was experienced in Sri Lanka and Nepal. In both these cases, India's involvement which was both invited and well meaning, boomeranged into much criticism and alienation.

Terrorism: Cross-border, Global and Internal Dimensions

Last but not the least, the major security challenge emerging from India's neighbourhood is of terrorism. India has been facing the threat of terrorism for a long time and this threat stands as one of the most worrisome aspect of security at present. Neighbours have contributed considerably to this threat. For a long time, much before the threat of terrorism became a major concern in Kashmir following the withdrawal of Soviet forces towards the end of the 1980s, Pakistan, China, and, later, Bangladesh (until recently), have been supporting insurgencies in India's Northeast. Theoretically, one can keep insurgencies separate from terrorism for analytical purposes, but there is a large overlap between the two as the insurgents, in their fight against the state, also attack innocent civilians and use violence for political purpose.

There are clearly three dimensions of the involvement of neighbours in causing, sustaining and inflating the terrorism threat in India. One is the role of cross-border terrorism; then, the use of neighbours by global terrorism forces in destabilising India and its neighbouring region and lastly, creation of domestic conditions that allow terrorism to grow and encourage neighbours for exploiting them to vitiate India's security situation. Pakistan constitutes the hub of cross-border terrorism for India, especially since 1989. Its initial aim was to disturb Kashmir and encourage separatism there but subsequently, in the post 1999 Kargil conflict years, terrorism against India has been turned into a strategy of "1000 cuts" to weaken India. This has become a well-planned war by other means, so to say, and its terrain has been expanded from land to the sea, and from Kashmir to the whole of India as became evident in the 26/11 attacks on Mumbai in 2008. Pakistan has also been using other neighbours like Nepal, Bangladesh and Sri Lanka, for sending terrorists and financial and material support for them into India.

India has changed its strategy in dealing with Pakistan. It has stopped talking to it on Kashmir and other issues and has mobilised considerable international pressure on Pakistan to stop cross-border terrorism. India has also resorted to punitive retaliation as is evident in surgical strikes in September 2016, escalation on the Line of Control and attack on Balakot terrorist training camp in 2019. There is no evidence that these moves have deterred Pakistan from continuing with the strategy of cross-border terrorism. Official statistics on casualties of terrorism in Kashmir clearly underline this, where both militancy and incidents of terrorism have marked an increase.[13] One of the reasons has been that the conditions of alienation and political uncertainty have encouraged Pakistan to carry on with its cross-border terrorism strategy. With the Indian move on August 6, 2019, of changing the constitutional status of J&K and removing its special status, Pakistan is trying its best to escalate conflict in Kashmir. It will not only infiltrate more terrorists but also help support militancy and religious radicalisation.[14] India needs to be prepared for dealing with this challenge until 2030 and beyond. Only a miracle can desist Pakistan from this strategy against India.

The character of global terrorism is changing. The Islamic State has been pushed out of its territory and there are indications that global terror attacks have been reduced in numbers and intensity. But there is not much comfort in India and its neighbouring region. There were hopes of a conflict resolution in Afghanistan through talks between the USA and the Taliban. But these hopes have been dashed for the time. The consequences of this may not be bad for India's security as the conflict in Afghanistan will keep Pakistan engaged on its north-western front. Then there were the Easter attacks in Sri Lanka which resulted in the death of more than 250 innocent people. The links of these terror attacks are not only spread out in India but go to the IS terror cells that are spreading out in South Asia as a whole.[15] The largest recruitment from South Asia for the IS went from the Maldives and terrorist groups in Bangladesh having links with the IS who have established a network of their operations in India as well. India's National Investigating Agency (NIA) seems to have interrogated nearly 104 Indians who returned from IS battlegrounds in Syria and Iraq. Events like attacks on the Rohingya Muslims of Myanmar and their displacement create conditions for the IS and other global terrorist organisations to expand and consolidate their position in the region.

To meet the challenge of an expanding network of terrorists in a region, the countries of the region need to cooperate with each other and coordinate their approaches. South Asia's experience in this respect has been frustrating so far. The South Asian Association for Regional Cooperation (SAARC) took up the issue of countering terrorism as early as in 1987 and adopted a Convention on Suppression of Terrorism. It never really worked on the ground. To improve the situation, an Additional Protocol to the Convention was adopted in 2004 but with little effect. The Bay of Bengal Initiative for Multi-Sectoral Technical and Economic Cooperation (BIMSTEC) has also moved in the direction of countering terrorism but concrete action and effect still seem far away.

At the bilateral level, loopholes in the counter-terrorism cooperation were starkly exposed on the question of the Easter terror attacks in Sri Lanka. India's intelligence agencies had shared critical information leads with their Sri Lankan counterparts weeks before the attacks took place but the Sri Lankan agencies simply did not act upon them. This was partly due to the confidence-deficit between the two countries at the highest levels and partly due to operational lethargy in the Sri Lankan security establishments, inflicted by rivalries and differences at the highest political levels within the ruling coalition of President Sirisena and Prime Minister Ranil Wickremasinghe. Malaysia has also refused to extradite Zakir Naik (Islamic preacher linked to extremism, radicalisation and terrorism) to India. To what extent cooperation at the bilateral level and coordination within a given country would improve in the context of counter-terrorism remains to be seen. However, by 2030, improvement at both the levels should be expected, though not to the extent it is evident in Europe or ASEAN.

In countering terrorism internally, India and all the other South Asian countries have been relying heavily on law and order methods, i.e., use of force.[16] Constitutional/political and developmental/economic aspects have also been, to some extent, built into respective counter-terrorism strategies and approaches. This has delivered results but not to the full satisfaction, because the terrorist groups and organisations have also been improving and redefining their approaches to assaults and aggression. It is on the front of countering the network mechanisms and ideological approaches of the terror organisation and their mentors (Pakistan-like sponsoring states and the flow of funding) that very little serious attention has been paid. What is softening the ground for radicalisation is increasing instances of alienation of Muslims in the countries where they are in a minority.

Politics in many of the South Asian countries such as India, Myanmar, Pakistan, Nepal and Sri Lanka is being played along religious and sectarian polarisation. This is also reflected in governance leading to alienation of minorities which then provides easy ground for the rise of and recruitment for terrorism. As a secular, civilisational country with a record of composite culture, maintaining unity in diversity, India should take the lead in countering alienation and radicalisation by reaching out to the communities that feel alienated, both within the country and also at the regional level. It should explore the possibilities of forging an ideological front with the cooperation of other countries in the region like Sri Lanka, Bangladesh, Indonesia, Malaysia and Thailand. The front should bear a multi-religious character comprising different religious preachers and faith leaders to project the moderate form of Islam that characterises South and Southeast Asian societies. This front should counter and present an alternative vision to what the Wahhabi/Salafi form of extremism and distorted jihad is spreading. Such an ideological offensive may not work immediately, but seems to be the need of the hour if the menace of terrorism is to be uprooted from its very foundations. A similar ideological front has also to be opened for countering extremism and radicalisation in other faiths like Buddhism and Hinduism.

Summing Up

India is facing multi-dimensional security challenges from the neighbourhood. No substantial reduction in these threats may be expected by 2030. Responding to them will need India's economic, military and diplomatic resources to be invested with discretion and careful planning. India should also streamline its ideological character encompassing its composite culture to meet the challenge of radicalisation and extremism which is going to grow and become formidable in the context of the increasing salience of social media.

NOTES

1. Lee Jeong-ho, "Beijing gives Pakistan its backing amid rising Kashmir tensions," *South China Morning Post*, 09 September 2019. https://www.scmp.com/news/china/diplomacy/article/3026308/beijing-gives-pakistan-its-backing-amid-rising-kashmir.
2. *The Indian Express*, September 18, 2019.
3. See for instance, *The Economic Times*, July 14, 2019; "Military Failure could push Pakistan to initiate nuclear attacks against India."
4. "Imran Khan warns of possibility of conventional war with India," *The Hindu*, September 15, 2019. https://www.thehindu.com/news/international/imran-khan-warns-of-possibility-of-conventional-war-with-india/article29422971.ece. For his interview with *Al Jazeera* news channel see, https://www.youtube.com/watch?v=SpfaJtrTMfc
5. Mansoor Ahmed, "Pakistan's Tactical Nuclear Weapons and their Impact on Stability"; Carnegie Endowment for International Peace, Regional Insight, June 30, 2016.https://carnegieendowment.org/2016/06/30/pakistan-s-tactical-nuclear-weapons-and-their-impact-on-stability-pub-63911; Kyle Mizokami, "Pakistan Has Lots of Nuclear Weapons: Should the World Worry", *The National Interest*, August 18, 2019. https://nationalinterest.org/blog/buzz/pakistan-has-lots-nuclear-weapons-should-world-worry-74516.
6. Sadia Tasleem, "Pakistani Nuclear Use Doctrine," *Regional Insight*, June 30, 2016, Carnegie Endowment for International Peace. https://carnegieendowment.org/2016/06/30/pakistan-s-nuclear-use-doctrine-pub-63913
7. Shyam Saran, "China in the twenty-first century: What India Needs to Know About China's World View", India International Centre, August 29, 2012. http://ris.org.in/images/RIS_images/pdf/Second%20Annual_K%20Subrahmanyam%20Memorial%20Lecture.pdf (This was the second K. Subrahmanyam Memorial Lecture).
8. //economictimes.indiatimes.com/articleshow/56324336.cms?from=mdr&utm_source=contentofinterest &utm_medium=text&utm_campaign=cppst
9. "China Bangladesh agree to advance cooperation under BRI", *Free Press Journal,* July 05, 2019, https://www.freepressjournal.in/business/china-bangladesh-agree-to-advance-cooperation-under-bri

10. The details of this discussion were presented by the author at the University of Shanghai and University of Copenhagen.
11. K.J.M. Varma, "China Pakistan troops launch 1st joint border patrols near Xinjiang," *Live Mint* (New Delhi), July 21, 2016, https://www.livemint.com/Politics/lcGoq0t78j5fS9tt8MHrdO/PLA-Pakistan-troops-launch-1st-joint-border-patrols-near-Xi.html
12. "China Increases Influence over Tibetan refugees in Nepal," *DW*, August 29, 2016, https://www.dw.com/en/china-increases-influence-over-tibetan-refugees-in-nepal/a-19511365
13. Vivek Chadha, "Are we winning the last gasp of terrorism in Kashmir", Commentary, *Institute for Defence Studies & Analyses,* July 11, 2017; Mukesh Rawat, "Pulwama Terror Attacks: In last five years, J&K saw 93% rise in death of security personnel in terror attacks", *India Today,* February 14, 2019, https://www.indiatoday.in/india/story/pulwama-terror-attack-jammu-kashmir-terrorism-data-last-5-years-soldiers-killed-1456427-2019-02-14; Abhinav Pandya, Militancy in Kashmir: A Study, VIF Paper, March 2019, Vivekanand International Foundation, https://www.vifindia.org/sites/default/files/Militancy-in-Kashmir.pdf.
14. Sharat Sabharwal, "Abrupt move in Valley feeds into already prevailing sense of alienation, religious radicalisation," *Indian Express*, September 17, 2019.
15. V.P. Malhotra, "Islamic State and South Asia," *Agni,* Vol. XIX, No.1, January 2016-April 2016; pp. 77-93; also Alok Kumar Gupta, "Islamic State in South Asia: Ramifications and Challenges for India", *AAKROSH*, Vol. 19, No.71, April 2016, pp. 23-41.
16. S.D. Muni (ed), *Responding to Terrorism in South Asia*, Manohar, New Delhi 2006; also S.D. Muni and Vivek Chadha (ed), *Asian Strategic Review 2016: Terrorism: Emerging Trends*, IDSA/Pentagon Press, New Delhi, 2016.

10

Problem of Illegal Migration from Bangladesh

S.K. Sood

The Bangladeshis have been migrating illegally to India since independence. Vested political interests have prevented successive governments in the past from taking serious action in the matter. The 1971 war of independence of Bangladesh led to a spurt in this phenomenon and many illegal migrants came and settled in the bordering districts in Assam and West Bengal. The main reason leading to the Assam agitation in the Eighties was identification and deportation of such illegal migrants. The issue has again gained prominence in the recent past mainly due to the promise of the NDA Government to identify all Bangladeshi nationals and deport them. The Army Chief, in February 2018, made a statement implying that there was a "planned" influx of people from Bangladesh into the Northeast and it was a part of proxy warfare by Pakistan with support from China with an aim to keep the area disturbed. He went on to refer to the growth of the AIUDF, a political party formed in 2005 to champion the cause of Muslims in the region, implying that the growth of the party was due to the support it enjoys amongst illegal migrants from Bangladesh.[1]

The issue of a "National Register of Citizens", and the recent influx of Rohingya tribals from Myanmar also brought focus to the problem. It also compelled the policy planners to consider and define the difference between illegal migrants and refugees.

Defining Illegal Migration

An illegal immigrant can be defined as a foreigner who enters a country without an entry or immigrant visa, especially a person who crosses the border by avoiding inspection or who overstays the period allowed as a visitor, tourist, or businessperson.

The US Department of Homeland Security Centre for Media and Democracy[2] states, "Illegal immigration (also referred to as unauthorised or undocumented immigrants) refers to the migration of people across national borders in a way that violates the immigration laws of the destined country."

Demetrios G. Papademetriou, PhD, Director of the Migration Policy Institute (MPI), in a 2005 essay[3] states, "Illegal immigration takes several forms, four of which are the most common: They are:

(a) Undocumented/unauthorised entrants: These are nationals of one state who enter another state clandestinely.
(b) Individuals who are inspected upon entry into another state, but gain admission by using fraudulent documents.
(c) Violators of the duration of a visa: These include individuals who enter another state properly but 'wilfully' overstay their period of legal stay, thus lapsing into irregular status.
(d) Violators of the terms and conditions of a visa: Nationals of one state who enter another state with proper documents and procedures, but at some point violate the terms of their visa. The most frequent such violation is the acceptance of employment. Violation of 'border crosser visas' that allow border residents from an adjacent country to reside and be employed in the other country within strictly prescribed time and geographic parameters is another example of violations of such terms and conditions.
The Cambridge Dictionary defines an illegal immigrant as "someone who lives or works in another country when they do not have the legal right to do this."

Suffice to say that those persons who are staying illegally in a country are called illegal immigrants. They are not the citizens of the country where they are staying and working and have no legal right to stay and work there.

The migration of population from one part of the world to another has been an age-old practice. Cross-migration of population is a universal phenomenon. Various studies establish beyond doubt that the population of the entire world is genetically related to each other. This is because the reproductive activity between the settlers and migrants after certain time becomes a norm.

The migration of the Aryan race to India from central and Western Europe is a historical fact. The Aryans, after a prolonged stay, have become naturalised and presently constitute a large portion of the population of the Indian subcontinent.

Historically, migration is known to have taken place in search of resources for sustenance. It may have also taken place from areas with hostile weather to areas more suitable for sustenance of life. Humans moving to far-flung areas with these aims settled there and merged with the local population. Migrations also occurred when marauders and rulers moved to far-flung areas in search of wealth, conquered those areas and decided to stay back because of logistical difficulties in returning or to exploit the resources of the conquered territory.

So we had Alexander travelling all the way from Greece to India. He left behind representatives to administer the areas conquered, settled permanently and became naturalised. The most recent example of migrants becoming naturalised is that of the Munhall who ruled a large portion of India for over 200 years before the British usurped power from them.

We are aware that the United States of America, Australia and Latin American countries are almost entirely populated by white migrants from Europe. The original inhabitants of these lands, known as Red Indians or Aboriginals, etc., are in a minority and have been reduced to the status of second-class citizens. Similar migration of whites took place to African nations. Large-scale migration of Chinese origin people has taken place in countries like Malaysia, Singapore, etc.

A lot of forced migration has also taken place in the past, especially from the 18th century onwards. In order to overcome a shortage of labour, black people from Africa and people of Indian origin were taken in large numbers to many Western countries and also to the West Indies and many island-nations all over the world. With hardly any means to return to their motherland, they became settlers and now from a substantial portion of the populations of those countries.

Wars and communal unrest have also led to large-scale migrations. The example of the partition of the Indian subcontinent in two separate nations led to wholesale migration of Muslims from Hindu-dominated parts of India to what are now Pakistan and Bangladesh and vice versa. Estimates of people who had to leave their homes in this tragedy of colossal proportions range up to 2 million.

The above however cannot be termed "Illegal Migration" because when these migrations took place there was no notion of territoriality and sovereignty in the strict sense that prevails today.

The advent of modern nation-states brought in the concept of territory and sovereignty of a nation over a particular land mass. With territoriality came the consciousness of cultural identity and a desire to maintain that particular cultural identity which was likely to be diluted if migration was allowed unhindered. Besides cultural identity, nations also realised that finite resources located within the territory under their control would become inadequate to sustain the pressure of increasing population by the onslaught of migration. The nations therefore started imposing restrictions on the free movement of persons between countries and allowed only those persons to come whom they thought would contribute gainfully to their society. Thus, the passport and visa regimes were introduced.

However, such restrictions were able to control only the legal modes of migration. The population however, keeps looking for greener pastures for a better future and to earn their livelihood. Many such people who want to migrate do not have adequate resources to undertake their journey through formal channels. For example, the Bangladeshi illegal migrants to India cannot afford to go through the expensive process of obtaining passports/visas, etc. Hence, they resort to exploiting the gaps in the border to cross over to India. Many such illegal migrants do not possess any special skills because of which they are not welcome in the country of their choice. Resultantly such persons adopt illegal means in order to migrate.

The illegal migrants sometimes adopt desperate means to reach their destination leading to tragic consequences. Many Bangladeshi nationals have fallen to the bullets of the Border Security Force in their attempt to cross over illegally to India. In the famous Komagata Maru incident involving a group of citizens of the British Raj, twenty Sikh illegal migrants lost their lives while returning from a failed attempt to migrate to Canada in 1914 after being fired upon by the Indian Imperial Police at Calcutta (now Kolkata). This was one of several incidents in the early 20th century in which exclusion laws in Canada and the USA were used to exclude immigrants of Asian origin.

Factors Leading to Illegal Migration to India

India has assimilated immigrants of different races and culture to build a composite civilisation. India therefore is often called a land of immigrants. Some immigrants are refugees escaping repression on political or religious grounds. The remaining Bangladeshi nationals cross over to India in search of better opportunities. However, unchecked immigration of Bangladeshi nationals in recent times has been a cause of conflict especially in Assam between the locals and immigrants over control of resources.

Sanjeev Tripathi, former head of R&AW, attributes India's geostrategic location, its relatively sound economic position vis-à-vis its neighbours, and its liberal democratic credentials for it to be an attractive destination for people of other parts of the region fleeing persecution in their countries of origin or looking for a better life.[4] He further opines that the influx of refugees/illegal immigrants from Bangladesh has largely been left unattended leading to an adverse impact on the interests of local populations in the area and India's national security interests. The absence of national refugee laws also adds to the problem resulting in denial of any assistance to even genuine asylum seekers.

While immigration from other countries of the region like Nepal and Bhutan into India continues, it cannot be termed as illegal because of the fact that we have open borders with these countries and bilateral agreements granting status similar to that of Indian citizens as to the subjects of these countries. The problem of illegal migration from Bangladesh is however more serious.

Illegal immigration from Bangladesh continues unabated and various estimates put the figure of such illegal migrants at anything between 15 to 20 million. Large numbers of these illegal migrants have settled in states bordering Bangladesh but many have also come to interior areas where the employment opportunities and levels of income are much better.

There are several factors contributing to illegal migration of Bangladeshi nationals to India. These factors can be generally categorised as "Pull" and "Push" factors. Push factors are those which compel people to seek better opportunities in another country. These would include factors like over-population and consequent pressure on land, lack of economic development and employment opportunities, communal or ethnic strife etc. The pull factors may include better economic opportunities, prevalence of peace and tranquillity, ethnic and cultural similarities and also ease of getting into the country and merging with the population in the country of destination.

In the context of India and Bangladesh, the pull and push factors can be described as under:

Push Factors

(a) The rate of growth of population in Bangladesh is very high at about 1.1 per cent per annum adding over 2 million people every year, leading to a heavy burden on already scarce land resource. The population density of Bangladesh was already very high at 1,252 persons per sq km in 2016. Such heavy increase of population every year adds further to the density and heavy burden on scarce land. The increasing burden on land leads to disguised unemployment and decreasing income in an economy which is mainly agriculture based. Lack of gainful employment and income thus leads the poor to cross over to India.

(b) One third of the land in Bangladesh gets inundated every year during monsoons. Frequent cyclones and storms further cause heavy damage to standing crops. Ab initio, burden of large population coupled with repeated destruction of crops due to the above natural calamities leads to economic distress and hunger causing them to migrate illegally.

(c) Although the economy of Bangladesh grows at 7.65 per cent per annum, which makes it one of the highest growing economies of the world, yet the per capita income is only about $4,200 (2017 est.) with over 12 per cent population living below 3 dollars per day as compared to the per capita income of India at $7,200 (2017 est.). This stark disparity of income and prospects of a better future encourages the Bangladeshi population to migrate to India illegally.

(d) Bangladesh abandoned secularism in 1978 and declared itself as an Islamic republic. This, coupled with persecution of ethnic minorities, especially Hindus, has led them to seek asylum in India by crossing over through porous borders. The Buddhists who are residents of the Chittagong Hills area have witnessed persecution from the very beginning and settlement of the majority Muslim community on the land in this tribal area have forced many of them to migrate to areas in Meghalaya and Mizoram.

(e) The population pressure being very heavy, it perhaps is an unstated Government policy to encourage people to migrate to other parts of world. India being a neighbour sharing over 400 km of porous border is a natural destination. The Bangladesh Government follows an unstated policy similar to what Nazi Germany referred to as "Lebensraum," implying that Bangladesh considers that the neighbouring Indian territory is needed for its natural development.

(f) Sheikh Mujibur Rehman wanted the population of the then East Pakistan to occupy the land of bordering states of India and stated that "*Because Eastern Pakistan must have sufficient land for its large population and Assam will give it full scope for expansion and because Assam has abundant forest and mineral resources such as coal, petroleum etc, Eastern Pakistan must include Assam to be financially and economically strong.*"[5] The only difference in the unstated "Lebensraum" followed by Bangladesh being that the territory for expansion is gained peacefully through illegal migration. The Bangladeshi settlers in border areas are in such large numbers that the cultural territory of Bangladesh extends well beyond the physical boundary into Indian Territory. The Bangladeshi Government also encourages its population to migrate to several Western countries also which they do both legally as well as illegally.

Pull Factors

(a) The most important pull factor is the better performing Indian economy and availability of better employment opportunities here. This coupled with the dismal state of industry and employment opportunities as discussed above contribute to a great extent to Bangladeshis trying to illegally migrate to India.

(b) Ethnic and linguistic similarity amongst people residing on both sides of borders is a major pull factor. Family ties go back to pre-partition days with some having migrated to East Pakistan after partition. There was large-scale influx of refugees to India during the 1971 war of liberation of Bangladesh. Some of these refugees continued to stay in India while most went back after the formation of Bangladesh. Thus, many have their relatives staying on both sides of the border. This facilitates easy merger of illegal migrants after they cross over to India.

(c) Riverine and porous nature of the borders makes it easy for the illegal migrants to cross over undetected. At several places, the population resides very close to borders and many towns and villages are located right at the International Border or even on both sides of the border with only a street separating the Indian side from the Bangladeshi one. There are places where a common mosque is used for prayers by residents of both sides. There are several other places where even a house is located on both sides of the boundary pillar. This population pattern along the borders has facilitated the generations-old familial ties to be maintained and nurtured through marriages and frequent interactions. This also facilitates illegal migrants to find easy shelter in border areas before moving forward to the interior parts of India after their identity papers have been procured. Another fact is that the population on the Indian side of the border too is very poor and they are willing to take in these illegal migrants for a few days for a consideration until their identity documents are prepared by middlemen.

(d) Ease of availability of essential identity documents like Aadhar, Voter ID, Ration card, etc., facilitates the integration of illegal migrants in India. This also encourages others to try their luck at crossing over and settling illegally in India. Government employees connive to facilitate these documents.

(e) Almost all political parties, because of vested interests and vote bank politics have ignored the issue of illegal migration, thus indirectly encouraging others.

(f) Another important reason is the definition of illegal migrants as per the Assam Accord. As per this Accord, an illegal immigrant is one who has migrated to India after 24 December 1971. However, many illegal immigrants are being granted refugee status thus opening the way for them to be finally granted citizenship.

Consequences of Illegal Migration

The illegal migration of Bangladeshi nationals has led to some serious problems. As stated by the Army Chief, and discussed above, the settlement of illegal migrants in border areas has led to a change in the demographic profile of these areas, resulting sometimes in communal tensions due to a clash of cultural and ethnic practices. This has been referred to as "demographic invasion of the North East" by many scholars. Illegal migration has serious implications on national security and limited resources.

To take the example of Assam, as a result of this influx, Bangladeshis have become majority groups in Dhubri, Barpeta, Goalpara and Hailakandi districts of Assam. They have become deciding factors in almost half the 126 assembly constituencies of Assam. This influx of illegal migrants led to a volatile situation in the early Eighties in the form of the Assam agitation. The subsequent Assam Accord signed in 1985 has not satisfied any of the parties to the conflict including the immigrants who now wield sizeable political power. The loopholes in the Illegal Migrants (Determination by Tribunals Act) 1983 applicable in Assam (as against the Foreigners Act applicable in other states) prevent forceful action to be taken against infiltrators. Till date, only a very few persons have been deported and the problem remains where it was with all its social, political, human and, security aspects begging attention. This Act was finally struck down by the Supreme Court in 2005.

The situation is somewhat the same in West Bengal and Tripura and a little better in other states of the Northeast. The impact of illegal immigrants has both external and internal dimensions.

Internal Dimensions

The Ethnic Divide: The eastern parts of India are less developed with very little industry, few jobs, and overpopulation in the fertile plains and limited scope for agriculture in the hills (of the Northeast). Infrastructural development is retarded with many areas still inaccessible. Amongst the common people, there is little cash flow. In short, there is very little to be shared by very many while the aspirations of the people have grown with greater exposure to the outside world. While economic deprivation in the age of liberalisation has given rise to discontent all over India, the situation is far more explosive bordering on ethno-linguistic cleavage in the Northeast because of the demographic imbalance and the perceived injustice created by the presence of a large number of illegal migrants.

Militancy: The demographic invasion of the Northeast by illegal immigrants from Bangladesh (coupled with economic deprivation, neglect by the Centre, opportunistic policies) was the flashpoint for of insurgency in Assam in the Eighties. Interestingly, perusal of the charter of demands of all the militant outfits in the Northeast reveals a common thread—ousting of foreigners or outsiders as their prime objective and demand. The popular movement (1979–1985) demanded deportation of illegal immigrants. The Indian Parliament passed the Illegal Migrants (Determination by Tribunal) Act in 1983 in an attempt to address the problem, but the measure failed to make any impact. The agitation culminated in the Assam Accord that was signed on August 15, 1985, by the central and state governments and leaders of the All Assam Students Union and All Assam Gana Sangram Parishad, which spearheaded the Assam movement. The Accord envisaged that all foreign nationals who had entered Assam on or after March 25, 1971—the day after the Pakistan Army began full-fledged operations against Bangladeshi civilians seeking independence, causing them to flee to India in large numbers—were to be detected, their names deleted from the electoral rolls, and subsequently deported under the Foreigners Act, 1946. But little headway has been made in that direction. The process of differentiating actual citizens from the fake ones is quite complex due to various reasons. Although the state has the Foreigners' Tribunal to identify fake citizens, it is far from being a foolproof one and often runs into controversies.

Social Aspects: At the time of partition, various people of the Northeast were traditional in their outlook and slow to adopt foreign ways. All that has greatly changed over the last 70 years, especially with large-scale influx of illegal immigrants. Massive corruption, drug menace, frequent communal clashes et al have links to the existence of illegal immigrants.

Unprincipled Politics: Unprincipled politicians treat illegal immigrants as vote banks and this has done more to undermine the integrity of the nation than all other factors put together. While paying lip service to their national obligations, politicians have often connived to secretly undermine the process of identification of illegal immigrants to remain in power. Others, like the Assom Gana Parishad (AGP) leaders who spearheaded the Assam agitation against foreigners in the Eighties and subsequently won landslide victories in the Assembly elections squandered the popular mandate and mired themselves in massive corruption.

The External Dimension

The Fifth Column: India does not have the best of relations with its neighbours. As a direct fallout of history, ethnicity as also the strategic location of the region, China and Bangladesh are two countries whose interests are directly affected by the happenings in India's East and the Northeast. The states of West Bengal and Assam are tenuously linked by the narrow Siliguri corridor. Illegal migrants today have maximum presence in the strategically located districts of Dhubri, Goalpara and Barpeta of Assam. The region therefore is a fertile ground to launch another proxy war against India. The consequences of such an action would be catastrophic for India. The entire Northeast would be cut off and along with it, all its rich human and natural resources. The magnitude of the problem can be envisaged by comparing just Assam's turnover of tea alone, amounting to three thousand crore rupees which would be lost to the nation.

The Chinese Factor: India and China see themselves as long-term adversaries in South Asia. In spite of various confidence-building measures, the Sino Indian border dispute continues to fester with the Chinese continuing to hold on to their territories in Aksai Chin while also claiming the whole of Arunachal Pradesh. They thus have a reason to foment trouble, especially so in the areas adjoining the territories under dispute.

The Future Threat: Illegal immigrants from Bangladesh along borders as well as within the country provide a fertile ground for recruitment by terrorist organisations inimical to the interests of India. The ISI has always targeted Indian interests worldwide using gullible co-religionists for furthering its aims. With Bangladeshi immigrants now spreading all over India into cities such as Jaipur, Delhi, Pathankot, Bikaner, the border towns and districts of West Bengal and Bihar and various other places, it has a ready pool of sympathisers already in position at different places whose potential for damage, starting from passing of information on security matters down to actively participating in sabotage and terrorist acts needs to be properly understood.

The Road Ahead

In spite of India taking up the issue with the Bangladeshi government on several occasions at the political and diplomatic levels, they refuse to acknowledge the problem and take any effective measures to control the flow of immigrants. The construction of a fence by India has only been partly successful.

The practice of pushing back infiltrators apprehended at the border or brought from the interior has not been effective as they re-enter from a different area or are being pushed back again by Bangladesh. Such practices do not have any legal backing and invites protests from Bangladesh.

Even the most committed hardliners realise that it is difficult to reverse the demographic invasion that has already taken place. The challenge is to ensure that no further migration takes place and those migrants already in the country, though permitted to earn their livelihood, are not granted privileges due to bona fide citizens. These could include the following:

Identifying Illegal Bangladeshi Migrants

Being from the same ethnicity, it is very difficult to distinguish between Indian nationals and Bangladeshi illegal migrants. Further, they are already in possession of necessary documents and this makes it virtually impossible to establish their illegal status.

The National Register of Citizens (NRC) is under preparation in Assam for the purpose of identifying illegal migrants residing in the Northeastern state who entered Indian territories after midnight on 24 March 1971 and to determine the citizenship of the applicants who have applied for inclusion of their names in the updated NRC. It is a register containing the names of all genuine Indian citizens residing in Assam. The register was first prepared after 1951.

The NRC is being updated as per the provisions of The Citizenship Act, 1955 and The Citizenship (Registration of Citizens and Issue of National Identity Cards) Rules, 2003 (as amended) and Ministry of Home Affairs (Office of Registrar General, India), Order No. S.O. 596(E), dated 15 March 2010, published in the Gazette of India, Extra, Part II. No. 504 S.3(ii), dated 16 March 2010, p. 1.). As per the two statutes, the eligibility status would be ascertained based on the NRC, 1951 Electoral Rolls up to 1971 and in their absence the admissible documents up to 24 March (midnight) 1971. The documents should be able to establish the presence of the applicant in Assam or in any part of India on or before 24 March 1971. The update process of the NRC started in the year 2013 under the strict monitoring of the Supreme Court of India.

Part of the draft NRC was released on 31 December 2017. The total number of people included in the Part Draft NRC was 19,010,932 members out of 3.29 crore applicants. Subsequently, on 30 July 2018, the Complete Draft NRC was released. A total of 4,070,707 applicants were found ineligible and the total number of persons included in the Complete Draft NRC is 28,983,677. The persons whose names do not appear in the Draft NRC may file claim applications within the stipulated period. A person may also have an objection against entry of any name in the draft NRC. Any person can also apply for correction of his name or any other entry in his respect as appearing in the Draft updated NRC.

Approximately four million people not finding their names in the NRC points towards the magnitude of the problem of illegal immigration. There have however been some lacunae in the entire process. The case of an Army subedar having served for over 30 years in the Indian Army and drawing pension is one such case. Such cases are being reviewed and may ultimately lead to inclusion of many more names in the list.

One very important issue connected with the NRC is what happens to those who are finally identified as illegal immigrants? Will they be deported? Will Bangladesh accept them? Have we signed or negotiating the signing of any such agreement with Bangladesh? If they continue to stay in India, how will they earn their livelihood—through some kind of work permit? Has the Government prepared for these contingencies?

The confusion about the status and disposal of those not included in the NRC is visible amongst the ruling party also. The then Home Minister, Raj Nath, on the floor of Parliament had stated that everyone not included in the list cannot be labelled an illegal migrant while the then BJP president and present Home Minister declared that all the 40 lakh missing names are "Ghuspathias" (illegal immigrants)!

Further, there would be many persons who are born in India to these illegal immigrants and thus are Indian citizens by birth. Such persons cannot be deported in any case.

What is the point of the entire exercise if these people are not to be deported and given the status of second-class citizens by withdrawing some rights like voting rights, etc., because they will continue to remain in India with incumbent security and other threats as discussed above?

Based on this detection process, some measures can be taken to distinguish them from bonafide citizens. These measures could include preparation of a comprehensive biometric database of Bangladeshi immigrants and their classification in two distinct categories: asylum seekers and illegal immigrants.

The Government will also have to decide on the restrictions to be imposed on illegal migrants. These could include denial of voting rights and restriction on employment with the Government and Armed Forces. They may be permitted to set up private industry but the profits should not be allowed to be repatriated to the mother country.

Further, migrants should not be permitted to own land except what has been already purchased for purely residential purposes within the laid down limits. Any land which they may be in possession of over and above this limit should be taken over by the government and given to the concerned person on lease for the duration of his lifetime. The lease should not transfer to his next of kin.

Children of persons identified as migrants may stay with their parents and avail of educational opportunities. However, they should not be eligible for government grants, scholarships or other reservations. Land held by their fathers on lease will not be transferred to them.

All migrants above the age of 18 should be issued with work permits and migrant identity cards. They should register themselves at the nearest police station and report there at periodic intervals.

The assistance of some NGOs dealing with Bangladeshis living in India, such as the Bangladesh Udbastu Kalyan Parishad, the Bangladesh Udbastu Unnayan Sangsad, Nikhil Banga Nagarik Sangha and Bangladesh Mohajir Sangha, might be useful in these efforts.

The NDA Government has shown its intent to extend the NRC to West Bengal also. However, there is a lot of resistance to this from the Trinamool Congress Government of the State

The provisions of The Citizenship (Amendment) Bill, 2016, have led to protests in the Northeast after its passage in the Lok Sabha early this year. The bill however lapsed with end of the term of the previous Lok Sabha. The Government has made its intentions clear to introduce the bill again. Opposition to the bill stems from fears that it will give legitimacy to illegal migrants in India.

The Bill had proposed to provide citizenship to those who had been forced to seek shelter in India because of religious persecution or fear of persecution in their home countries. They are primarily Hindus, Sikhs, Jains, Buddhists, Parsis and Christians from Afghanistan, Pakistan and Bangladesh. This is a drastic change from the provisions of the Citizenship Act of 1955 that label a person an "illegal immigrant" if he or she has entered India without travel documents or has overstayed the date specified in the documents.

Passage of the bill in the Lok Sabha, it led to a political backlash and unrest in the Northeast and protests by ethnic Assamese groups. Assamese organisations contend that as a result of the bill, the burden of illegal migrants will be passed on to the state alone. The bill was opposed by opposition parties in the Rajya Sabha for excluding Muslims from countries such as Nepal and Sri Lanka and they pushed for the bill to be referred to a select committee before discussion in the Rajya Sabha.

The stand of the Centre is that the amendment is for migrants who came through the eastern and western borders and are staying in India. The burden will be shared by the entire country, with the Centre willing to help to implement it.

The proposed amendment is at cross-purposes with the National Register of Citizens (NRC). The NRC was updated under the Citizenship Act to weed out illegal immigrants from Bangladesh and other countries. The legacy data—the collective list of the NRC data of 1951 and the electoral rolls till 24 March 1971—have been analysed to update the NRC. The amendment paves the way for non-Muslim minorities who came to Assam from Bangladesh between 1 January 1966 and 24 March 1974 to get citizenship. This negates the NRC exercise as it is against the spirit of the Assam Accord according to ethnic Assamese groups and regional parties.

Preventing further migration can be done through stricter surveillance at the borders specially on riverine borders which cannot be fenced and Inter-agency cooperation in identification and ensuring that these illegal migrants do not get access to identity documents.

India can also assist the Bangladesh Government to introduce a unique identity system in that country starting with their border areas.

As discussed above, a major push factor for illegal migration to India is poverty in Bangladesh. Therefore, we may consider providing economic assistance to them in order to create better employment opportunities, and develop infrastructure there. This can prove to be a more effective and long-term solution to the problem.

Formulating a National Refugee Law

Most of the Bangladeshi migrants in India do not get covered under the internationally accepted definition of "Refugees". Formulating a policy on refugees will thus make it easy to distinguish illegal immigrants from refugees.

The "eminent persons' group" set up by UNHCR had proposed a model refugee law for South Asian countries in 1997. The refugee law along with such other appropriate laws to distinguish asylum seekers and refugees from illegal migrants should be so framed that illegal migrants are not able to exploit any loopholes in order to prolong and finally attain legitimacy for their stay in India. The refugee policy of India not being based on any formal law is not cohesive. People from Tibet, Afghanistan, Myanmar and Sri Lanka are given the status of asylum seekers, but this does not apply to Bangladesh.

Bilateral Agreement with Bangladesh

A wide-ranging agreement with Bangladesh to prevent migration from there is also mandatory. The consent of the Bangladesh government in this regard will be difficult as the solution outlined above hits at the very root of Indo Bangladesh tensions. Sanjeev Tripathi in the article referred to above argues that such agreements should provide for the two countries to take back their nationals staying illegally in the other country after due verification process. India should also agree to consider giving work permits to certain specified categories and numbers of Bangladeshis living in India after their Bangladeshi nationality is established and the Bangladeshi government provides them necessary travel documents. Such an agreement is essential to tackle the problem. The key to its success would be a joint verification procedure acceptable to both countries.

Developing a SAARC Convention/Declaration on Refugees

Signing of the 1951 Refugee Convention and its 1967 Protocol by India besides enacting its own refuge laws could help identification of illegal migrants and the manner of dealing with them.

International Cooperation

India has so far adopted a policy of treating the problem as a bilateral one. As a country at the receiving end of the problem, it can also consider involving international organisations like UNHCR to resolve the problem. The precedent of utilising the good offices of UNHCR in the repatriation of Sri Lankan refugees is already there. They are also involved in the problem of Afghan refugees in India. India can at least take advisory assistance from these organisations.

Conclusion

The Group of Ministers set up in the wake of the Kargil episode identified illegal migration as a major threat to India's security and amongst many other suggestions recommended introduction of a National Register of Citizens. Implementation of this recommendation will facilitate the task of identifying and dealing with such illegal migrants.

The problem could have been nipped in the bud in its very infancy but due to a variety of reasons such as a sense of misplaced idealism, political chicanery and sheer lack of will, it has festered for over seventy years, occasionally coming to the boil. A stage has now reached when it is threatening the very integrity of the Indian Union. The need now is to display the will to take decisions which the situation so obviously mandates. The challenge of stemming this flow and repatriating the illegal immigrants back to Bangladesh is indeed daunting. A bundle of multipronged, well-coordinated strategies pursued under an appropriate legal framework as suggested above might be able to address this problem in a more effective manner.

This being one of the issues that the NDA Government vowed to resolve, it is expected that concrete steps will be taken to tackle the problem in a holistic manner. Even in the state elections in Assam, this was identified as a priority area for action.

The prospects indicate that the problem of illegal Bangladeshi immigration in India will be tackled more vigorously now than ever before.

NOTES

1. *The Economic Times*, February 3, 2018.
2. "Illegal Immigration US," sourcewatch.org, August 21, 2008.
3. "The Global Struggle with Illegal Migration: No End in Sight," Migration Policy Institute, September 1, 2005.
4. Sanjeev Tripathi, "Illegal Immigration From Bangladesh to India: Toward a Comprehensive Solution," Carnegie, June 29, 2016, https://carnegieindia.org/2016/06/29/illegal-immigration-from-bangladesh-to-india-toward-comprehensive-solution-pub-63931
5. "Eastern Pakistan: Its Population, Determination and Economics."

11

India-Afghanistan Partnership, Counter Terrorism and Security in South Asia

Vinay Kaura

India and Afghanistan share a long history of cultural and societal ties. New Delhi's engagement with Kabul has however become multidimensional in recent years, particularly after the overthrow of the Taliban regime. India believes that a close partnership with Afghanistan is vital for its national security interests, defined in terms of territorial security, counter-terrorism, and regional connectivity. As Afghanistan's stability is considered a significant factor for India's own security, India has been supportive of the spread of democratic institutions in Afghanistan. Most of the mainstream Afghan political leaders also view India as an important regional partner against Pakistan's intrusive influence and persistent interventions in Afghanistan. Given their long history of friendly ties, both India and Afghanistan have benefitted by expanding the areas of cooperation between them since the arrival of democracy. As the USA tries to disentangle itself from the Afghan conflict by implementing a negotiated settlement with the Afghan Taliban, it will have long-term implications on the fight against terrorism, India's strategic interests as well as regional security.

An Overview of India-Afghanistan Partnership

India's most important objective in its relationship with Afghanistan is to make sure that Islamabad does not dictate the terms of Indo-Afghan partnership; Pakistan has been bitterly vehement against India's diplomatic and developmental presence in Afghanistan. Since Pakistan's manipulation of Afghan internal political dynamics has always worried Indian policymakers, New Delhi has desired a regime in Kabul that does not permit Pakistan's security establishment to run training camps for anti-India terrorist groups. Afghanistan-Pakistan territorial disputes and strained bilateral ties have also brought New Delhi and Kabul closer to each other.

After independence in 1947, India began to enjoy amicable relations with Afghanistan until the Soviet intervention of the country in 1979. India's special partnership with the Soviet Union, in particular, New Delhi's "gratitude for Soviet support during the Bangladesh war,"[1] and the logic of Cold War politics led India to take a neutral position on Soviet intervention, which adversely affected India's image among the Afghans and the West. But before Mikhail Gorbachev withdrew the Soviet troops from Afghanistan, he ensured the installation of a Soviet-friendly regime of Mohammed Najibullah, a former head of the Afghan Intelligence agency KhAD. However, India experienced troubled ties with Afghanistan when the latter witnessed civil war, emergence of Islamist extremism and jihadist terrorism in the last decade of the twentieth century. During 1987 to 1992, when Najibullah was the president, official relations between India and Afghanistan were warm as Najibullah was apprehensive of Pakistan's growing influence in Afghan affairs. But due to the fierce resistance of Afghan Mujahedeen, who were backed by the USA and Pakistan in their fight against the Soviets, Najibullah had no option but to endorse the UN peace proposal, surrendering his power to a coalition of Islamic parties. Disintegration of the Soviet Union in 1991 precipitated the collapse of his regime, as Moscow could no longer provide Kabul with financial and military assistance. Under these circumstances, India too did not have the resources to safeguard the Kabul regime. Najibullah agreed to leave Afghanistan and settle in India. But his plan of living a life in exile in India could not materialise, as he was not allowed to leave Afghanistan. But his family members were able to reach New Delhi in time.[2]

India's influence fluctuated, waning with the ouster of the Najibullah regime and temporarily rising when Burhunuddin Rabbani's regime ruled during 1992-96. Bringing about a shift in India's Afghan strategy, the Narasimha Rao government soon reached out to various Mujahedeen factions. Rabbani and his associate, Ahmad Shah Masoud, a powerful member of the Jamiat-e-Islami also became close to India, making Islamabad angry with Tajik dominance in Afghanistan. Rabbani and Masoud also realised the benefits of Kabul's ties with New Delhi as an effective counterweight to balance Pakistan. Thus, Rawalpindi began supporting Pashtuns for political domination of the country. Pashtuns, who comprise more than 40 per cent of the Afghan population, believe that they are the rightful rulers of the country, basing their claim on the history of the previous three centuries when Pashtun dynasties ruled Afghanistan. With the coming to power of the Pakistan-supported Taliban regime in 1996, New Delhi's influence in Afghanistan was entirely eclipsed by Islamabad. New Delhi "was forced to close its embassy and all its consulates and, with ISI encouragement, Afghanistan quickly became the base for a whole spectrum of anti-Indian groups, including Lashkar-e-Taiba."[3] It was first time in the modern history of Afghanistan that Pakistan had a government in Kabul that was extremely friendly to Islamabad, having no links with India.

This period also witnessed India providing support to the Northern Alliance, an anti-Taliban resistance group comprising mostly Tajiks, Uzbeks and Hazaras. Russia and Iran also supported the Northern Alliance. But India faced increased challenges from Pakistan's 'deep state' on the Kashmir front. As underlined by Ayesha Jalal, "tactic of pushing battle-hardened militants from Afghanistan across LOC [Line of Control between India and Pakistan] to wage a low-intensity war against Indian security forces in Kashmir was designed to keep the subcontinent's most contentious dispute in the international gaze."[4]

With US Intelligence and airpower support, the Northern Alliance was able to chase the Taliban away from Afghanistan. Following the fall of the Taliban regime in 2001, India began to rebuild its bilateral ties with Afghanistan's new rulers. Hamid Karzai, a Durrani Pashtun, was appointed the president of Afghanistan and a Constitution was adopted following the Loya Jirga in 2004. India wholeheartedly supported President Karzai, who reciprocated the gesture in equal measure. As the trust deficit widened between Islamabad and Kabul, Karzai often blamed Pakistan for supporting cross-border terrorism during his entire term as president.

India has emerged as the most important regional power, investing in reconstruction and institution building in Afghanistan. Since 2001, New Delhi has provided $3 billion in economic aid to Kabul. However, Pakistan's ideological fixation with anti-Indianism and its operational prerequisite of gaining 'strategic depth' in Afghanistan has cast a negative shadow over India's role in reconstruction and development of war-ravaged Afghanistan. Indian diplomatic missions, engineers and aid workers have been repeatedly targeted by the Taliban in Afghanistan.[5] New Delhi has deployed a mountain-trained paramilitary force, the Indo-Tibetan Border Police (ITBP), to guard the Indian Embassy in Kabul and its four consulates in Jalalabad, Mazar-e-Sharif, Kandahar and Herat.[6]

Kabul is therefore an important security and strategic partner for New Delhi as common interest in combating terrorism and building democratic stability ensure strong mutual ties between the two countries. On the other hand, Afghanistan and Pakistan view each other with suspicion, as there is very little trust between them. Pakistan deeply fears the emergence of Pashtun nationalism within its borders as well as in Afghanistan which has tried to promote Pashtun nationalism in Pakistan due to its vision of itself as the home of all Pashtuns. The idea of Pashtunistan dates back to the partition of India and Pakistan in 1947, when many Pashtuns did not accept the newly created country of Pakistan. Pashtun nationalists led by Khan Abdul Ghafar Khan, also known as "Frontier Gandhi" due to his long association with Mahatma Gandhi and his non-violent political ideology, demanded a separate country independent of Pakistan, named Pushtunistan.[7] As Pashtun nationalists were close allies of India, Pakistan has always been suspicious of their intentions and objectives.[8] The most important reason for Pakistan's support to the Taliban is that it has represented a distorted form of Pashtun nationalism which is also couched in Islamist terminology,[9] thereby blunting the potency of Pashtun nationalism. Thus, Pakistan's policy of 'strategic depth' in Afghanistan is seen as serving two purposes: it solves the Pashtun problem and also functions as an insurance policy against a potential Indian military offensive.[10] In the words of an Afghan analyst, "Kabul has been a victim of Islamabad's 'strategic depth' policy that sees Afghanistan as the fifth state of Pakistan. India too has been a victim of Pakistan's proxy wars. The shared threat from Pakistan, home to the Taliban and Lashkar-e-Taiba, has strengthened India-Afghanistan ties."[11]

The 2011 Strategic Partnership Agreement is an important framework of India's deep-rooted association with Afghanistan. After a power-sharing agreement was signed between two leading contenders for power, Ashraf Ghani and Abdullah Abdullah, in the aftermath of the bitterly contested presidential election in 2014, Ghani was appointed as the president and Abdullah became the chief executive officer (CEO) of the national unity government. The ceremony was attended by India's then Vice President, Hamid Ansari.[12] Responding to India's concerns on the growing warmth between Kabul and Islamabad under the Ghani administration, Abdullah insisted that Afghanistan's engagement with Pakistan must never suggest that relations with India would ever be sacrificed.[13] President Ghani came to India in April 2015 on his first official visit to the country. During Ghani's interactions with the Indian leadership, the discussion ranged on cooperation and assistance in various sectors including health, education, agriculture, disaster management, power sector and electoral management. Moreover, both sides "expressed determination to work together, along with the international community, to combat and defeat the scourge of terrorism in all its forms and manifestations." They called on the international community to deal severely with the safe havens for terrorists that continue to threaten regional and global security."[14] The Afghan Embassy in Delhi proposed building a sister-city relationship between Delhi and Kabul, Mumbai and Kandahar, Ajmer Sharif and Herat, Hyderabad and Jalalabad, Ahmedabad and Asadabad, as well as the State of Assam and the Province of Helmand.[15]

India's Prime Minister, Narendra Modi, paid an unannounced visit to Kabul in December 2015. This was his first visit to Afghanistan after becoming India's Prime Minister. During his visit, Modi unveiled two of India's most important initiatives in Afghanistan: the inauguration of the Afghan parliament building, and the handing over ceremony for four Mi-25 attack helicopters. The supply of helicopters signalled a subtle shift in India's position on supplying 'offensive' military equipment. India began to shed its earlier hesitation on only giving non-lethal assistance like transport vehicles and military training to Afghanistan.[16] According to the joint statement, it was "agreed that groups and individuals that perpetrate violence on the people of Afghanistan and challenge by use of violence and terror against the Government of Afghanistan cannot be allowed to exercise control or wield influence over any part of Afghanistan's territory in any manner whatsoever." It was also decided to conduct the first Strategic Partnership Council meeting headed by Foreign Ministers in early 2016 along with four joint working group meetings.[17]

Afghan CEO Abdullah Abdullah visited India in early 2016, and held discussions on bilateral, regional and global issues including the security situation and reconciliation process in Afghanistan.[18] He also addressed the Counter Terrorism Conference in Jaipur in February 2016. Modi visited Herat in western

Afghanistan in June 2016 and jointly inaugurated with Ghani. The Afghan-India Friendship Dam, earlier known as the Selma Dam. It was his second Afghan visit in a span of six months. The importance of Indo-Afghan ties was further underlined by Afghanistan's decision to award Modi its highest civilian honour, Amir Amanullah Khan Award. During his speech after inaugurating the dam, Modi invoked iconic Sufi saint Khwaja Moinuddin Chishti, whose home village lies near the dam and who had settled in Ajmer: "Khwaja Moiunuddin Chishti, the first of the Chishti saints in India, said that human beings must have the affection of the sun, the generosity of the river and the hospitality of the earth."[19]

As Pakistan has continued to refuse to allow any Indian goods to travel over land to Afghanistan, New Delhi and Kabul are working on strengthening alternative routes, including the air cargo corridor launched in June 2017, as well as the Chabahar sea route. India's first major shipment of 130,000 tonnes of wheat to Afghanistan through Chabahar Port was dispatched from the western seaport of Kandla in October 2017, launching a trade route bypassing Pakistan. India's growing interest and influence in Afghanistan was reflected in Modi's announcement of providing Kabul with $1 billion in economic aid, when President Ghani held talks with him in New Delhi in September 2016. India's assistance to Afghanistan also extends to rebuilding of air links, power plants and investing in the health and education sectors. India helps train Afghan civil servants, diplomats and police personnel. Building on strong historical links, India has been open to the Afghan people, facilitating cooperation in diverse fields. Thousands of Afghans visit India every year for tourism, medical care and education. India has allowed Afghan government telecommunication through Indian satellites.

Afghanistan is a landlocked country which has been dependent on Pakistan's Karachi port for access to the sea. This advantage has given Islamabad considerable influence over Kabul that it has periodically utilised to pressure Afghan governments. This unfavourable situation is likely to change as India-funded construction work of a 135-mile road connecting Afghanistan's Nimroz province with the Iranian port of Chabahar has been completed.[20] India has already signed a three-nation deal with Iran and Afghanistan to develop the Chabahar port and build a transport-and-trade corridor through Afghanistan that could substantially reduce the time and cost of doing business with Europe.[21] New Delhi's commitment for the development of Afghanistan has already crossed

$3 billion since 2001. As informed by India's ambassador to the USA, Harsh Vardhan Shringla, in an event in Washington in November 2019, India has played an active role in the reconstruction and development of Afghanistan as reflected in the fact that it has successfully completed 400 social infrastructure projects and another 150 are under way.[22] India's role in Afghanistan has also acted as an exertion of its 'soft power'. The Afghan government believes that Bollywood and cricket are the two "real stars" of Afghanistan's close ties with India.[23] To promote cricket in Afghanistan, India has declared a stadium near Delhi as official training facility of the Afghan team besides providing coaching and other technical facilities.

India has two major strategic objectives in Afghanistan which it seeks to achieve through aid. First, India does not want the reassertion of the fundamentalist brand of political Islam as represented by the Taliban. Second, India does not want Pakistan to achieve 'strategic depth' in Afghanistan and exploit its advantage to harm India's security interests. India has therefore provided assistance for the Afghan national defence and security forces in fighting terrorism, organised crime, trafficking of narcotics and money laundering.[24] India's agenda is to build the capacity of the Afghan state as well as of Afghan security forces, enabling them to fight more effectively against terrorism. This is in tune with the requirements of the Afghan government as well as the international community.

India closely coordinates its diplomatic position with Afghanistan on issues of counter terrorism. For instance, when 140 Afghan soldiers were killed in a deadly terror attack claimed by the Taliban on the army base near Mazar-i-Sharif in April 2017, India strongly condemned the terror attack, asserting that it was a stark reminder of the need to dismantle safe havens sustaining terrorism from Pakistan. The statement by the MEA had stated that "India remains steadfast in its support to Afghanistan in fighting all forms of terrorism and bringing perpetrators of terrorist violence to justice, wherever they maybe."[25] Similarly, when a lethal terror attack took place in Pulwama in Jammu and Kashmir in February 2019, the Afghanistan Foreign Ministry condemned the attack with President Ghani saying that "terrorism is a cancer in the region, and it requires collective efforts to root it out."[26] In a move to combat terror, India and Afghanistan formalised the extradition treaty in November 2019 that would enable extradition of Pakistani terrorists operating out of Afghanistan.[27]

Conflict Landscape in Afghanistan

Ever since the Soviets marched into Afghanistan in 1979, the people of Afghanistan have not experienced peace. If modern Afghanistan is characterised by a low level of modernisation and development, there is sufficient historical evidence to support the view that the government in Kabul has been quite ineffective in exercising power throughout a large country with mostly inhospitable terrain. Politics and power in Afghanistan are strongly influenced by the ethnic complexities characterising it. Thus, the deep ethno-linguistic divisions and the fairly decentralised nature of the Afghan polity provide convenient fault lines ready for exploitation. Even after the ousting of the Taliban in 2001, a fundamental problem has been the failure of the Afghan government institutions to provide good governance and socio-political development to many parts of Afghanistan.

Similarly, there are unending layers of geopolitical complications with far-reaching strategic implications. The presence of the erstwhile Soviet Union or America in today's context has only served as a legitimisation tool for insurgents and jihadists of various hues to spread terror across Afghan territory. And Russia's and Iran's contrasting stances have only added to the already bewildering complexities of conflict. All parties are inclined to escalate military campaigns in the hope of compelling their rivals to negotiate on more suitable terms.

Another dimension worth noticing is the production of whopping 9,000 tons of opium in Afghanistan[28] which contributes to the generation of employment in most of the Afghan provinces as well as creation of vested interests. The role it plays in generating profits for the Taliban, local warlords and criminal networks also cultivates spoilers who wish the conflict scenario to continue in Afghanistan. The drug trade is estimated to finance around sixty per cent of the Taliban's total annual budget.[29] However, the drug money is not the Taliban's exclusive funding machine as they also mobilise finances from diversified sources including extortions, 'protection tax' from Afghan telecom companies,[30] donations from Gulf-based individuals and covert support from states amenable to their strategy.[31] President Donald Trump's August 2017 announcement of a new Afghan strategy was centred on pressurising Pakistan to take more action against terrorists.[32] Within this framework, the USA had announced the suspension of some $2 billion in aid to Pakistan until Islamabad took decisive action against the Taliban and the Haqqani Network.[33] But the policy soon lost its relevance with the USA making a U-turn to ensure its early withdrawal from Afghanistan.

The USA has spent around $900 billion in direct costs on the Afghan war so far. More than 2,400 American soldiers have died in the war, coupled with a casualty figure of around 100,000 Afghan civilians and security personnel.[34] Terror attacks on Afghan and foreign troops as well as Afghan civilians are being carried out by the Taliban and Haqqani network on a regular basis. As per the estimates of the UN Assistance Mission in Afghanistan (UNAMA), there have been about 32,000 civilian deaths since UNAMA started to keep formal records in 2009.[35] Despite nearly two decades of extensive US military aid and training, the Afghan security forces continue to remain plagued by serious operational problems that have enabled the Taliban to contest more than half of Afghan districts.[36] The Taliban-led insurgency remains a lethal force drawing sustenance from a variety of sources in Afghanistan as well as Pakistan, always attempting to coalesce with a number of anti-government elements and criminal networks.

The Afghan Taliban take pride in calling themselves the Islamic Emirate of Afghanistan, which is a conscious attempt to underscore their desire to establish a unitary state to impose its version of the Islamic Sharia they had built during 1996-2001 primarily through military conquests. That is why the Taliban are always eager to showcase their Islamist credentials while resisting all nationalist currents in Afghan politics. Before the 9/11 attacks, the Taliban were part of a global terrorist syndicate because of hosting al-Qaeda-linked terrorists. Therefore, India's biggest worry associated with their coming to power in Afghanistan is about turning the country into a hub of terrorism. Indians have strong reasons to believe that the Afghan Taliban is Pakistan's proxies who are being exploited to weaken the Afghan state from within.

The Afghan Taliban have been remarkably patient to wait for the withdrawal of American troops from Afghanistan in order to be able to establish 'peace' on their own terms. The tactics they have adopted remain very clear: their deadly terror attacks, especially in Kabul, seek to undermine the authority of the elected government, while demoralising the Afghan people. Caught in the brutal conflict, Afghans continue to suffer. Under the Trump Administration, the USA recognised the impossibility of a military solution to the Afghan war.

US-Taliban Peace Deal

Proponents of the US-Taliban peace deal argue that this is a follow-through on President Trump's 2016 campaign commitment to drawdown American forces before the 2020 presidential elections. However, there is a bipartisan consensus on the issue of withdrawal from Afghanistan. Sensing this broad consensus in domestic political circles, the USA has begun preparations to withdraw troops from Afghanistan following a peace deal with the Taliban signed in Doha in February 2020.

The opening talks between Zalmay Khalilzad and the Taliban were held in October 2018. The next round of interaction took place in December in which Pakistani and Saudi officials were also present. The Afghan government was reported to have despatched a team to Doha but despite attempts from the Saudis, the Taliban refused to meet them.[37] After six days of talks in late January 2019, Khalilzad was quoted as informing that the "Taliban have committed, to our satisfaction, to do what is necessary that would prevent Afghanistan from ever becoming a platform for international terrorist groups or individuals," in return for which American troops would withdraw from the country.[38] After more than two-week long negotiations in March 2019, there was no major breakthrough in talks. However, Khalilzad announced that an agreement "in draft" had been reached on counterterrorism guarantees by the Taliban for prohibition on the use of Afghan territory to mount terror attacks against the USA, and the troop withdrawal from Afghanistan. Even as talks were going on, the Taliban stepped up violence in the country to demoralise the Afghan security forces. Though Khalilzad also noted that after the agreement was finalised, "the Taliban and other Afghans, including the government, will begin intra-Afghan negotiations on a political settlement and comprehensive ceasefire."

As the Taliban continued to insist on the exclusion of the Afghan government from the talks, the USA also preferred to keep it away. But the Ghani government was unhappy at its marginalisation from the talks which were deciding the fate of the country. Venting his anger, Hamdullah Mohib, the Afghan National Security Adviser, even went on to accuse Khalilzad of undercutting the Afghan government to propel his own political ambitions. While accusing him of legitimising the Taliban and downgrading the legitimacy of the Afghan government, Mohib said that "we don't have the kind of transparency that we should have.... Knowing Ambassador Khalilzad's own history, personal history, he has ambitions in Afghanistan.... The perception in Afghanistan and the people in the government think, perhaps, perhaps all this talk is to create a caretaker government of which he will then become the viceroy."[39]

At the end of the sixth round of talks in May 2019, an Indian observer rightly mentioned that the Afghan peace process was faltering and that Khalilzad may "have only emboldened the Taliban and given the group undue legitimacy while undermining the elected government in Kabul," while also raising concerns about Khalilzad's negotiating strategy which may "have sent the wrong signal—one of desperation, which the Taliban leaders have read as victory. So high is their confidence—they fly around in ISI planes—and so malleable the US stand."[40] The eighth round of talks was concluded in August 2019 without any agreement. Taking a swipe at the US-led peace effort, President Ghani said that the Afghan "future cannot be decided outside, whether in the capital cities of our friends, nemeses or neighbours."[41] By August 2019, the talks appeared to be reaching their final state, with multiple reports detailing the outlines of an emerging deal. Khalilzad confirmed in an interview in September 2019 that the USA in principle had agreed to withdraw around 5,000 of its 14,000 troops from five bases within 135 days if the Taliban reduced violence in two key Afghan provinces. By the end of 2020, all American troops would be withdrawn.

But instead of a long-awaited announcement about the details of a US-Taliban peace deal, Trump tweeted on September 7 that the talks were off adding shortly afterwards that the Afghan peace process was "dead." The ostensible reason for the termination of talks was the Taliban's claim of responsibility for a terror attack that also led to the death of one American soldier. In addition to calling off the peace process, Trump also cancelled his planned meeting with Taliban leaders and Afghan President Ghani at Camp David.[42] The meeting would have generated bad publicity as it was set to be held just days before the anniversary of the 9/11 attacks.

While the breakdown of the Khalilzad-Taliban talks was certainly advantageous for India, the Trump Administration soon picked up the threads of negotiations as there was broad convergence of the USA and Pakistan's policies around the preference for a negotiated political settlement, each for their own reasons. Eventually, after over two years of dramatic back and forth, a deal was signed between the USA and the Taliban on February 29. The deal includes a timeline for the conditional withdrawal of US troops from Afghanistan and the Taliban's commitment to not allow global terror outfits to make Afghanistan their base. Representatives from India and Pakistan were also part of this gathering. Soon after the deal, New Delhi said that it would continue to extend support to the Afghan government and the people in realising their aspirations for a peaceful, democratic and prosperous future. However, it was Pakistan which played the key role in facilitating the talks between Washington and its former enemy, the Taliban.

Pakistan's Role and India's Concerns

Pakistan was forced to join the Bush Administration in the 'global war on terror' in 2001, but this commitment was never translated into action. Though Pakistan provided some tactical help to international troops led by the USA in fighting the al-Qaeda, however its attitude towards other jihadists remained ambiguous and controversial. Pakistan's ISI has continued to support Islamist terrorists including the Afghan Taliban and the Haqqani Network in fighting Afghan and American security forces. Supporting Islamist extremists has been a useful instrument in Pakistan's asymmetric strategy against India. Given this background, Pakistan's role in the current peace talks invites much scepticism in New Delhi as Rawalpindi has vastly different priorities in Afghanistan. Rawalpindi has often demonstrated that it can go to any extent to frustrate friendly relations between India and Afghanistan.

Islamabad had brokered the first round of direct talks between the Afghan government and the Taliban in July 2015, and it has also been part of the four-nation group comprising Pakistan, Afghanistan, the USA and China, but all such efforts have been unsuccessful. An Afghan analyst rightly terms Pakistan "the wrong moderator with the wrong actors in the wrong place."[43] Even though Pakistan faced tremendous pressure from the Trump Administration to deny safe haven to terrorist outfits, it continued to bet on a US withdrawal from Afghanistan. Getting the Afghan Taliban political legitimacy would help Pakistan's security establishment gain a much bigger political role in Afghan affairs. Its calculations seemed correct when the Trump Administration decided to pull out of Afghanistan at the earliest. Pakistan would do as much as it could to exploit the 'exit hurriedness' of the USA to ensure a favourable political outcome.

While Pakistan wants the world to believe that the Afghan Taliban is an autonomous entity which is completely free from Pakistani influence, the reality of Pakistani political and military patronage to the Taliban is not in doubt. The Afghan Taliban's reliance on Pakistan for military logistics, medical care and sanctuary for the insurgents remains crucial. Islamabad still holds the key to getting the Taliban to the table; a fact that has been underscored by Pakistan Prime Minister's Imran Khan's public claims of facilitating the US-Taliban talks. One important step taken by Islamabad in this regard was the release of Taliban co-founder Mullah Abdul Ghani Baradar in October 2018. Baradar was captured in Karachi in a joint US-Pakistan operation in 2010. Khalilzad remarked in

February 2019 that Baradar who "has a reputation of being more open, more pro-peace" was released at "my request," and also thanked the Pakistani leadership for facilitating the travel of many Taliban leaders to talks in Doha.[44]

India has backed Afghan political leadership in its endeavours to end the decades-long conflict. However, New Delhi does not want Islamabad to be brought back into the Afghan endgame without adequate safeguards, as Pakistan's 'deep state' has its own agendas for Afghanistan. Pakistani policymakers link developments in Afghanistan to Islamabad's relations with its traditional rival, India. In fact, it has become a received wisdom in Pakistan that the Kabul regime must have 'good' relations with Islamabad and that close relations between New Delhi and Kabul must be prevented at all costs. In response to Pakistan's statement that "India has no role in Afghanistan," India's MEA issued a strongly-worded statement in January 2019 asserting that "it is not for Pakistan to decide as to what role another country has in regional or global affairs. Pakistan also cannot decide on behalf of an independent and sovereign country Afghanistan and dictate to them as to how to conduct their foreign policy."[45]

Explaining Pakistan's approach to Afghanistan, a recent report by the Congressional Research Service (CRS) has pointed out that "Pakistan's security establishment, fearful of strategic encirclement by India, apparently continues to view the Afghan Taliban as a relatively friendly and reliably anti-India element in Afghanistan."[46] The report also argues that Pakistan's security services maintain ties with Afghan insurgent groups, particularly the Haqqani Network that has become a semi-autonomous component of the Taliban. Similarly, the US Department of State in its latest annual 'Country Report on Terrorism 2018', has criticised Pakistan for its lack of seriousness on countering terrorism; on the one hand, Pakistan claims to support political reconciliation in Afghanistan, while on the other, it does not prevent the Afghan Taliban and the Haqqani Network from operating in Pakistan-based safe havens.[47] The report also found that the Pakistani "government failed to significantly limit Lashkar-e-Tayyiba (LeT) and Jaish-e-Mohammad (JeM) from raising money, recruiting, and training in Pakistan—and allowed candidates overtly affiliated with LeT front organisations to contest the July [2018] general elections."[48] Pakistan does not mend its ways even though it has been placed in June 2019 on the "grey list" of Financial Action Task Force (FATF) for deficiencies in implementing UN sanctions related to designated entities, specifically citing concerns over Pakistan's failure to fully implement the UN Security Council's ISIL (Daesh) and al-Qaeda sanctions regime.

New Delhi does not want the Taliban to monopolize Afghan power at the behest of Pakistan and to allow safe havens for radical Islamist groups. Any government that emerges from the Afghan peace process should not be allowed to replicate the Islamic Emirate. One of the biggest challenges facing India in its Afghan strategy is growing divergence with the position adopted by Russia and Iran, its erstwhile partners, to prop up the Northern Alliance against the Taliban. India, Russia and Iran all want to make sure that peace and stability prevail in Afghanistan. But the problem lies in the ways to achieve this goal. If New Delhi would like the Afghan government to have the final authority to dictate the terms of peace talks with the Taliban, Russia and Iran differ in the sense that they would like the Taliban to be a partner in the fight against the ISIS which is seen by Moscow and Tehran as a greater threat than the Taliban.[49]

From a Russian perspective, the issue of Afghanistan demonstrates the opportunities and challenges to regional cooperation between New Delhi and Moscow. India's ties with Russia have traditionally been positive; however, Russia has become increasingly suspicious of the growing partnership between India and the USA. The geopolitical implications of the withdrawal of American troops from Afghanistan seem to be weighing heavily on the Kremlin. It has been observed that after withdrawal, if "India emerges as the regional proxy of the United States, this will raise concerns, not only in Moscow, but also in Islamabad and Beijing.... Moscow has therefore linked the drawdown of troops from Afghanistan to the role of India in its own regional security concerns."[50]

India expects more pressure on Pakistan but there are limits to American influence in forcing Pakistan to end its dependence on jihadist forces. India has been consistently telling the USA that the return of the Taliban to Kabul should not translate into endangering Afghan political and constitutional structures. India continues to support an Afghan-led, Afghan-owned and Afghan-controlled peace process, and has maintained a policy of no direct engagement with the Taliban. That is why India had sent two former diplomats in a "non official" capacity to a conference on the Afghan peace process in Moscow in November 2018 which was attended by a high-level Taliban delegation.

Several prominent Afghans, a few secretly, have visited New Delhi for discussions. As New Delhi is perceived as close to the Tajik-dominated Northern Alliance, India has ensured that its engagement with the Pashtun leadership dispels this perception that it has any favourite. In January 2019, the Indian Army Chief, Bipin Rawat, emphasised the need for India to open a channel of communication with the Taliban. He asserted that if India has interests in Afghanistan "then you cannot be out of the bandwagon. Unless you are sitting on that table, you will not know what is being discussed."[51] This was the first time when one of the senior-most voices in the Indian establishment echoed demands calling for India's greater participation in the peace process. There has been no change in India's policy though. One of the probable reasons for India's reluctance stems from the fact that doing so would legitimize marginalisation of the Afghan government from the process; New Delhi does not want to give this impression that it is abandoning its Afghan allies. There is no doubt that Afghans have viewed India's unequivocal support very favourably, the hurdles being created by the dynamics of Indo-Pak relationship should not come in the way of more military assistance to the Afghan government.

Security in South Asia after the US Exit

Afghanistan today resembles a failed state divided by decades of internal conflict and external interference. The situation in terms of improvements in Afghan governance and rule of law has lagged behind the uncertain tactical gains being made in the peace talks between the USA and the Afghan Taliban. International donors face the daunting challenge: massive amount of aid has not brought about the desired level of progress, and unlikely to do so in the future. At the same time, outside aid will be very critical to the survival of the new Afghan government if it is to maintain security and stability. India will need to invest huge amounts of continuing developmental and military assistance.

While it is certainly not in a position to rule over the whole of Afghanistan, the Taliban does control a large territory in the rural areas in the Pashtun-dominated provinces of eastern and south-eastern Afghanistan. The sudden withdrawal of American forces will only provide it greater opportunity to expand its area of activities. The US-Taliban peace deal neither seems to have helped the Afghans restore an Afghan government on Afghan terms nor has it inspired any confidence on taming the Taliban's innate extremist impulses fuelled by Pakistan. Hence, the deal is the not the panacea for the problems that Afghanistan faces; there are so many issues to be addressed without which the country cannot witness lasting peace. Based on past precedents, a forcible imposition of a stringent Islamic-based justice system is likely to be resisted by people of many ethnicities in Afghanistan. Many educational restrictions for females including restrictions on movies, mobile phones and enforcement of daily prayers will not be welcomed. It needs to be understood that a desire for stopping the violence in Afghanistan cannot be equated with a desire for a long-term peace. Do the Taliban really long for permanent peace? Will the Taliban honour its commitment to stop supporting those who encourage global jihad?

Pakistan opposes a permanent presence of the US military in Afghanistan, but is also afraid of a sudden exit that could aggravate problems in its own tribal areas and cause another wave of Afghan refugees across the border. However, Pakistan may hope that even when the Trump Administration withdraws troops and chaos descends in Afghanistan, its ongoing fortification of the Durand Line will help it stop cross-border terrorism and the uncontrolled movement of Afghan people towards Pakistan. Pakistan has claimed to have completed a major portion of the border wall with Afghanistan, while the remainder is to be completed soon. Though the utility of the border wall in checking the cross-border flow of insurgents seems suspect, it will however hamper the historical and cultural exchanges between the people on both sides of the Durand Line. As no Kabul government, including the brief Taliban regime in 1996-2001, has ever recognised the border with Islamabad, a future Afghan government, including the one with representation from the Taliban, is likely to oppose the construction of the wall. Thus, the Pakistani government is sure to lose goodwill among the Afghan people after peace returns. This bilateral tension will thwart peace along the border areas.

The Doha deal clearly indicates that the Trump Administration is totally fed up with America's 'longest war'. However, the US desperation to end the war without a convincing narrative could have debilitating consequences for South Asia. Without American presence in Afghanistan, the odds are that a civil war would break out in the country. Such a conflict would encourage the need for the Taliban to maintain links with jihadist groups, including al-Qaeda. A perceived Taliban victory would even provide the motivation for jihadists to seek refuge in the Taliban-controlled Afghanistan and emulate its ideology in their own struggle elsewhere.[52]

Pakistan has been counting on the Taliban's return which it deeply believes gives it strategic depth in Afghanistan vis-à-vis India. If the Taliban are back in Kabul soon, Pakistan's ability to control the Taliban for tactical gains against India will likely get a boost. As a result, India's investments in Afghanistan will also be at a huge risk of being wiped out. Besides losing Kabul to Islamist fundamentalists, New Delhi may also be forced to get more involved in Afghan affairs, which will have both domestic and regional consequences.

Ripples formed by Afghan turbulence will inevitably affect Kashmir which will be at the centre of how India responds to the emerging geopolitical situation in Afghanistan. Thus, further destabilisation in Afghanistan is likely to provide more space for Kashmir-focussed Islamist forces. If there is an increase in violence in Jammu and Kashmir, New Delhi's attempts to reshape and restructure grassroots politics will also receive a setback.

NOTES

1. Mohammed Ayoob, "India's options and the Pashtun factor," *The Hindu*, January 7, 2019.
2. Hafizullah Emadi, *Dynamics of Political Development in Afghanistan; The British, Russian, and American Invasions*, New York: Palgrave Macmillan, 2010, p. 167.
3. "A deadly triangle: Afghanistan, Pakistan and India," *Brookings*, June 25, 2013.
4. Ayesha Jalal, *The Struggle for Pakistan: A Muslim Homeland and Global Politics*, London: The Belknap Press of Harvard University Press, 2014, p. 298.
5. "Terrorist Attacks and Threats on Indians in Afghanistan since 2003," *South Asian Terrorism Portal*, June 2017.
6. PTI, "Indo Tibetan border police seeks upgrading command level in Afghanistan," *The Indian Express*, October 1, 2016.
7. Thomas H. Johnson, Barry Zellen, in *Culture, Conflict, and Counterinsurgency*, Stanford: Stanford University Press, 2015, p. 154.
8. Amanullah Ghilzai, "Why Pakistan Fears Indo-Afghan Ties," *Foreign Policy*, April 1, 2014.
9. Ayoob, "India's options and the Pashtun factor." *The Hindu*, January 7, 2019.
10. Vinay Kaura, "Implications of Afghan-Pakistani Clashes Along the Durand Line," BESA Center Perspectives Paper No. 1355, The Begin Sadat Center for Strategic Studies, November 26, 2019.
11. Abdul Rahman Rahmani, "India's soft power is very effective in Afghanistan," *Hindustan Times*, January 25, 2019.
12. "Ghani Inaugurated As New Afghan President," *Radio Free Europe, Radio Liberty*, September 29, 2014.
13. Asit Jolly and M.G. Arun, "We need realistic dialogue with Pakistan: Dr Abdullah Abdullah," *India Today*, March 13, 2015.
14. "Joint Statement during the State Visit of President of Islamic Republic of Afghanistan to India," Ministry of External Affairs, Government of India, April 28, 2015.
15. M. Ashraf Haidari, "India and Afghanistan: A Growing Partnership," *The Diplomat*, September 16, 2015.
16. Suhasini Haidar, "Modi reaches Kabul," *The Hindu*, December 25, 2015.
17. "Joint Statement between India and Afghanistan," Ministry of External Affairs, Government of India, December 25, 2015.
18. Suhasini Haidar, "India in the loop on Taliban talks: Abdullah," *The Hindu*, February 4, 2016.
19. PTI, "PM Modi awarded Afghanistan's top civilian honour," *Times of India*, June 4, 2016.
20. Thomas Barfield, *Afghanistan: A Cultural and Political History*, New Jersey: Princeton University Press, 2010, p. 344.

21. "India, Iran and Afghanistan sign Chabahar port agreement," *Hindustan Times*, May 24, 2016.
22. PTI, "India finishes 400 social infra projects in Afghanistan, US praises effort," *Hindustan Times*, November 22, 2019.
23. PTI, "Bollywood cricket two real stars of Afghanistan's relationship with India Envoy," *The Week*, November 22, 2019.
24. Ministry of External Affairs, "Joint Statement on the 2nd Strategic Partnership Council Meeting between India and Afghanistan, New Delhi," Government of India, September 11, 2017.
25. PTI, "Afghan army base attack toll 140: India says time to dismantle terror havens," *Hindustan Times*, April 22, 2017.
26. ANI, "Afghanistan President condemns Pulwama terror attack, says terrorism needs to be rooted out," *Business Standard*, February 15, 2019.
27. Dipanjan Roy Chaudhury, "India, Afghanistan agree to extradite Pakistani terrorists," *Economic Times*, November 25, 2019.
28. "Opium cultivation in Afghanistan at all-time high," *Dawn*, November 17, 2017.
29. "US Department of Defence, "Department of Defence Press Briefing by General Bunch via teleconference from Kabul, Afghanistan," December 12, 2017, https://www.defense.gov/News/Transcripts/Transcript-View/Article/1395077/department-of-defense-press-briefing-by-general-bunch-via-teleconference-from-k/
30. Gabriel Domínguez, "How the Taliban get their money," *Deutsche Welle,* January 21, 2016, http://www.dw.com/en/how-the-taliban-get-their-money/a-18995315
31. Abubakar Siddique, "Taliban Strategy In Afghanistan: 2017 And Beyond," *Gandhara*, December 24, 2017, https://gandhara.rferl.org/a/afghanistan-taliban-strategy/28936181.html
32. Vinay Kaura, "US–Pakistan relations in the Trump era: Resetting the terms of engagement in Afghanistan," ORF Occasional Paper, No. 128, December 2017.
33. Seema Sirohi, "US Suspends $2 Billion in Aid to Pakistan For Failure to Take Action Against Terror Groups," *The Wire*, January 6, 2018.
34. Kelly Magsamen and Michael Fuchs, "The Case for a New U.S. Relationship with Afghanistan," Center for American Progress, July 29, 2019.
35. United Nations Assistance Mission in Afghanistan, "Afghanistan: Protection of Civilians in Armed Conflict Annual Report 2018," Kabul, 2019, p. 1.
36. Shoaib Sharifi and Louise Adamou, "Taliban threaten 70% of Afghanistan, BBC finds," *BBC*, January 31, 2018.
37. Secunder Kermani and Sami Yousafzai, "Taliban talks: Pakistan arrest 'sends militants message'," *BBC News*, January 15, 2019.
38. Mujib Mashal, "U.S. and Taliban Agree in Principle to Peace Framework, Envoy Says," *New York Times*, January 28, 2019.
39. Jennifer Hansler and Kylie Atwood, "Senior Afghan official accuses US envoy of 'delegitimizing' Afghan government," *CNN*, March 14, 2019.
40. Seema Sirohi, "Is the Afghan peace process going anywhere?" Observer Research Foundation, May 25, 2019.
41. Ayaz Gul, "Taliban, US End Latest Round of Talks Without Announcing Outcome," *VOA*, August 12, 2019.

42. Peter Baker, Mujib Mashal and Michael Crowley, "How Trump's Plan to Secretly Meet With the Taliban Came Together, and Fell Apart," *New York Times*, September 8, 2019.
43. Mohammad Shafiq Hamdam, "A peace agreement in Afghanistan would be 'victory for all, defeat for none'," *The Hill*, March 30, 2018.
44. PTI, "Mullah Baradar released by Pakistan at the behest of US: Khalilzad," *The Hindu*, February 9, 2019.
45. Government of India, "Official Spokesperson's response to media query," (January 18, 2019).
46. PTI, "Pakistan views Afghan Taliban as reliable anti-India element in Afghanistan: U.S. Congressional report," *The Hindu*, November 6, 2019.
47. United States Department of State, "Country Reports on Terrorism 2018," Bureau of Counter-terrorism, October 2019.
48. Ibid.
49. Ahmad Majidyar, "Iran and Russia Team up with Taliban to Undermine U.S.-led Mission in Afghanistan," Middle East Institute, March 24, 2017.
50. Natasha Kuhrt, "Russian Views of India in the Context of Afghanistan," in Kate Sullivan (ed.). *Competing Visions of India in World Politics*: *India's Rise Beyond the West*, Palgrave Macmillan, 2015, p. 176.
51. Shaurya Karanbir Gurung, "'Cannot be out of the bandwagon': Army Chief General Bipin Rawat on talks with Taliban," *Economic Times*, January 10, 2019.
52. Ioannis Koskinas, "Don't sign a death warrant for Afghan democracy," *War on the Rocks*, August 26, 2019.

CONTRIBUTORS

Brigadier General Alain Lamballe (Retd.) has served important military and diplomatic assignments in Western Europe (United Kingdom), Central Europe (Hungary, Austria), Balkan (Bosnia and Herzegovina) and South Asia (India, Pakistan, Sri Lanka, Maldives), besides various short term missions all over the world.

He holds Ph.D. in political sociology and diplomas of the Paris School of Oriental Languages and Civilisations in Hindi, Urdu and Hungarian. He is member of the Société d'Histoire Générale et d'Histoire Diplomatique (Society for General and Diplomatic History), Paris; the association of the Centre des Hautes Etudes sur l'Afrique et l'Asie Modernes (association of the Center of Higher Studies on Modern Africa and Asia), Paris; and affiliated with various think tanks including Athéna, Forum du Futur (Forum for the Future), and Asie 21 (Asia 21). He is also the former chairperson of the association Institut des Hautes Études de Défense Nationale/Asie Moyen-Orient (IHEDN/AMO).

He has authored four books and contributed various chapters in edited books and numerous articles, mostly on political, economic and military issues of South Asia and surrounding areas.

Admiral Arun Prakash (Retd.) served as India's 20th Naval Chief and Chairman Chiefs of Staff. An aviator by specialisation, during his 40 year career, he commanded a carrier-borne fighter-squadron, a naval air station and four warships; including the aircraft-carrier INS Viraat. He has also logged over 2500 hours in fighters, patrol aircraft and helicopters. In flag rank he commanded the Eastern Fleet, the National Defence Academy, the Andaman & Nicobar

Joint Command and the Western Naval Command. On staff, he served as the head of the Aviation and Personnel Branches of the navy and as the Vice Chief of Naval Staff.

During his tenure at the helm, the Indian Navy saw many initiatives being launched in the fields of doctrine, strategy, transformation and foreign maritime cooperation. He is a graduate of the IAF Test Pilots School, Defence Services Staff College and the US Naval War College. During the 1971 War, he was awarded the Vir Chakra while flying with an IAF fighter squadron in Punjab.

Post-retirement, he served two terms as a member of the National Security Advisory Board and was Chairman of the National Maritime Foundation. He served on the 1999 Arun Singh Task force as well as the Naresh Chandra Committee on national security reforms. He lives in Goa, and writes and speaks on strategic and security related topics.

Dr. Christian Wagner is Senior Fellow at the German Institute for International and Security Affairs (SWP) in Berlin. He was head of the Research Division Asia at SWP, from 2007 to 2014. Prior to joining SWP in 2003, he was a Senior Fellow at the Institute for Development Research at the University of Bonn (2001-2002), and Assistant Professor at the Institute of Political Science and Administrative Studies at Rostock University (1996-2001).

Dr Wagner is also a member of the European Association for South Asian Studies. He was a member of the board of directors of the German Association for Asian Studies (DGA), from 2007 to 2013. He was a Visiting Fellow at the Observer Research Foundation, the Jawaharlal Nehru Institute for Advanced Studies (JNIAS) and at the Institute for Defence Studies and Analyses (IDSA) in New Delhi in 2015/16. He obtained his M.A. and Ph.D from Albert-Ludwigs-University Freiburg. His area of interest includes Indian Foreign Policy, Regional Cooperation in South Asia, and Democracy in South Asia.

Maj. Gen. Dhruv C. Katoch (Retd.) is an alumnus of Sherwood College, Naini Tal, National Defence Academy, Khadakvasla, Defence Services Staff College, Wellington, Higher Command Course, Mhow and National Defence College, New Delhi. He holds MSc and MPhil degrees in Defence Studies from Madras University and is a Doctor of Philosophy (Honoris Causa) from Indira Gandhi University, Rewari.

A third-generation Army officer, he took part in 'Operation Pawan' for two years as part of the IPKF in Sri Lanka. He has also served and participated in operations against terrorists and insurgents in J&K and various states of North East India. He commanded his battalion on the Line of Control in Jammu and Kashmir, a sector in Mizoram and a division in Arunachal Pradesh where he was responsible for the defence of Kameng Sector. Before retiring from the Indian Army on 31 January 2009, he was the Chief of Staff of an Operational Corps on the Western Sector. Post retirement, he joined the Indian Army's premier think-tank, Centre for Land Warfare Studies, later rising to be its Director till November 2014.

He has authored innumerable papers and study reports on defence and security-related issues and edited/co-edited six books. He speaks on these issues on television news channels and at military training establishments and universities across India. Based in the NCR, he is currently Director, India Foundation; Editor, SALUTE magazine and Secretary-General, Indian War Veterans Association.

M. J. Akbar is a distinguished writer and Member of Parliament for BJP. During his long career in journalism, he launched, as editor, India's first weekly political news magazine, *Sunday* in 1976, and two daily newspapers, *The Telegraph* in 1982 and *The Asian Age* in 1994. He has also been editorial director of *India Today* and *The Sunday Guardian*.

He first served as an elected Member of Parliament between 1989 and 1991, and returned to public life in March 2014. In July, 2015 he was elected to the Rajya Sabha from Jharkhand. In July, 2016 he was elected for another term, this time from Madhya Pradesh. He has also served as Minister of State for External Affairs in the government led by Prime Minister Narendra Modi.

He is the author of several internationally acclaimed books, including *India: The Siege Within*; *Nehru: The Making of India*; *Kashmir: Behind the Vale*; *The Shade of Swords: Jihad and the Conflict between Islam and Christianity*; *Tinderbox: The Past and Future of Pakistan*; and *Gandhi's Hinduism: The Struggle Against Jinnah's Islam*. In addition there have been four collections of his columns, reportage and essays.

In 2004, he was named a member of the committee set up by Saudi Arabia's King Abdullah to draft a ten year charter for Muslim nations at a special conference in Mecca. In March 2006 he joined The Brookings Institution, Washington, as a Visiting Fellow in the Brookings Project on U.S. Policy towards the Islamic world. He also serves as chairman of the trust for the Calcutta Muslim Orphanage.

M L Kumawat, IPS (Retd.) is a former Director General of the Border Security Force (BSF), and the founder Vice Chancellor of Sardar Patel University of Police, Security and Criminal Justice, Jodhpur. He has held important assignments while working in the Police for over thirty seven years such as the chief of Greyhounds, Andhra Pradesh; Joint Director, CBI; Additional Director General (Law and Order), Andhra Pradesh; the chief of CID, Andhra Pradesh; Special Secretary (Internal Security), MHA, Government of India. He also served as the Chairman of Rajasthan Public Service Commission (RPSC).

His two pathbreaking proposals – establishment of a Police University and creation of 'Commando Battalion for Resolute Action' (COBRA) for tackling the Maoist challenge – were accepted by the government. He has been awarded Police Medal for Meritorious Service in 1989 and the President's Police Medal for Distinguished Service in 1997.

He is a Distinguished Fellow and Trusty at the Observer Research Foundation, New Delhi. He has been sitting on selection committees for appointment of Vice-Chancellors and faculty members in various Universities in India. He has authored several monographs and chapters in edited books on security related themes. Spending time in both Delhi and Jaipur, he writes and speaks on policing and internal security issues.

Dr. R.K. Arora is a serving officer of the Border Security Force, presently working on deputation as Professor in the Department of International Affairs and Security Studies, Sardar Patel University of Police, Security and Criminal Justice. He has more than two decades of experience as a field practitioner of border security, counter-narcotics, counter-insurgency and counter-terrorism in various parts of India and as an international peacekeeper at the UN Mission. His Doctoral research on Indo-Pak Border has been well received by relevant stakeholders. His area of interest includes Border Security, Counter-Terrorism and Cyber Security. His articles and monographs are published regularly by eminent publishing houses.

Lt. Gen. Syed Ata Hasnain (Retd) Through most of his 40 year illustrious career, he has served in turbulent environment and hot spots. From Sri Lanka to Siachen Glacier, from the North East to Jammu & Kashmir (J&K), and in UN operations from Mozambique to Rwanda, he has seen it all in crucial appointments. He commanded the Indian Army's Srinagar based 15 Corps.

He is a sought after speaker and writes for major Indian newspapers besides being a regular participant in television debates on mainstream television. With a strong academic background from Sherwood College Nainital, St Stephen's College Delhi, the Royal College of Defence Studies, Kings College London and the Asia Pacific Centre for Security Studies, he has been at the forefront of encouraging the adoption of the US initiated Scholar Warrior concept in the Indian Army. He has spoken at the Lee Kwan Yu School for Public Policy, the Rajaratnam School for International Studies and the Indian Institute for South Asian Studies, and at the International Institute of Strategic Studies (IISS), London. He is associated with the Vivekanand International Foundation and Centre for Joint Warfare Studies, as Distinguished Fellow and is on the Governing Council of the Indian Council of World Affairs (ICWA) and Institute of Peace & Conflict Studies (IPCS).

Since 2014, he has attended over 30 meetings of the Track-2 groups relating to Indo-Pak relations. He is a member of the India Afghanistan Foundation under aegis of Ministry of External Affairs and was also on the Committee for promotion of India-Indonesia relations. In 2018, he was appointed by the President of India as Chancellor of the Central University of Kashmir. In addition, in February 2020, he has been nominated by the Prime Minister as Member of the National Disaster Management Authority (NDMA). He has six decorations awarded by the President for India and two by the Army Chief.

Professor S.D. Muni is a member of Manohar Parrikar Institute for Defence Studies and Analyses (IDSA) Executive Council. For nearly forty years, he taught, conducted and supervised research, in International Relations and South Asian Studies at Jawaharlal Nehru University (1974-2006), National University of Singapore (2008-2013), Banaras Hindu University (1985-86), and University of Rajasthan (1972-73). He served as India's Special Envoy to SE Asian countries on UNSC Reforms (2005) and represented India's Minister of External Affairs at the 50th Anniversary celebrations of the Paris Peace Conference, held in Phnom Penh, Kampuchea. He was also India's Ambassador to Lao People's Democratic Republic (1997-99). Prof. Muni was nominated to the first ever constituted National Security Advisory Board of India during 1990-91. He was the founding executive member of the Regional Centre of Strategic Studies, Colombo, Sri Lanka, and also served on the Executive Council of the Institute for Defence Studies and Analyses (IDSA), New Delhi, India. In 2005 he was bestowed with 'Sri Lanka Ratna', Sri Lanka's highest national honor for a foreign national.

The Jawaharlal Nehru University, where he held the prestigious Appadorai Chair of International Politics and Area Studies, conferred on him the status of Professor Emeritus in 2014. He has been sitting on selection committees for appointment of Vice-Chancellors and Faculty members in various Universities. He was invited to address the UN Special Committee on Indian Ocean as a Zone of Peace at Sochi, then as part of the Soviet Union, in 1985. Author and editor of nearly thirty books & monographs and more than 200 research papers, Prof. Muni was also the founder editor of two prestigious quarterly Journals in India, The South Asia Journal (Subsequently renamed as South Asian Survey, launched by Indian Council for South Asian Cooperation), and Indian Foreign Affairs Journal (For Association of Indian Diplomats). He lives in New Delhi, and writes and speaks on neighbourhood and security related issues.

Sanjiv Krishan Sood is a retired Additional Director General (ADG) of the Border Security Force. Having put in over 38 years of meritorious ervice, he has served along all the borders of India with Pakistan and Bangladesh including eight years on LC and in the sensitive Samba Sector of Jammu & Kashmir. His interests include border management, security-related issues and the role of security forces in security matrix of India, politics and humour. He has authored a book and contributed several chapters on border security. He is a regular participant in television debates on mainstream news channels.

Dr. Vinay Kaura is an Assistant Professor in the Department of International Affairs and Security Studies, Sardar Patel University of Police, Security and Criminal Justice. Having a Master's degree in both History and Political Science, he obtained his PhD on Afghanistan- Pakistan relations with special reference to Islamic fundamentalist terrorism. His research interests include Indian Foreign Policy, Indo-Pacific Region, Afghanistan-Pakistan Relations, Counter-Terrorism and Counter-Insurgency. His articles are being regularly published in national and international papers and his research has also been published in reputed journals and edited books.

Index